D1556689

The Canterbury and York Society

GENERAL EDITOR: DR P. HOSKIN

ISSN 0262-995X

CANTERBURY AND YORK SOCIETY VOL. CVII

Proctors for Parliament

Clergy, Community and Politics, *c.*1248–1539

(The National Archives, Series SC 10)

VOLUME I: *c.*1248–1377

EDITED BY

PHIL BRADFORD & ALISON K. McHARDY

The Canterbury and York Society

The Boydell Press
2017

First published 2017

A Canterbury and York Society publication
published by The Boydell Press
an imprint of Boydell & Brewer Ltd
PO Box 9, Woodbridge, Suffolk IP12 3DF, UK
and of Boydell & Brewer Inc.
668 Mt Hope Avenue, Rochester, NY 14620-2731, USA

website: www.boydellandbrewer.com

ISBN 978-0-907239-80-2

A CIP catalogue record for this book is available
from the British Library

Details of previous volumes are available from Boydell & Brewer Ltd

The publisher has no responsibility for the continued existence
or accuracy of URLs for external or third-party internet websites
referred to in this book, and does not guarantee that any content
on such websites is, or will remain, accurate or appropriate

This publication is printed on acid-free paper.

Typeset in Monotype Baskerville by Word and Page, Chester, UK
Printed and bound in Great Britain by TJ International Ltd.

Dedicated to
David and Elaine Bradford
and to the memories of
Barbara M. Wilson of The Mount School, York
and
Denis Hay of Edinburgh University

This book is produced with the generous assistance of a grant from Isobel Thornley's Bequest to the University of London.

The Society is grateful for the generous financial support of the Lincoln Record Society in the production of this volume.

CONTENTS

ILLUSTRATIONS

ACKNOWLEDGMENTS

Many years ago the late Katherine Longley, then archivist of York Minster, suggested to AKM that she should expand her notes on SC 10 to include the whole series, but it was Mark Ormrod, PB's doctoral supervisor, who brought us together and so made this project possible. Our thanks are due to him, both for this and for reading the entire manuscript and making detailed comments. Gwilym Dodd read the draft introduction and gave other assistance to AKM. Our general editor, Pippa Hoskin, has offered advice and kindly encouragement. Others who have helped us in various ways are Elizabeth Biggs, Sam Drake, Maureen Jurkowski, Rob Wheeler and Patrick Zutshi; we are grateful to them all.

Our final thanks go to the forbearing staff of Drucker's Viennese Patisserie at the Bullring Centre in Birmingham, the unlikely but productive location for many of our editorial meetings.

ABBREVIATIONS

C&Y	Canterbury and York Society
CCR	*Calendar of Close Rolls*
CPR	*Calendar of Patent Rolls*
ODNB	*Oxford Dictionary of National Biography*
PROME	*Parliament Rolls of Medieval England*
PW	*The Parliamentary Writs and Writs of Military Summons*, ed. Francis Palgrave, 2 vols. in 4 parts (London, 1827–34)
RDP	*Reports from the Lords Committees Appointed to Search the Journals of the House, Rolls of Parliament, and Other Records and Documents, for All Matters Touching the Dignity of a Peer of the Realm*, 5 vols. (London, 1820–9)
RS	Rolls Series (The Chronicles and Memorials of Great Britain and Ireland during the Middle Ages)
TNA	The National Archives

INTRODUCTION

The clergy are the forgotten men of the medieval English parliament. The main reason for this probably lies in the structure of England's national political assembly and the way in which parliament evolved. In other political assemblies of medieval western Europe there were usually three, though occasionally four, estates: clergy (always first in seniority), nobility (who were sometimes divided into greater and lesser) and commons.[1] This was never the case in England, where the two 'houses' of Lords and Commons developed during the fourteenth century. This was by no means a natural or preordained development. The *Modus Tenendi Parliamentum*, written in the 1320s, divided parliament into six grades or estates: the king, the higher clergy, the clerical proctors (representing the lower clergy), the nobility, the knights of the shires, and the citizens and burgesses.[2] Although the idealistic provisions of the *Modus* depart from the reality of the early-fourteenth-century parliament in several respects, its approach is interesting both for demonstrating that there were alternative understandings of parliament in its early years which could have led it to develop in different directions, and for the prominence it gives to the clergy, including viewing the clerical proctors (lower clergy) as an estate in their own right. Yet the final result of the struggles over parliament during the fourteenth century was the emergence of two houses of which the clergy formed parts, rather than becoming a separate estate. Lost among the crowds of laity, they have left no distinctive mark on the national consciousness.

Another reason for the neglect of the parliamentary clergy lies in the development of the two convocations, of Canterbury and of York, as purely clerical representative institutions. It was the evolution of the convocations as tax-granting bodies which seemed to sideline the clergy politically, and which has misled some scholars into believing that the lower clergy went only to meetings of convocation, but not to parliament, whereas they actually attended both assemblies.[3] Study of

---

[1] C. H. McIlwain, 'Medieval Estates', in J. R. Tanner, C. W. Previté-Orton and Z. N. Brooke, eds., *The Cambridge History of Medieval Europe, vol. VII: The Decline of Empire and Papacy* (Cambridge, 1932), pp. 665–715; A. R. Myers, *Parliaments and Estates in Europe to 1789* (London, 1975).

[2] *Parliamentary Texts of the Middle Ages*, ed. Nicholas Pronay and John Taylor (Oxford, 1980), pp. 78–9, 91. The dating of the *Modus* remains a controversial topic. Most historians take as their starting point W. A. Morris, 'The Date of the "Modus Tenendi Parliamentum"', *English Historical Review* 49 (1934), 407–22, and M. V. Clarke, *Medieval Representation and Consent* (London, 1936). A majority would accept that the *Modus* was composed at some point between 1316 and 1324, as suggested by V. H. Galbraith, 'The *Modus Tenendi Parliamentum*', *Journal of the Warburg and Courtauld Institutes* 16 (1953), 81–99. The assumption here is that the *Modus* was composed at the end of this period, around 1324: P. J. Bradford, 'Parliament and Political Culture in Early Fourteenth-Century England', University of York Ph.D. thesis (2007), pp. 186–98.

[3] For example, A. F. Pollard, *The Evolution of Parliament* (London, 1926), p. 74: 'the clerical proctors preferred to give their answers to the king's proposals in convocation, and absented themselves from the parliament chamber'.

the clergy's place in parliament is also hampered by the lack of comprehensive records of their attendance and activities, although the presence of some clerical peers can be observed from the lists of triers of petitions which were recorded in the parliament rolls.[4] By contrast there exist for members of the lay commons both the election returns from sheriffs and the writs *de expensis* which enable the representatives of counties and boroughs to be identified, even though their parliamentary (and other) activities may remain obscure.[5]

Yet the numbers of clergy involved were not negligible. All twenty-one bishops of England and Wales were summoned to parliament from the thirteenth century onwards. From 1295 the bishops were also commanded, via the *praemunientes* clause in the writs of summons, to warn the deans of their cathedral churches (or the priors, in the case of monastic cathedrals), one representative of every cathedral chapter, all sixty archdeacons, and two representatives of the lower clergy of each diocese, to attend.[6] This made a total of 169 (almost entirely secular) clergy.[7] The religious are much harder to quantify, for the numbers of parliamentary abbots varied widely, as will be seen, but by the later fourteenth century the number summoned was normally twenty-seven. Thus some forty-eight men, the bishops and abbots, were called by individual writs of summons, and constituted the clerical peers, while 148 lower clergy were called indirectly, through their bishops. In theory, therefore, the number of clergy in a 'typical' late-medieval parliament was 196; sometimes in the late thirteenth and early fourteenth centuries the numbers were much greater. How could this group of almost 200 clerical parliamentarians have become almost invisible to many later historians?

For most of the time when medieval parliaments were being studied, from the seventeenth to the nineteenth century and beyond, the interest of historians was in parliament as a critic of the crown, and later in its growing legislative power. This initially meant the study of challenges to royal acts and policies mainly led by members of the lay aristocracy, and often most vividly described in narrative

---

[4]   Taking the 1340s as an example, we have the lists for five parliaments, which demonstrate the clerical involvement. In April 1341, the bishops of Durham and Salisbury were among the auditors for English petitions, with the bishops of Ely and Hereford assigned to petitions from elsewhere. In April 1343, the bishops of Salisbury and Carlisle were triers for England, and the bishops of Durham and Norwich for the rest of the British Isles and the continent. June 1344 saw the bishops of Chichester and London dealing with English petitions and those for other places handled by a group including the bishops of Coventry and Lichfield, Bath and Wells, and Ely, as well as the abbots of Westminster and St Augustine's, Canterbury. The triers for September 1346 included the bishop of Chichester and the abbot of Westminster for England, and the bishop of Norwich and the prior of Rochester for elsewhere. The division in January 1348 was different: the auditors of English and Scottish petitions included the bishops of London, Lincoln and St Davids, the abbots of St Albans and Waltham, and the prior of Rochester; among those assigned to clergy petitions were the bishops of Winchester and St Davids; while the bishops of Norwich and Ely were on duty for Gascony, Wales and Ireland.

[5]   *Return of the Name of Every Member of the Lower House of the Parliament of England, Scotland and Ireland*, 2 vols. (London, 1878).

[6]   *RDP*, III, p. 67.

[7]   Two dioceses had two cathedrals: Bath and Wells, and Coventry and Lichfield. Each of these four chapters, as well as their dean or prior, was entitled to be represented.

sources.[8] Later efforts took the form of detailed study of the members of parliament, especially the lay commons.[9] Medieval parliamentary peers as a group
have had less attention; the one notable exception was the work of a former clas-
sicist turned politician.[10] From the 1920s to the 1960s, the prevailing view was
that parliament was a court of justice and some historians reminded us that this
institution was one of the crown's instruments of government, not primarily
a forum for complaint.[11] Scholars of the later twentieth century did not reject
this view outright, but did qualify it considerably. The 'royal instrument' view
of parliament was especially important to the study of England's late-medieval
warfare, but also involved a reassessment of the relationship between king and
parliament.[12] These functions coalesced in the way that kings in parliament
received petitions and dispensed justice and benevolence to their subjects, not
least to members of the clergy.[13] Researchers can now freely access and search
the texts of these petitions through The National Archives' online catalogue. The
central source for medieval parliamentary history, the parliament rolls, have been
translated and subjected to new scholarly scrutiny, with the results now widely
disseminated.[14]

---

[8] Classic examples of this include William Stubbs, *The Constitutional History of England in
its Origin and Development*, 3 vols. (Oxford, 1875); T. F. Tout, *The Place of the Reign of Edward
II in English History* (Manchester, 1914); and James Conway Davies, *The Baronial Opposition to
Edward II, its Character and Policy: A Study in Administrative History* (London, 1918).

[9] A pioneering work was Josiah C. Wedgwood and Anne D. Holt, *History of Parliament:
Biographies of Members of the Commons House 1439–1509* (London, 1936). The History of
Parliament Trust was established in 1940 and published its first volumes (covering the period
1750–90) in 1964. The Trust sponsors and publishes research into the history of parliament
in all periods.

[10] J. Enoch Powell and Keith Wallis, *The House of Lords in the Middle Ages* (London, 1968).

[11] Foremost amongst the literature is the substantial (and often combative) output of
H. G. Richardson and G. O. Sayles, whose collected papers were published as *The English
Parliament in the Middle Ages* (London, 1981). They also published a collection of sources for
parliament missed by the eighteenth-century compilers of the printed parliament rolls:
Rotuli Parliamentorum Hactenus Inediti, MCCLXXIX–MCCCLXXIII, Camden Society, 3rd
Series, 51 (London, 1935). Sayles continued to write after Richardson's death, most notably
The King's Parliament of England (London, 1975) and his edited selection of translated sources
for parliament, *The Functions of the Medieval Parliament of England* (London, 1988). It is worth
noting that Sayles is one of the few who explicitly recognised the continuing presence of the
lower clergy in parliament beyond 1340: *King's Parliament*, pp. 114–15.

[12] Michael Prestwich, *Edward I* (London, 1988), pp. 436–68; Phil Bradford, 'A Silent
Presence: The English King in Parliament in the Fourteenth Century', *Historical Research*
84 (2011), 189–211; Gwilym Dodd, 'Parliament and Political Legitimacy in the Reign of
Edward II', in *The Reign of Edward II*, ed. Gwilym Dodd and Anthony Musson (York,
2006), pp. 165–89; W. Mark Ormrod, *Edward III* (New Haven, CT, 2011); Gwilym Dodd,
'Conflict or Consensus: Henry IV and Parliament, 1399–1406', in *Social Attitudes and Political
Structures in the Fifteenth Century*, ed. Tim Thornton (Stroud, 2000), pp. 118–49; Christopher
Allmand, *Henry V* (London, 1992), pp. 366–83; John Watts, *Henry VI and the Politics of Kingship*
(Cambridge, 1996).

[13] Gwilym Dodd, *Justice and Grace: Private Petitioning and the English Parliament in the Late
Middle Ages* (Oxford, 2007); *Petitions to the Crown from English Religious Houses c.1272–c.1485*, ed.
Gwilym Dodd and Alison K. McHardy, C&Y 100 (2010).

[14] *PROME*, available in printed form and electronically.

In all this endeavour the clergy might have seemed entirely neglected, but this was not quite the case. Politically active bishops, for example, have never lacked academic biographers.[15] For the other clerical peers a pioneering study by Aloyse M. Reich not only drew attention to the parliamentary abbots as a group, but described in some detail the fluctuating numbers of those who were summoned.[16] More recently J. R. Maddicott has given due, and welcome, attention to the roles of bishops and the religious in parliamentary business.[17]

The lower clergy have not only received less scrutiny, but their very right to attend parliament has been doubted.[18] Ironically, it was the work of four historians investigating monastic accounts which rescued the diocesan or lower clergy from this oblivion. In 1927 Elizabeth Levett showed that the accounts of Gamlingay (Cambridgeshire) and Wooton (Hampshire), two St Albans Abbey manors, pro-vided evidence for the attendance of clerical proctors in parliament in the early fourteenth century;[19] in 1933 Edith Lowry published similar material from Gamlin-gay for the later fourteenth century,[20] and the following year Frances Page produced evidence for the same period from another Cambridgeshire manor, Oakington.[21] Finally, Marjorie Morgan, in *The English Lands of the Abbey of Bec*, showed that the manor of Combe in the bailiwick of Ogbourne (Wiltshire) made payments towards the expenses of clerical proctors for parliament in the years 1306–7 and 1308–9.[22]

Despite this neglect, there exists a substantial body of evidence concerning the parliamentary importance of the clerical estate, at every level, which has never been systematically exploited and which, notwithstanding some individual efforts (not least the material on the lower parliamentary clergy which has been examined by J. H. Denton and J. P. Dooley for the period 1295–1340, and A. K. McHardy for the post-1340 period),[23] remains almost unknown. The contents of TNA series SC

---

[15]   All the medieval bishops of England (and most Welsh bishops) now have entries in the *ODNB*, where further references may be found.

[16]   Aloyse Marie Reich, *The Parliamentary Abbots to 1470: A Study in English Constitutional History*, University of California Publications in History 17 (Berkeley and Los Angeles, 1941). Sister Reich consulted only printed sources, but doubtless a world war prevented further investigation in English archives.

[17]   J. R. Maddicott, *The Origins of the English Parliament, 924–1327* (Oxford, 2010).

[18]   For example, Pollard, *Evolution of Parliament*, p. 122: 'the clergy of the two provinces preferred […] to abandon parliament except in so far as they were represented there by prelates.' Clarke, *Medieval Representation and Consent*, p. 150, argued that 'by 1337 the proctors of the clergy had, for all practical purposes, ceased to be an estate of parliament.' Edward Miller states that by 1340, 'the clerical proctors had withdrawn to their convocations': *Historical Studies of the English Parliament, Volume I: Origins to 1399* (Cambridge, 1970), p. 17.

[19]   A. E. Levett, 'The Financial Organisation of the Manor', *Economic History Review* 1 (1927), 65–86; reprinted in A. E. Levett, *Studies in Manorial History* (Oxford, 1938), p. 48.

[20]   E. C. Lowry, 'Clerical Proctors in Parliament and Knights of the Shire, 1280–1374', *English Historical Review* 48 (1933), 443–55.

[21]   Frances M. Page, *The Estates of Crowland Abbey* (Cambridge, 1934), p. 63.

[22]   Marjorie Morgan, *The English Lands of the Abbey of Bec*, (Oxford, 1946), p. 58.

[23]   A. K. McHardy, 'The Representation of the English Lower Clergy in Parliament during the Later Fourteenth Century', in *Sanctity and Secularity: The Church and the World*, ed. Derek Baker, Studies in Church History 10 (1973), pp. 97–107; J. H. Denton and J. P. Dooley, *Representatives of the Lower Clergy in Parliament, 1295–1340*, Royal Historical Society Studies in History 50 (Woodbridge, 1987).

10 (Special Collections: Parliamentary Proxies), printed in this and a subsequent volume, will make available the last great unexploited source for the history of the medieval English parliament. Ignorance of this material has led to the undue neglect of an important element of the community of the realm and its relations, both within itself, and with the laity. It is this neglect which, we hope, these volumes will redress.

PROCTORIAL REPRESENTATION IN THE MIDDLE AGES

The proctors named in the documents in SC 10 were the heirs of two Roman law traditions. One concerned the representation of individuals. Someone choosing a deputy to represent him was following the Roman practice of appointing a *procurator*: an individual who acted on behalf of another, especially in legal proceedings.[24] The growth of litigation at the papal court ensured that the practice of appointing proctors was perpetuated and developed throughout western Europe during the eleventh and twelfth centuries. This concept of the chosen representative entered into many aspects of public life, not only in litigation, but in general business (especially for individuals travelling to distant places), diplomacy, diocesan administration, and even in marriage.[25] Those named in SC 10 to represent individuals – bishops, abbots, cathedral deans or priors, and archdeacons – were the heirs of this tradition.

The other tradition, that one individual could represent a group, arose from Justinian's maxim *quod omnes tangit ab omnibus approbetur* ('what concerns all should be approved by all').[26] At the end of the twelfth century the clergy began to be taxed, and by about 1200 lawyers understood the maxim to mean, in effect, 'no taxation without representation'. During the early and middle years of the thirteenth century a perfect storm of events and traditions came together to produce the concept of representative government as embodied in the English parliament.

The earliest, strongest and most influential developments were in the church.[27] In April 1213 Innocent III summoned the Fourth Lateral Council, which convened on 15 November 1215. Although primarily concerned with faith and renewal the council also had a financial aspect; Pope Innocent wished to raise a tax to support a crusade, and for that reason he summoned proctors from cathedral chapters, on the principle of *quod omnes tangit*. The Fourth Lateran Council might have remained a unique occasion in the history of representation had it not been for a decision by Innocent's successor, Honorius III (1216–27). In 1216 a provincial council was convened at Sens, at which the presiding archbishop wished to exclude proctors from its deliberations. The capitular representatives appealed to the pope, arguing that, if they were summoned, they should be admitted to the council's discussions. The pope agreed with them, and in 1217 (25 February) his decretal *Etsi membra corporis Christi* for the first time gave proctors of cathedral chapters attending church

---

24 'Procurator', in David M. Walker, *The Oxford Companion to Law* (Oxford, 1980), p. 1004.
25 See, for example, Froissart's account of the marriage of Philippa of Lancaster and João I of Portugal in 1387: J. Froissart, *Chronicles*, trans. T. Johnes, 2 vols. (London, 1855), II, p. 221.
26 The original runs '. . . quod omnes similiter tangit ab omnibus comprobetur', V. 59–2–3, *Corpus Iuris Civilis*, vol. 2, *Codex Justinianus*, ed. Paul Krueger (Berlin, 1929), p. 231.
27 The next three paragraphs draw heavily on Richard Kay, *The Council of Bourges, 1225: A Documentary History* (Aldershot, 2002).

councils the right to participate in conciliar discussions and decision-making. Cathedral chapters needed separate representation because their endowments were distinct from those of their bishops.

Honorius III was no democrat. He needed the chapters' representatives at church councils to give binding consent to his plan to tax their revenues at the rate of 10 per cent to support the running of the curia, as well as to fund a crusade. In 1225 his legate Romanus convened a council at Bourges to confront the Albigensian challenge, and to approve his financial scheme. The summons to the archbishop of Rouen ordered him to call, indirectly, the abbots, priors, deans, archdeacons and the chapters in his province. The attending proctors had become aware of the planned permanent 10 per cent levy and, armed with the power to give binding consent to taxation, they secured a debate on this proposal. It was the proctors who opposed Honorius's plan, and secured Romanus's agreement to postpone the matter until it had been considered by a council in England.

Then, in contravention of the protocol which regarded conciliar proceedings as confidential, one of those present at Bourges wrote an account of the events there to an English counterpart, in effect giving instructions on how to resist the papal proposal.[28] So when two councils were summoned in England in 1226, to discuss papal financial demands, proctors were included each time. Both gatherings took place in London. The first council, held in May, included cathedral proctors; in addition, monastic chapters were called to the second, in October.[29] These councils rejected Honorius's plan for permanent funding of the work of the curia, though the second granted the pope a subsidy of a sixteenth.[30] The legate Otto called proctors to a council in 1237, and to a series of councils in 1240 which met to grant papal subsidies.[31] Subsequent church councils in England cemented the connection between the presence of proctors and the voting of papal taxation, and by the later thirteenth century the body now called convocation was coming into being.[32]

Meanwhile, financial necessity was forcing English kings to make concessions and reassure their subjects through representative gatherings.[33] The start of this process came in 1215 with Magna Carta,[34] while the reign of Henry III saw the clerical ideas utilised and expanded by the political elites. General taxation by the crown in 1225, 1232 and 1237, coinciding with papal tax demands, developed the ideas that all affected groups should be consulted (*quod omnes tangit*) and that whole classes could give consent through their elected proctors. Bishops, who collectively

---

[28]   'Almost certainly a proctor': Kay, *Council of Bourges*, p. 175.

[29]   *Councils and Synods with Other Documents Relating to the English Church, II: A.D. 1205–1313*, ed. F. M. Powicke and C. R. Cheney (Oxford, 1964), pp. 155–64.

[30]   Jane E. Sayers, *Papal Government and England during the Pontificate of Honorius III (1216–1227)* (Cambridge, 1984), p. 191; William E. Lunt, *Financial Relations of the Papacy with England to 1327* (Cambridge, MA, 1939), pp. 178–86, 607; John Le Neve, *Fasti Ecclesiae Anglicanae 1066–1300. Volume 4: Salisbury*, ed. Diana E. Greenway (London, 1991), Appendix 1, pp. 139–41.

[31]   *Councils and Synods*, ed. Powicke and Cheney, pp. 285–92.

[32]   R. L. Storey, 'The First Convocation, 1257?', in *Thirteenth Century England III: Proceedings of the Newcastle upon Tyne Conference 1989*, ed. P. R. Coss and S. D. Lloyd (Woodbridge, 1991), pp. 151–9.

[33]   Maddicott, *Origins of the English Parliament*, which restores the clergy to their rightful place in the development of parliament, is the basis of these two paragraphs.

[34]   'The notion of virtual representation implicit in the Charter.' *Ibid.*, p. 206.

had great political and administrative expertise, as well as legal and economic power, were always central to the growth of parliament. But proctors of the lower clergy also were summoned to parliament in 1247, the bishops promising to try to persuade them to vote a tax. In January 1254 the bishops in parliament said that they could not commit the lower clergy to a tax grant, and four months later, in another parliament, the lower clergy proctors made a tax grant, but under such strict conditions as negated their offer.[35]

Two other developments were taking place during these early and central decades of the thirteenth century. One was that bishops and abbots who were unable to attend meetings of parliament were starting to send deputies in their stead.[36] The other was that, as laymen noted the tax-granting power of the lower clergy, they copied the church's practice of having elected representatives of other groups than magnates, beginning with the knights in 1248, 1253 and 1254, with the burgesses following in 1265.[37]

Thus by the middle years of the thirteenth century ideas of representation, by both the clergy and laity, were well established, a situation brought about by a conjunction of financial demands from the rulers in church and state, with an awareness of the principles of law, essentially Roman law, by educated members of the clergy. These developments were coming to fruition at much the same time as the material in the series SC 10 begins. At the same time bishops began to send letters excusing their non-attendance at national meetings, to appoint proctors to appear in their stead, and to record these letters in their registers.[38]

Though the documents in this series arose, in theory, from two distinct concepts or legal bases, in practice the distinction soon became blurred. For example, a cathedral dean might act in collaboration with his chapter to appoint parliamentary proctors. More obviously, the kind of proctors appointed by individuals or elected by groups might be not just similar, but actually identical. Discussion of the personnel of the proxies will appear in the next volume.

THE HISTORY OF SC 10 AND PARLIAMENTARY PROXIES

The National Archives Series SC 10 consists of individual letters, nearly all of them from the clergy, although with a handful from lay peers. They are the letters of authorisation for those who attended parliament, either as the deputies for individuals, or as the chosen representatives of electing groups, and they were presumably the means by which deputies and delegates were able to gain entrance to the meeting-places of parliament. It seems likely that proctors were given two proxy letters when sent to parliament. One was handed to the clerks of parlia-

---

[35]   *Ibid.*, pp. 211–16.

[36]   *Ibid.*, pp. 159, 461.

[37]   *Ibid.*, pp. 213, 469–70.

[38]   Walter Bronescombe of Exeter recorded under the heading 'Proctorship for Parliament' a letter to the bishop of London, the other bishops of Canterbury and York provinces, and to the lower clergy, explaining his absence from a meeting of parliament at St Albans in December 1264 because of his poor health and other misfortune, and giving notice of the appointment of Masters John Wyger and J[ohn] de Bradley as his proctors, dated at Bishop's Nympton on 23 November 1264: *The Register of Walter Bronescombe Bishop of Exeter 1258–1280*, ed. O. F. Robinson, 3 vols., C&Y 82, 87 and 94 (1995, 1999 and 2003), II, no. 573.

ment, while the other was retained by the proctor as proof of his credentials.[39] In a very few cases both letters have survived.[40] The submitted letters were filed by the chancery clerks, but the evidence suggests that the names of proctors were also enrolled, since proxy rolls existed and are known to have survived into the eighteenth century.

An indication of the lost information contained in the proxy rolls is the *Vetus Codex*, the collection of parliamentary documents assembled during Walter Stapeldon's reform of the exchequer as treasurer in the 1320s,[41] which includes a list of 103 proxy appointments for the Carlisle parliament of 1307.[42] Since there are no corresponding letters in SC 10 for that parliament, this is a reminder that the proxy appointments in the series represent only a proportion of the total number made during the Middle Ages, with the list in the *Vetus Codex* being a fortuitous survival. The largest number of appointments found for a single parliament in SC 10 is sixty-three, for the parliament of May 1322. Even allowing for the reduction in the numbers summoned to parliament over time, it is safe to assume that some, perhaps many, letters of proxy appointment have been lost in the intervening years, along with the rolls on which these appointments were recorded. If rolls were indeed produced, it is not entirely clear why the original letters were also kept. Luck rather than judgement may be responsible for their survival. However, it may also be an indication of the importance contemporaries attached to proctors, leading them to preserve both the original appointment letters and the enrolled lists. Certain parliamentary clerks seem to have had tidier minds than others: the letters for the parliament of 1318, for example, have the name of the sender noted on the back, presumably for filing purposes; those for the parliament of February 1351 all have the name of the sender written at the top in the same contemporary hand. Presumably this aided filing, an indication that the originals remained an important part of the nascent parliamentary archives.

There are major gaps in the parliamentary archives in the second half of the fifteenth century, with no material in SC 10 between 1447 and 1523. The survival of part of the journal from the parliament of 1461–2, the so-called 'Fane Fragment', does demonstrate that by Edward IV's reign the attendance of the Lords was being recorded;[43] as this was Edward's first parliament, it is very likely that

---

[39]   This is the practice dictated in the *Modus Tenendi Parliamentum: Parliamentary Texts*, ed. Pronay and Taylor, pp. 67–8, 80–1. It is also possible that in some cases, proctors were only given a single letter. The abbot of Reading's appointment for the Good Parliament in 1376 (31/1520) notes that the exhibitor of the letter is the proctor: 'dilectos nobis in Christo dominum Petrum de Barton clericum et Thomam Seynt Alban presencium exhibitores nostros procuratores et excusatores'.

[40]   Examples include 4/182 and 5/225, for the bishop of London (1316); 5/224 and 5/226, bishop of Rochester (1316); 7/322 and 7/325, prior of Ely (1321); 8/354 and 8/355, abbot of Crowland (1322); 8/396 and 8/398, abbot of Lesnes (1322); 12/558 and 12/559, prior and chapter of Ely (1328); 23/1146 and 23/1146, chapter of York (1344); 30/1452 and 30/1453, archbishop of Canterbury (1371); 33/1640 and 33/1641, prior of Durham (1380).

[41]   Mark Buck, *Politics, Finance and the Church in the Reign of Edward II: Walter Stapeldon, Treasurer of England* (Cambridge, 1983), pp. 163–96; M. C. Buck, 'The Reform of the Exchequer, 1316–1326', *English Historical Review* 98 (1983), 241–60.

[42]   TNA C 151/1, ff. 130*v*–132*r*, printed in *PW*, I, 185–68, and *PROME*. The list can also be found in Appendix 3 of this volume.

[43]   W. H. Dunham (ed.), *The Fane Fragment of the 1461 Lords' Journal* (New Haven, CT, 1935);

the practice was already current under Henry VI and may have commenced earlier. In survivals from 1514 onwards, the attendance record is the standard way of beginning daily entries in the journal of the House of Lords. By this stage, proxies were also being entered in the journal. Those of the parliament which commenced on 21 January 1510 are the first we know to have been thus recorded, with further entries surviving for 1512 and 1515 before a gap until 1534.[44] Unfortunately, the few surviving letters in SC 10 which date from the reign of Henry VIII are for sessions of parliament for which there is no extant journal, so the two cannot be compared. However, the laconic entries in the journal differ notably from the more expansive text of the letters of appointment, not least in typically noting that the appointer was absent with royal permission, and often giving the name of the person presenting the proxy.

During the Tudor and Stuart periods the proctorial system changed significantly. Prior to the sixteenth century, only a handful of proxy appointments by secular peers exist. Although it is unwise to argue from absence of evidence, it does not seem likely that a vast number of such appointments ever existed. During Henry VIII's reign, this began to change, largely as a result of the Reformation. With the dissolution of the monasteries at the end of the 1530s, only the bishops remained in parliament (although the lower clergy officially continued to be summoned through the *praemunientes* clause), meaning most extant proxy appointments thereafter were made by lay peers. Significant changes were then enacted under Charles I. From at least 1626, appointments were recorded in special proxy books alongside the journals. These books then replaced the journal entries from 1628, with 146 surviving volumes compiled before the abolition of proxy voting in 1868.[45] Changes to the proxy system in 1626 additionally introduced the rule that no peer could receive more than two proxies, and dictated that spiritual peers should only name other spiritual peers as their proctors, and lords temporal other lords temporal.[46] By this stage, in marked contrast to the fifteenth century in particular, those appointing proctors were naming just a single representative.

These enrolled versions of proxies are the only evidence we have for appointments, since with one exception, there are no surviving letters between the final letter in SC 10 from 1536 and the first printed proxy deed in the sequence in the Parliamentary Archives, which dates from 1767. The exception is a handwritten survival from George I's reign, which demonstrates that forms were being circu-

R. Virgoe, 'A New Fragment of the Lords' Journal of 1461', *Bulletin of the Institute of Historical Research* 32 (1959), 83–7; Powell and Wallis, *House of Lords*, 512–15.

[44]   *Journal of the House of Lords, 1509–1793*, 39 vols. (London, 1767–1830), vol. 1, pp. 3–6, 11–13, 19–25, 33, 43–6, 58, 83–4 and 103.

[45]   Parliamentary Archives, HL/PO/JO/13. See also Clyve Jones, 'Further Proxy Records for the House of Lords, 1660–1720', *Parliamentary History* 28 (2009), 429–40; J. C. Sainty, 'Proxy Records of the House of Lords, 1510–1733', *Parliamentary History* 1 (1982), 161–5; V. F. Snow, 'The Reluctant Surrender of an Absurd Privilege: Proctorial Representation in the House of Lords, 1810–1868', *Parliamentary Affairs* 29 (1976), 60–78. Proxy voting was abolished by Standing Order 54 on 31 March, 1868; this practice remains explicitly prohibited in Standing Order 61 of the current Standing Orders of the House of Lords: 'The ancient practice of calling for proxies shall not be revived except upon the suspension of this Standing Order; and not less than two days' notice shall be given of any Motion for such suspension.'

[46]   *Journal of the House of Lords*, vol. 3, p. 507.

lated to allow the appointment of proxies. Dating from 1715, the letter from the bishop of Norwich, naming the bishop of Salisbury his proctor, is a template for bishops, in wording not that dissimilar to the format used in medieval letters patent in SC 10, with the necessary gaps completed.[47] The individual letters of appointment gave way to printed proxy deeds, the wording still recognisably based on the medieval format, which contained blanks – with one form for secular peers and a different one for spiritual peers – for the name of the appointer and his proxy.[48] There are a large number of these surviving from the reigns of George III and Victoria, although by the 1850s and 1860s the majority of the printed deeds (which were still in Latin) had the spaces for details left blank, the senders simply signing and sealing them.

As the proctorial system changed over the years, the old letters were forgotten. Bundles of the medieval proxy letters and the proxy rolls were left to moulder in the Tower of London. In 1642, the jurist and MP John Selden referred to rolls of parliamentary proxies found in the Tower, noting that they were already in an advanced state of decay.[49] By the beginning of the following century, it appears that most of this material had been lost. In 1701, Humphrey Hody noted that 'In a Record of the Tower, much defac'd and almost rotten, I found a short List of Proxies sent to the Parliament of Northampton' in October 1307.[50] He proceeded to provide details of the list.

> The Clergy of the Diocese of Durham constituit loco suo 2, of the Diocese of York, 1; of Carlisle, 3; of Ely, 2; of the Archdeaconry of Salop, 2; of the Diocese of Bath and Wells, 2. The Chapter of York constituted 2; of Hereford, Pauls and Wells, but 1. There are also the Proxies of 3 Abbots. The Abbot of Waltham, 2; of Bella Landa, 1; of Abington, 1.

Equivalent letters in SC 10 can be found today for all thirteen of these proxy appointments. However, twenty-five letters of appointment are extant in SC 10 for Edward II's first parliament, which indicates that the proxy list must either have been inaccurate or (more likely) badly decayed. The state of the public records in the Georgian period was parlous, and in the review prompted by the burning down of the Palace of Westminster in 1834 chaotic archives were discovered dispersed across London, some containing the skeletons of animals intermingled with the documents, with the Record Commission by 1836 widely viewed as 'a byword for profligate spending, chaotic management, and out-of-control staffing'.[51]

Clearly, in these circumstances the disintegration of the proxy rolls had not been a matter of concern for those charged with preserving the records, given that the archives in general were in such a bad state. That some of the original proxy letters themselves had survived appears to have been a result of good for-

---

[47]   Parliamentary Archives, HL/PO/JO/12/1/162.

[48]   Surviving deeds are contained in the Parliamentary Archives, HL/PO/JO/12. There are also two deeds, signed but with the names left blank, in TNA PRO 30/70/7/481.

[49]   John Selden, *Privileges of the Baronage when They Sit in Parliament* (London, 1642), pp. 1–7.

[50]   Humphrey Hody, *A History of English Councils and Convocations and of the Clergy's Sitting in Parliament* (London, 1701), p. 390.

[51]   Caroline Shenton, *The Day Parliament Burned Down* (Oxford, 2012), pp. 55–7, with quotation on p. 175.

tune rather than design. Writing in the 1820s, in the preface to *Parliamentary Writs*, Francis Palgrave explicitly referred to Selden and Hody as he noted the probable demise of the proxy rolls.

> It is stated by Selden and Hody, that Proxy Rolls were formerly extant in the Tower. The Editor has been informed that none can now be found; and, as it appears from these writers that the Records were much decayed, it is to be apprehended that they have since perished. About fifty original Proxies, principally of the Reign of Edw. II., have been preserved among the Parliamentary Petitions, and they will appear in their proper order.[52]

Palgrave duly printed transcripts of these letters, noting in each case that the original was in the Tower of London. These proxies had clearly been separated from the others which had survived, the existence of which apparently escaped Palgrave's notice at this stage. However, some 2,500 proxy appointments were still in existence. In 1843, Appendix II of the report of the Deputy Keeper of the Public Records (none other than Sir Francis Palgrave) listed miscellaneous bundles of documents then stored in the White Tower at the Tower of London. This 'Inventory of Writs and other Documents returned into or kept upon the Files of the Chancery, and other Miscellaneous Records deposited in the White Tower' included reference to thirteen bundles of parliamentary proxies.[53] The first bundle was recorded as containing an assortment of documents, including writs, petitions, assent to clerical elections and memoranda of works as well as parliamentary proxies, dating from the reigns of Henry III and the first three Edwards. There were then two bundles of proxies for Edward II's reign, four for Edward III's reign, three for Richard II's (including one listed as being only for his thirteenth regnal year), and one each for the reigns of Henry IV, Henry V and Henry VI. These were all recorded as 'Parliamentary Proxies from the Clergy', except for those of Henry IV, which were listed as 'Parliamentary Proxies, principally from the Clergy.' The following year's report, continuing to calendar the collection of Royal Letters held in the Wakefield Tower at the Tower of London, included the following two entries.

> W[illiam], Bishop of Bath and Wells, to the King – on account of sickness, he cannot come to London to treat of matters touching the King and the realm, and prays to be excused. 1st September, 1263. [*Partly decayed.*][54]

> R., Abbot of Abbotsbury, to the King – praying to be excused for not having come, as summoned, to London, on the Quinzaine of the Feast of St John, which sickness had prevented his doing.[55]

These are the letters now filed as SC 10/1/5 and SC 10/1/4.

---

[52]   *PW*, I, item II in the Preface (the Preface is unpaginated).
[53]   TNA PRO 43/4 (*Fourth Report of the Deputy Keeper of the Public Records, 1843*), Appendix II, pp. 113, 116, 117, 120, 122, 123, 124 and 127.
[54]   TNA PRO 43/5 (*Fifth Report of the Deputy Keeper of the Public Records, 1844*), Appendix II, p. 65 (no. 477).
[55]   *Ibid.*, p. 67 (no. 521).

Whether further proxy letters not held in the Tower were consumed by fire in 1834 is an open question, but given the imprecise knowledge of the contents of the records held in the Palace of Westminster, it is more than likely that this was the case.[56] The fire did at least result in an inquiry into the state of the public records, which led to the Public Record Office Act 1838 and the construction of a new Public Record Office on Chancery Lane. In the 1850s, records (including the proxy letters) were moved from the Tower of London to Chancery Lane.

During the 1890s, the Royal Letters and other chancery documents were divided into artificial special collections, one of which became series SC 10, containing these parliamentary proxies. What is not clear is whether these letters were originally kept all together, or whether they were removed from related documents in order to fit contemporary ideas of archival tidiness. Many letters in file 1 have 'R.L.' and a number written on the guard, presumably designating their previous number amidst the bundles of Royal Letters. These numbers are non-sequential (for example, what are now documents 1/2, 1/3, 1/4 and 1/5 are designated R.L. 546, 50, 521 and 477 respectively), which does suggest that even if the letters were kept together, they were sorted and rearranged. Nevertheless, despite some misfiling, and some omissions, the contents of SC 10 present nothing like the problems caused by being ripped out of context which beset some of the other special collections, the Ancient Petitions (SC 8) being a prime example.[57] The proxy letters were bound together in bundles of fifty, inside black covers. A draft manuscript list from *c.*1894 indicates that these files had been created by 1893.[58] Already by this stage it was realised that errors had been made, and that five of the letters were filed under the wrong date. A later list in the same file identifies four of these five errors, plus another two mistakes.[59] Some proxy letters (and one entire file) found their way into the wrong series, an error which has never been corrected. There were a few later additions to SC 10, especially in the 1970s,[60] but it seems that by the early 1930s the files had largely assumed the form in which they can still be found today.

THE CONTENTS OF SC 10

SC 10 contains 2,646 letters bound into fifty-two files.[61] It was clearly the intention of the creators of the special collection that each file should contain fifty documents, but in reality the totals range from a minimum of forty-six letters in file 51 to a maximum of sixty-seven in file 48. Files containing more than fifty letters are

[56]   Shenton, *The Day Parliament Burned Down*, pp. 180–2.

[57]   Gwilym Dodd, 'Parliamentary Petitions? The Origins and Provenance of the "Ancient Petitions" [SC 8] in the National Archives', in *Medieval Petitions: Grace and Grievance*, ed. W. Mark Ormrod, Gwilym Dodd and Anthony Musson (Woodbridge, 2009), pp. 12–46.

[58]   TNA OBS 1111.

[59]   As discussed in the next section, there are actually considerably more errors in the dating sequence than this record would suggest.

[60]   For example, on the inside cover of file 3 is a note in blue biro, 'No 150B added to this file (+150 renumbered 150A) 20/5/74 [Selby, August 1312]'. 29/1422B contains a note on the guard that it was 'Added here 8.8.72', noting 'old ref: C 47/20/4/23'.

[61]   One document (21/1003) is included in the numbering sequence but no longer exists, with a note dated 26 January, 1932 indicating that it has been united with 21/1031. This document is discounted in the discussion which follows.

a result of the later addition of documents, most easily identified in the sequence by the 'A' or 'B' suffix after their number (although there are a few unnumbered later insertions). Of the two files containing fewer than fifty letters, file 51 has only forty-six because it is at the end of the sequence and there were presumably insufficient documents to create a full file, while file 21 has forty-nine because the letter originally filed as 21/1003 was only a fragment which was later reunited with its other half (21/1031). Theoretically, the letters are filed and numbered in date order, with a scribbled, nineteenth-century note in the binding margin identifying the sender. Whilst the identification, when present, is usually (although by no means always) correct, there are several significant errors in the dating. In some cases, odd letters have been misfiled (for example 1/16, which is for a great council in 1340 but has been placed between the last letter of Edward I's reign and the first of Edward II's). In other instances, letters relating to a parliament have been kept together but placed in the wrong place. The letters for the parliament of May 1335, for example, consist of documents 18/900 and 19/901–19/944, a sequence placed between the letters for the parliament of March 1336 (18/875–18/899, 19/945–19/950 and 20/951).

The first fifty-one files of these letters are overwhelmingly proxy appointments by the clergy to parliament, or in a few cases to convocation. File 52 contains forty-eight appointments from secular peers dating from three distinct periods: 1307–39, 1400–42 and 1529–36. As a group, this is a remarkably disappointing collection which adds little to our knowledge of the workings of parliament. Three other documents (13/601, 14/672 and 50/2481) are also from secular peers but have been misfiled among the letters from the clergy. Four other letters have been misfiled in SC 10, being a letter from Edward II about his father's body (1/40), a note from the bishop of Hereford that he has executed the *praemunientes* clause (2/98), an election return for burgesses from Bristol (14/687), and an appointment of proctors by the bishop of Exeter for an appearance before the king and council over a legal battle.[62] There are forty-six documents which cannot be dated with certainty.[63] In two of these the sender has not provided a date or any other evidence which would allow a date to be deduced; in two more, a regnal year can be established but not the exact parliament. In most instances, the documents are stained or damaged, or only a fragment has survived. In several cases, the name of the sender or the proctor(s) permits a rough date to be estimated, such as in the sequence of fourteenth century letters in file 51, but the damage prevents a precise date being determined. However, the vast majority of documents can be dated and their sender identified, as shown in Table 1.

Some documents from other series in The National Archives must also be considered with SC 10. There are the 103 appointments for the Carlisle parliament of 1307, the last of Edward I's reign, enrolled and preserved (as already mentioned) in the *Vetus Codex*.[64] Amidst the election returns in C 219 is a file containing proxy appointments for the parliament of September 1334 (C 219/5/17). How this ended up being filed as a collection of election returns is a mystery, but the file seems to have been in this box since it was created. It is clearly an error, and the twenty-six letters have been calendared in this volume, as have fourteen additional letters for

---

[62] These five letters are calendared in Appendix 1 of this volume.
[63] For details of these, see Appendix 2 of this volume.
[64] See Appendix 3.

TABLE I. DOCUMENTS IN SC 10 BY REIGN AND SENDER

	Henry III	Edward I	Edward II	Edward III	Richard II	Henry IV	Henry V	Henry VI	Henry VIII	Unknown	Total
Bishops	1	7	97	224	85	30	22	27	8	5	506
Abbots	5	3	258	585	252	117	89	104	34	16	1463
Deans	0	0	33	46	31	12	5	9	3	1	140
Deans & Chapters	0	0	18	44	15	22	12	8	0	1	120
Chapters	0	0	41	61	21	15	4	6	0	1	149
Archdeacons	0	0	18	26	1	7	14	2	0	0	68
Clergy	0	0	34	39	9	2	3	2	0	0	89
Other	0	0	4	7	1	1	3	2	0	0	18
Unknown	1	0	2	6	4	1	1	1	2	19	37
Secular Peers	0	1	2	15	0	6	7	3	17	1	52
Misfiled	0	0	2	2	0	0	0	0	0	0	4
Total	**7**	**11**	**509**	**1055**	**419**	**213**	**160**	**164**	**64**	**44**	**2646**

'Abbots' also includes priors of religious houses which were not cathedrals.

'Deans' also includes cathedral priors, as well as subdeans and subpriors, acting alone.

'Deans & Chapters' includes cathedral priors, subdeans, subpriors or other named chapter officials sending a proxy jointly with the chapter.

'Archdeacons' includes one combined letter from an archdeacon and clergy.

'Other' includes deans of collegiate chapels, the master of the Order of Sempringham, the Prior of St John of Jerusalem in England, and a fifteenth-century clerical peer.

TABLE 2. PROXY APPOINTMENTS IN TNA BY REIGN AND SENDER

	Henry III	Edward I	Edward II	Edward III	Richard II	Henry IV	Henry V	Henry VI	Henry VIII	Unknown	Total
Bishops	1	17	97	228	86	30	22	27	8	5	521
Abbots	5	38	258	614	252	117	89	104	34	16	1527
Deans	0	6	33	47	31	12	5	9	3	1	147
Deans & Chapters	0	4	18	46	15	22	12	8	0	1	126
Chapters	0	10	41	62	21	15	4	6	0	1	160
Arch-deacons	0	15	18	26	1	7	14	2	0	0	83
Clergy	0	20	35	42	9	2	3	2	0	0	113
Other	0	3	4	7	1	1	3	2	0	0	21
Unknown	1	0	2	6	4	1	1	1	2	19	37
Secular Peers	0	1	2	15	0	6	7	3	17	1	52
Total	**7**	**114**	**508**	**1093**	**420**	**213**	**160**	**164**	**64**	**44**	**2787**

This table includes all the documents from SC 10, as well as 145 appointments from elsewhere in TNA which belong in SC 10 but have been filed in the wrong series or for which the letters themselves do not survive: the enrolled list of 103 senders of proxies in C 151/1, one letter each from C 146 and C 270, twenty-six letters from C 219 and fourteen letters from C 49. The four documents which belong in other series but have been misfiled in SC 10 have been omitted.

'Abbots' also includes priors of religious houses which were not cathedrals.

'Deans' also includes cathedral priors, as well as subdeans and subpriors, acting alone, as well as one joint proxy from a dean and archdeacon.

'Deans & Chapters' includes cathedral priors, subdeans, subpriors or other named chapter officials sending a proxy jointly with the chapter.

'Archdeacons' includes one combined letter from an archdeacon and clergy.

'Other' includes deans of collegiate chapels, the master of the Order of Sempringham, the Prior of St John of Jerusalem in England, two proctors of the clergy who sent their own proctors in their stead, and a fifteenth-century clerical peer.

the parliament of September 1353 which have found their way into a file in C 49,[65] along with one stray letter located in C 146 and another in C 270.[66] In total, if we add these appointments to those in SC 10 and deduct the four misfiled therein, this gives 2,787 appointments which should be in SC 10. As the *Vetus Codex* names are an enrolled list, this means there are 2,684 surviving letters of appointment, a minimum figure as documents may also lie undiscovered in other series.[67] That SC 10 represents only a partial record of proxy appointments can be demonstrated not only by the large list of proxies found in the *Vetus Codex* for which there are no corresponding survivals in SC 10, but also by reference to other ecclesiastical sources, such as bishops' registers, which contain details of appointments for which there is no corresponding document in The National Archives.[68] Denton and Dooley also calendared appointments surviving from other sources for the lower clergy in the period 1295–1340, such as cathedral and university libraries, county record offices and the British Library.[69] Sometimes a bishop or abbot appointing proctors would send a letter to the king to excuse his absence, making no mention of the names of his proctors.[70] In some cases, these have survived whilst the proxy appointments have been lost.[71] It is worth noting that SC 10 also contains evidence which fills out other sources. When we have bishops' registers, for example, letters in SC 10 have not often been entered in the register. Even where this was done fairly conscientiously, there are omissions: only six of Roger Martival's eight SC 10 letters can be found in his register.

The first three letters in SC 10 are undated but almost certainly relate to the parliament of February 1248 in London, making these amongst the earliest parliamentary records we possess, predating parliament rolls by many years. There is also a document which is probably from July 1260, although the first dated letter in the series (1/5) is from 1 September 1263. The final letter is from 18 February 1536, meaning that the documents in SC 10 span a period of 288 years. However, no proxy appointments survive between Henry VI's parliament in February 1447 and Henry VIII's in April 1523, a gap of seventy-six years. SC 10, in common with certain other parliamentary sources, contains no records from the reigns of Edward IV, Richard III and Henry VII.

Discounting the names from the *Vetus Codex* and the fifty-two appointments by secular peers, we have eleven letters from the thirteenth century, 2,014 from the fourteenth (including four from Henry IV's first parliament in 1399), 517 from the

---

[65] This is an indication that the proxy letters might not have all been together when created into a special collection, since four letters from the 1353 parliament are filed in SC 10.

[66] C 49 is King's Remembrancer: Parliamentary and Council Proceedings; C 146 is Ancient Deeds; and C 270 is Ecclesiastical Miscellanea.

[67] It should be noted that this does not equate to 2,683 proxy appointments, since duplicate letters for the same assembly survive in some cases.

[68] These will be listed in an appendix to the second volume.

[69] See the list of proctors in Denton and Dooley, *Representatives of the Lower Clergy*, pp. 103–21. Although a search of various county archives and cathedral record offices may turn up other 'lost' appointments, that is beyond the scope of this work.

[70] See 1/21 and 1/41, 2/58 and 2/59, 3/112 and 3/115, 3/117 and 3/118, 4/189 and 4/190, 4/200 and 5/221, 5/233 and 5/234, 6/700 and 7/701, 11/519 and 11/527, and 29/1442 and 29/1445.

[71] See 1/1, 1/3, 1/4, 1/16, 1/36, 2/72, 2/90, 3/116, 4/180, 6/287, 8/374, 9/408, 9/411, 11/512, 21/1024, 26/1228 and 51/2516.

fifteenth, and forty-seven from the sixteenth. Some four-fifths of the collection is thus from the fourteenth century, with around 42 per cent of the datable letters which survive coming from the reign of Edward III. There are no extant letters from some parliaments, and for several assemblies just a single letter survives, with ten or fewer letters extant for forty parliaments. Thirty or more letters survive for twenty-two assemblies (mainly under Edward II and Edward III). The 508 letters from Edward II's reign come from twenty-three assemblies, an average of twenty-two letters per meeting, the highest of any monarch in SC 10. It is perhaps no coincidence that the greatest number of letters surviving from a single parliament (sixty-three) is for the assembly of May 1322 at York. Although it opened after the battle of Boroughbridge, the writs of summons had been sent out before the king's decisive clash with the earls of Lancaster and Hereford. In the tense climate, it is entirely possible that many of the higher clergy in particular wished to avoid becoming embroiled in national politics.

More than twice as many letters survive from Edward III's reign than from his father's, but they come from nearly three times as many assemblies (sixty-two), an average of between seventeen and eighteen per assembly, lower than both Richard II (twenty-one assemblies, averaging just under twenty) and Henry IV (eleven assemblies, averaging over nineteen). Those averages then drop steadily, from between fourteen and fifteen for Henry V (eleven assemblies), to between twelve and thirteen for Henry VI (thirteen assemblies). An average of between six and seven letters then survive for Henry VIII's seven assemblies. These figures are calculated only for parliaments for which one or more letter survives in SC 10; including parliaments for which there are no survivals would change the figures dramatically, especially in the later period.

The majority of clerical letters come from the higher clergy; the documents from the reigns of Henry III and Edward I (and all but three from that of Henry VIII) are all from bishops and abbots. In the rest of the collection, the proxy appointments of abbots and (non-cathedral) priors form by far the largest group of surviving documents, accounting for around 56 per cent of the identifiable letters in SC 10. The next largest group is the appointments of the bishops, accounting for just under a fifth of the surviving documents. Combined, the proxy appointments of bishops and heads of religious houses (excluding cathedral priories) account for three-quarters of all surviving letters in SC 10. Certain individuals among the bishops and abbots merit mention for the number of proxy appointments for which they were personally responsible, with the following twenty-six men having fifteen or more surviving proxy appointments to their name.

Walter Fifehead	Abbot of Hyde near Winchester (1319–62)	30 letters
Dafydd ap Bleddyn	Bishop of St Asaph (1314–45)	27 letters
Adam of Boothby	Abbot of Peterborough (1321–38)	25 letters
Roger Yatton	Abbot of Evesham (1379–1418)	25 letters
Ralph de Borne	Abbot of St Augustine's, Canterbury (1310–34)	24 letters
Thomas de la Mare	Abbot of St Albans (1349–96)	24 letters
William Chiriton	Abbot of Evesham (1316–44)	23 letters
Richard of Draughton	Abbot of Bury St Edmunds (1312–35)	22 letters
Matthew of Englefield	Bishop of Bangor (1328–57)	21 letters[72]

---

[72]   This assumes 24/1165, which is damaged, comes from Englefield.

John Chynnok	Abbot of Glastonbury (1375–1420)	21 letters
John of Sherburn	Abbot of Selby (1369–1408)	21 letters
Roger of Thame	Abbot of Abingdon (1335–61)	20 letters
John of Aylsham	Abbot of St Benet of Hulme (1326–47)	20 letters
Richard of Charlton	Abbot of Cirencester (1320–35)	19 letters
Simon of Eye	Abbot of Ramsey (1316–42)	19 letters
William Methwold	Abbot of St Benet of Hulme (1365–96)	19 letters
Walter of Winforton	Abbot of Winchcombe (1360–95)	19 letters
John Deeping	Abbot of Thorney (1365–97)	19 letters
Thomas of Moulton	Abbot of St Mary's, York (1331–59)	19 letters
Walter Camme	Abbot of Malmesbury (1361–96)	18 letters
Richard Yateley	Abbot of Reading (1378–1409)	18 letters
Ralph of Shrewsbury	Bishop of Bath and Wells (1329–63)	17 letters
Henry of Overton	Abbot of Peterborough (1361–91)	17 letters
Thomas Chellesworth	Abbot of Malmesbury (1396–1424)	15 letters
Thomas Charwelton	Abbot of Thorney (1402–26)	15 letters
John Deeping	Abbot of Peterborough (1410–38)	15 letters

Although these 536 letters do not represent 536 appointments, since in a handful of instances more than one letter survives from the same individual for a parliament, it is noteworthy that just twenty-five individuals are responsible for almost a fifth of the documents found in SC 10. It is also telling that only three of the names on this list are bishops, all the others being abbots of the major houses. The list is overwhelmingly a fourteenth-century one; only Thomas Charwelton served his entire abbacy in the fifteenth century, with the tenures of four others beginning in the fourteenth century and ending in the fifteenth. Several of these men had long periods in office, in some cases more than thirty years, so it is perhaps unsurprising that a large number of letters have survived from them. This makes the example of Adam of Boothby, the third most prolific appointer of proxies surviving in SC 10, especially glaring, since he was abbot of Peterborough for only seventeen years. Several of these cases will be discussed in more detail below.

Amongst the lower clergy, around 16 per cent of the SC 10 letters relate to cathedrals (deans, priors and chapters). The remainder come either from archdeacons or from diocesan clergy. The majority of letters from the lower clergy are from the fourteenth century, but a handful date from the fifteenth century. Aside from the abbots' letters, there is considerable variation in the number of survivals from each of the twenty-one dioceses in England and Wales. At one end of the spectrum, 112 letters of appointment survive from the diocese of Worcester: twenty-three from bishops, forty from the priors of Worcester Cathedral, three from the subprior and chapter, thirty-nine from the chapter alone, three from archdeacons, and four from the clergy. 110 documents survive from the diocese of York: thirty-five from the archbishops (including one from the keeper of spiritualities *sede vacante*), two from the deans of York Minster, nine from the dean in combination with his chapter, thirty-six from the chapter alone, ten from archdeacons and eighteen from the clergy. 106 letters survive from the diocese of Durham, meaning that Durham, Worcester and York together account for almost a third of the extant letters from diocesan bishops and clergy. At the other end of the scale, almost nothing survives from the diocese of Canterbury, with just five letters from the archbishops and a single document from a prior of Canterbury Cathedral. Only seventeen letters can be found from Winchester (six from the bishops, five relating to the cathedral, one from an archdeacon and five from the clergy) and eighteen from Norwich (of which fifteen are from the bishops and the other three from the cathedral). Of the twenty-seven Salisbury survivals, a lone appointment – that of the cathedral chapter – is not from the bishop. Exeter (five) and Chichester (six) have a similar paucity of lower clergy appointments. The twenty-nine letters from Llandaff are all from the bishops, with no letters from the lower clergy surviving from that diocese. From Lincoln diocese there are appointments by bishops, by deans, subdeans and the cathedral chapter (in various combinations), and by archdeacons, but there are no letters from the clergy of the diocese.

Proportionately, the survival rate of the letters from the northern province is significantly better than of those from the southern one. Fifty-eight of the letters from diocesan clergy, or nearly two-thirds of the total, come from the dioceses of Carlisle (twenty-two), Durham (eighteen) and York (eighteen). Almost a third of cathedral-related appointments also come from the northern dioceses, along with more than a third of extant letters from archdeacons. Although numerically insignificant, the survival of lower clergy proctors from the three Welsh dioceses of Bangor, St Asaph and St Davids is especially interesting, since this was the only representation of Wales in the medieval parliament. Given the great losses among the medieval registers of the Welsh bishops,[73] SC 10 also makes available information about these dioceses which can be found nowhere else.

Even without the unanswerable question of how representative the survivals are of the total number of appointments originally made, the raw figures do not necessarily give the complete picture. Worcester Cathedral alone accounts for a fifth of surviving cathedral letters. However, the evidence suggests that this is because the priors of the cathedral invariably made their proxy appointments separately from the chapter, even if both appointed the same proctor(s). As a result, the forty appointments by the priors and the thirty-nine from the chapter have considerable overlap. The priors of Coventry Cathedral, on the other hand, almost always seem to have made their appointments jointly with the chapter, so that there are thirty-four joint appointments and just a single letter from the chapter alone. Similarly, there is only one letter from a dean of Bangor alone, alongside twenty from deans jointly with the chapter and none from the chapter by itself. Had Bangor or Coventry followed the Worcester practice, considerably more documents would survive from the two dioceses and the statistics would look quite different. Durham and Ely have a roughly equal split between letters from the dean or prior alone and appointments made in combination with the chapter. Differences in local practice thus have an influence on the number of letters emanating from individual dioceses.

The condition of the letters in SC 10 is highly variable. That the documents were not always stored with care is evident from the stains caused by water and other damage found on several letters. Some are fragments or very badly damaged, but there are actually very few from which no information whatsoever can be retrieved, even if an ultraviolet light is often required, and a good proportion

---

[73] On bishops' registers, see David M. Smith, *Guide to Bishops' Registers of England and Wales: A Survey from the Middle Ages to the Abolition of Episcopacy in 1646* (London, 1981); David M. Smith, *Supplement to the Guide to Bishops' Registers of England and Wales: A Survey from the Middle Ages to the Abolition of Episcopacy in 1646*, C&Y Centenary Supplement (2004).

of the letters remain in excellent condition. Several of the letters in file 51 are in a very poor state, with many of these being undatable. As was standard practice, letters were sealed. The strip by which the seal was attached survives on quite a few letters, although only in a handful of cases does the seal itself or a portion of it remain. The only one in good condition is that of the abbot of Peterborough on a letter sent in 1532 (51/2502), with a reasonable proportion of the abbot of Thorney's seal surviving on his letter of 1536 (51/2519); otherwise, the remaining few seals are badly worn or fragmented.[74] In the reign of Henry VIII, the practice of the sender personally signing the letters seems to have become fairly common.[75] Otherwise, all we have is the text of the letter, occasionally with an address written on the back. The writing and legibility of the letters varies greatly. Most were clearly penned fairly quickly as a functional text, and some require considerable effort to decipher, but a few of the letters are beautifully presented and presumably intended to impress. The letters of the bishop of Winchester in April 1309 (3/112 and 3/115) are elegantly written in a clear hand, with an unusual number of words (including place names) written out in full rather than abbreviated. One of the abbot of Crowland's letters from 1442 (50/2452) opens with an enormous, elaborate letter 'e' for the 'Excellentissimo', with similarly extravagant, oversized letters for the words 'domino', 'Henrico', 'Francie', 'Illustri', 'Domino' and 'Hibernie' in the course of the first line. This stands out against the neat but otherwise unremarkable text of the rest of the letter. The abbot of Winchcombe's letter in 1536 (51/2519) looks more like part of a book, written out impeccably on carefully ruled lines. There are other examples of elaborate opening letters and embellishments, but these were functional documents and for the most part the presentation of the letters reflects this fact.

Nearly all of the letters are in Latin, although a tiny number are in French (and two of the sixteenth-century letters from secular peers – 52/31 and 52/41 – are in English). With the exception of 4/187, which is the appointment of two proctors by the abbot of St Albans in 1316, the French letters are personal letters from bishops or abbots to the king, excusing their absence but not naming proctors; as noted above, these presumably complemented the appointment letters given to the proctors.

Most of the documents are letters close to the king, using similar wording. They are addressed 'to the most excellent lord prince' (*excellentissimo principi domino*), recite the royal titles in the relevant style, identify the sender, give a reason that the sender cannot attend parliament (which is usually identified by place and date, or by a direct quotation from the writ of summons), appoint proctors and outline relevant powers ceded to them, and are then dated in varying styles. Occasionally the king was addressed in a different form. 'To the most serene prince' (*serenissimo principi*) is the most frequently used (if still uncommon) alternative; this was the standard opening of Abbot William de Chiriton of Evesham, for example. 'To the noble prince' (*magnifico principi*) is also found on occasion. Sometimes the address bears

---

[74]   Fragments of seals are particularly numerous in the sixteenth-century letters in file 51: 51/2505, 51/2506, 51/2507, 51/2508, 51/2510, 51/2515, 51/2516, 51/2518, 51/2520 and 51/2521.
[75]   See 50/2481, 50/2482, 50/2485, 50/2489, 50/2490, 50/2492, 50/2496, 50/2498, 51/2504, 51/2505,51/2506, 51/2512, 51/2113, 51/2516, 51/2543 and 51/2524. The practice is also found in the letters of the secular peers: 52/30, 52/31, 52/32, 52/33, 52/34, 52/36, 52/39, 52/40 and 52/45.

hints of flattery or excessiveness. The letter of the bishop of Ely in May 1335 (19/943) was addressed 'to the most victorious and most excellent lord' (*victoriosissimo ac excellentissimo domino*), although most of Edward III's victories (save Halidon Hill in 1333) lay in the future. This is rare; for the most part, the letters are sober and formulaic.

A handful of letters are addressed to the archbishop of Canterbury, six of them from St Davids diocese for the parliament of May 1322.[76] In April 1309, the abbot of St Augustine's, Canterbury, addressed his excuses to the bishop of Chichester as chancellor (2/58). Occasionally, if it was known that a parliament would be held or started in the king's absence, the proxy letters are addressed to others. In 1313, Edward II summoned a parliament on 23 May to meet at Westminster on 8 July; on 1 July, while he was still in France, the king appointed the earls of Gloucester and Richmond and the bishops of Bath and Wells and Worcester to open and proceed with parliament until he returned.[77] The proxy appointment of the bishop of Norwich (3/114) and the letter of excuse for absence of the bishop of Winchester (3/115),[78] dated 10 June and 8 June respectively, are addressed to three of these four (the earl of Richmond is overlooked by both bishops), three weeks before the king gave them responsibility for parliament. The other letters for this assembly show no such knowledge, and this perhaps tells us something about the relationship of John Salmon of Norwich (a trusted royal counsellor) and Henry Woodlock of Winchester (the man who, although rarely at court, had crowned Edward and was unsympathetic towards the Ordainers) with the king and the place it gave them in royal counsel. On other occasions, the king was known to be out of the realm, as in July and November 1338 and February 1339, when Edward III was at Antwerp during meetings of parliament or great councils, in October 1339 when he was at Mont-Saint-Martin, and January 1340 when he returned to England after the planned opening date of parliament.[79] Many letters were addressed to the king as normal, but several were sent to Prince Edward as custodian of the realm.[80] Some indecisively addressed their letters to both the king and Prince Edward (21/1012), or to the king or Prince Edward (21/1026, 21/1050 and 22/1069), or 'to the king or the one holding his place in England' (21/1019), or 'to the king or the custodian of the realm' (21/1043).

A significant minority of the documents (just over a fifth) are letters patent. The majority of letters from cathedral chapters and diocesan clergy fall into this

---

[76] 8/358 (chapter of St Davids), 8/367 (clergy of St Davids), 8/373 (archdeacon of Carmarthen), 8/376 (archdeacon of St Davids), 8/377 (bishop of St Davids), 8/387 (archdeacon of Brecon) and 8/397 (archdeacon of Cardigan).

[77] *CCR, 1313–1318*, p. 66; J. R. Maddicott, *Thomas of Lancaster, 1307–1322: A Study in the Reign of Edward II* (Oxford, 1970), p. 150; J. R. S. Phillips, *Aymer de Valence, Earl of Pembroke 1307–1324: Baronial Politics in the Reign of Edward II* (Oxford, 1972), pp. 64–5; Seymour Phillips, *Edward II* (New Haven, CT, 2010), pp. 213–14.

[78] Interestingly Henry Woodlock's proxy appointment (3/112), in the same hand and bearing the same date and place, is addressed to the king.

[79] Edward's movements are taken from Ormrod, *Edward III*, p. 618. `

[80] 'Prince Edward, duke of Cornwall, earl of Chester and custodian [or keeper] of the realm': 21/1009, 21/1023, 21/1034, 21/1042; 'Prince Edward, duke of Cornwall and custodian of the realm': 21/1013, 21/1014, 21/1020; 'Prince Edward': 22/1077; 'Prince Edward, keeper of the realm': 22/1079.

category. As these were summoned indirectly and required to elect proctors rather than attend in person, there was no need to send excuses to the king, although surviving letters close from this source suggest that it was also customary to notify the king about the appointments. Where letters patent survive from abbots and bishops, these are probably the letters given to the proctors themselves to act as their credentials. There are some unusual examples. The bishop of Bangor (in 1344) and the abbot of Peterborough (in 1383) began with normal letters close to the king, but ended by making them letters patent (23/1141 and 35/1713). In 1414, the archdeacon of Huntingdon sent a witnessed notarial instrument (45/2201A).

In some cases, the documents can give us clues about the way in which proctors were appointed. There are instances of proxy letters for a parliament from the same person in which different proctors were appointed. In 1315, for example, Thomas of Sherborne, abbot of Winchcombe, appointed Hugh of Bristol in one letter (3/135), and Brother William of Gloucester and William de Boys in another (3/136). On 25 April 1322, Prior John Crauden of Ely issued a letter (8/392) appointing Brother John of Conington and Nicholas of Stockton as his proctors; the following day, another letter (8/359) named Brother John of Conington and John of Spanby. Several documents show evidence of indecision about proctors, or that the letters were sometimes written before the identity of the proctors had been determined. In 1371, the abbot of Winchcombe's letter of appointment (29/1448) names just one proctor, but this is followed by a large gap which closed with the plural 'clerks', clearly indicating the intention to appoint more than one man. The names of the two proctors in the letter of appointment from the prior and chapter of Carlisle in 1410 (43/2144) have been written in a different hand from the main text, using a darker ink than is found in the rest of the letter. For the same parliament, the abbot of Bardney's letter (43/2147) has three proctors, of which the middle name has been written in different writing into the middle of a space which is far too big. In 1423, the abbot of Ramsey appointed two proctors (48/2356). After the second name, Robert Poleyn, is a large gap with a faint line drawn across it. Since there is no change in handwriting or ink and no obvious break in the flow of the letter before this, it is possible that the option was left to appoint more proctors before the letter was sent. The abbot of Evesham's letter from 1432 (49/2412) has obviously had the names of the three proctors written into a space at a later stage in a different, neater hand, maybe indicating a degree of indecisiveness. In 1439 (49/2446), either the abbot of St John's, Colchester, or his scribe did not know the first name of the chancery clerk, John Bate, as this name has been written in later in a gap which was too large, the resulting space faintly scribbled through. There are also examples of errors or ignorance in the names of the proctors. The bishop of Winchester's appointment for July 1313 (3/112) simply has two dots where the initial of the prior of Southwark should be, indicating that the identity of the prior was probably not known to the scribe. In 1382 (34/1690), the archbishop of York's scribe named 'Thomas de Shirburn, abbot of Selby' as one of the archbishop's proctors; the abbot was in fact John de Sherburn, who had been in office since 1369.

For the parliament of May 1322, the letter from John de Canyng, abbot of Abingdon (8/385), was sent with a large gap before the year, clearly intended for the place and date but never filled in. Later in the year, for the November parliament, Canyng's letter (9/401) provided a date but no year, which was to become something of a habit for the scribes writing the letters of the abbots of

Abingdon; four out of the eight letters of Canyng's successors, Robert of Garford and William Cumnor, failed to supply years in the dating clause (13/626, 13/650, 14/678 and 18/853). Some letters have no date at all (3/136, 10/455 and 11/512), presumably intentionally. However, the letter from Louis de Beaumont, bishop of Durham, for the November 1322 parliament (9/420) simply ends 'dated at', with no place or date given, so clearly this was sent before anyone managed to fill in the missing details. Although other internal evidence, such as the date and place of the parliament, the name of the abbot or the names of the proctors, normally allows the letter to be dated, this is not always the case. It does not help that the date is sometimes recorded erroneously. 13/610 is a letter from the abbot of Bury St Edmunds for a parliament of Edward III at Westminster dated 'seventeenth day of the month of January in the third year of your reign', which is 17 January 1330. The problem with this is that this does not relate to any assembly; the first parliament of 1330 was held at Winchester in March and the writs for it were not issued until 25 January. It seems likely that the clerk has miscalculated the regnal year, perhaps unaware of exactly when in January Edward II was officially replaced by his son, and that this should actually read 'the second year of your reign' and relate to the February 1329 meeting. Similarly, 18/874A, from the abbot of Glastonbury, is dated 'sixth ides of February in the year of our Lord one thousand, three hundred and thirty-four [8 February, 1335 NS]'. The parliament referred to in the letter is clearly that of February 1334 at York, so unless the scribe has deviated from the practice of the year changing on 25 March, this is obviously a dating error.

More puzzling are the cases of mistaken identity in the names of the senders of proctors. In 1353, the bishop of Rochester was identified in his letter (C 49/46/39) as Thomas, whereas the new bishop was actually John of Sheppey. The last Thomas to hold the post had been Thomas Wouldham, who had died in 1317, after which Hamo Hethe had been in office for thirty-three years. It is hard to know who wrote this letter and how they made such a mistake. There are several instances of a space being left unfilled for the initial of a prior or abbot.[81] It is telling that these examples are all from individuals among the higher clergy. It could be envisaged that upon receiving the summons, a bishop or abbot might instantly decide whom to appoint and then have the letter written, but these occasional errors, alongside the evidence for uncertainty about the names of proctors, suggest that the appointment process was not always a tidy one. Presumably it was sometimes necessary to determine who might be willing to serve or who might be at parliament anyway, which may have created time pressures and caused the letters to be written before the decision about proctors had been taken. That the identity of the sender could be mistaken raises interesting – although unanswerable – questions about where and by whom some of these letters were written, although the simple fact of human fallibility should never be discarded. The demand for tidy theories says more about modern historians than about the medieval clergy.

THE HIGHER CLERGY IN SC 10

Clergy were summoned to parliament in two ways: directly by individual writ, and indirectly via the *praemunientes* clause on the writs sent to the bishops.

---

[81] Examples include 3/134 (prior of Bath, 1315), 9/430 (abbot of Ramsey, 1322) and 23/1101 (prior of Worcester, 1339).

Although the concept of peerage and the notion of a house of Lords was only in a developmental stage in the fourteenth century, it was those summoned by individual writ – the bishops and the heads of religious houses which were not cathedrals – who came to be seen as the clerical peerage, and who are considered here as the higher clergy. As already noted, it is from this group that the majority of documents in SC 10 derive.

The Bishops

The bishops were an integral part of the medieval parliament, with key officers of state usually drawn from amongst their number. For that reason, at least some bishops were usually present in every parliament and great council, their presence occasionally confirmed by a mention in the chronicles or parliament rolls, or by their appointments as triers of petitions. It is perhaps noteworthy that little survives in SC 10 from the three principal bishops of the southern province, the archbishop of Canterbury and the bishops of London and Winchester. The important place of the archbishop of Canterbury as both primate of the church and major counsellor to the king presumably explains why SC 10 contains evidence for only five occasions on which an archbishop sent proxies in his stead: Walter Reynolds in 1319 (6/282), Simon Meopham in March and October 1330 (13/640 and 13/649) and in 1333 (17/830), and Simon Sudbury in 1371 (30/1452 and 30/1453). The archbishops of York were less assiduous in personal attendance at parliament, with their appointments for thirty-three assemblies extant in SC 10. Geography could have played a part in the archbishops' reluctance to travel, with Salisbury, Winchester and Westminster an arduous journey from York in the Middle Ages. However, it is worth noting that all of these are in Canterbury Province, and most of the assemblies concerned took place at Westminster. It is more likely that ecclesiastical politics were a significant factor, with the question of precedence between the two archbishops a perennial source of tension.[82] It is notable that four of the five times on which the archbishop of Canterbury is known to have sent proxies were for assemblies in York Province. The fact that most parliaments took place within their diocese may explain why there is rarely evidence for the absence of the bishops of London; eight of the nine documents from them in SC 10 relate to parliaments away from London or Winchester (most at Lincoln or York). Only Robert Braybooke excused himself from a Westminster assembly, a few months before he died in 1404. A mere five documents concerning four parliaments survive from the incumbents of England's richest see, Winchester.

Generally speaking, as a body the episcopate appear to have taken their parliamentary duties seriously, although there was something of a division between conscientious bishops who almost never left their dioceses and episcopal officers of state who rarely saw fit to visit theirs. Foremost in the former category were men like Richard Swinfield of Hereford, a conscientious diocesan who spent most of his time on local affairs (especially his successful attempt to have his predecessor, Thomas Cantilupe, canonised) and visited London so rarely that in 1311 he let out his house there to Hamo Chigwell.[83] It can be questioned whether Swinfield ever

[82]   Roy Martin Haines, *Ecclesia Anglicana: Studies in the English Church of the Later Middle Ages* (Toronto, 1989), pp. 69–105.

[83]   The agreement was for two years at a rent of £10 a year: *Registrum Ricardi de Swinfield*

bothered to attend parliament, given that proxy appointments by him survive in the *Vetus Codex* and for nearly every parliament of Edward II's reign before the bishop's death in 1317. No letters from him survive for Edward I's reign, but given his complete lack of interest in parliament in later years this is more likely to be a result of the loss of the evidence than any sudden change of heart or disagreement with the new king. Roger Martival of Salisbury missed a minimum of eight assemblies in his fifteen years as bishop of Salisbury (1315–30), all of which were held at York or Lincoln. Like Swinfield, Martival spent little time outside his diocese, beyond a brief period as a negotiator between Edward II and the earl of Lancaster in 1319.[84] Of a completely different mentality were bishops like John Droxford of Bath and Wells. In 1309, Archbishop Winchelsey, a veteran of disputes with the crown, attempted to consecrate Droxford at the same time as Edward II had called a parliament at Stamford. Several bishops informed Winchelsey that they would be going to parliament rather than attending the consecration, including Droxford himself.[85] Even so redoubtable a man as Robert Winchelsey was unable to consecrate someone who declined to be present. Droxford was among the class of bishops who saw their state obligations as paramount, with ecclesiastical roles of secondary concern. The division between pastors and courtiers persisted throughout our period.

If SC 10 is not a complete record of proxy appointments, it probably gives a fairly accurate picture of how individual bishops related to parliament, at least in the fourteenth century. Except when an individual was noted as a trier of petitions, discovering whether a particular bishop attended a named parliament is rarely possible. A rare instance of the record of attendance is found in the register of John Grandisson of Exeter. This includes the writ of summons to a parliament at Winchester on 11 March 1330, a meeting for which no parliament roll survives. A marginal note tells us that this parliament was where 'where the Lord [Bishop] was present in person and the earl of Kent was beheaded'.[86] Clearly the execution of Edmund of Woodstock, tricked into believing Edward II was still alive, made a great impression of the bishop. In the case of Henry Woodlock of Winchester some information provided by the bishop was misleading. In answer to a writ ordering collection of money owed to the crown, and dated 16 November, 1306, Woodlock replied that he had received this on Christmas Eve but was now making his way to parliament; it was summoned to meet at Carlisle. In fact, he got no further north than his manor of Witney, in west Oxfordshire, and appointed proctors for this meeting.[87] On the other hand, following the parliament of April 1308, Woodlock wrote a friendly letter to Henry de Bluntesdon, archdeacon of

Episcopi Herefordensis 1283–1417, ed. William W. Capes, C&Y 6 (1909), pp. 467–8.

[84]   C. R. Elrington, 'Martival, Roger (*c*.1250–1330)', *ODNB*.

[85]   *Registrum Henrici Woodlock, Diocesis Wintoniensis, A.D. 1305–1316*, ed. A. W. Goodman, 2 vols., C&Y 43 and 44 (1940–1), vol. 1, p. 382; *Registrum Roberti Winchelsey, Cantuariensis Archiepiscopi A.D. 1294–1313*, ed. R. Graham, 2 vols., C&Y 51–2 (1952–6), vol. 2, p. 1113.

[86]   'Ubi Dominus personaliter interfuit et Comes Kancie decollatus est.' *The Register of John de Grandisson, Bishop of Exeter (A.D. 1327–1369): Part I, 1327–1330, with Some Account of the Episcopate of James de Berkeley (A.D. 1327)*, ed. F. C. Hingeston-Randolph (London and Exeter, 1894), p. 43.

[87]   *Reg. Woodlock*, vol. 2, p. 919. The appointment (vol. 1, pp. 158–9) is undated. For Woodlock's itinerary, see vol. 1, p. xviii.

Dorset, expressing disappointment that the two had not met up in London at the parliament after Easter.[88]

Perhaps unsurprisingly, the Welsh bishops are well represented in SC 10, the four dioceses in Wales accounting for more than a fifth of the letters from bishops overall. The Welsh cathedral cities – especially Bangor and St Davids – were a long, difficult journey from any English city in which parliament was held. All the major venues (London/Westminster, York, Lincoln, Winchester and Salisbury) were in the southern or eastern parts of the country furthest from Wales, requiring an expensive and hazardous journey for the Welsh bishops. The difficulties they encountered are highlighted by one of the letters in SC 10 from Henry Gower, bishop of St Davids, dating from 1336 (20/951). In a departure from the formulaic excuses of such letters, Gower explained that he had not had time to make arrangements to travel to parliament since the messenger had only found him at Llawhaden on the last day of February, with a writ for an assembly which commenced on 11 March in distant Westminster. The image this creates, of a royal messenger desperately roaming south-west Wales in search of a bishop, encapsulates the problem for the Welsh bishops. Their dioceses were remote, often with difficult terrain, and they had multiple castles and manors. Their sees were relatively poor, so repeated summons to parliament in a short period of time would have taken their toll, making it understandable that they frequently sent proctors rather than journey to England with an expensive episcopal retinue. SC 10 has plenty of examples from two long-serving Welsh bishops, Dafydd ap Bleddyn of St Asaph and Matthew de Englefield of Bangor. That saving money was a consideration in Wales is suggested by the way in which the various clerical elements within a diocese often combined to send the same proctor or proctors to represent them. For the parliament of May 1322, David Fraunceys, the rector of Johnston in Roose, was given the St Davids proxy appointments of the bishop, the cathedral chapter, and the archdeacons of Brecon, Cardigan, Carmarthen and St Davids (8/358, 8/373, 8/376, 8/377, 8/387 and 8/397).

There were occasions when individual bishops were not summoned or actually commanded not to attend parliament by the king. In the former case, the was usually because the king had fallen out with a particular bishop, as happened with Edward I and Robert Winchesley of Canterbury, Edward II and both Walter Langton of Coventry and Lichfield and Henry Burghersh of Lincoln, and Edward III and Adam Orleton of Hereford, Worcester and Winchester. On other occasions, bishops might be spared a summons because their services were required elsewhere. In 1313, for example, the bishops of Carlisle and Durham were both explicitly ordered to stay in their dioceses to defend the north against the Scots and to send proctors to parliament in their stead, although only Richard Kellaw of Durham's proxy appointment now exists in SC 10 (2/97).[89] Sometimes bishops were granted life exemptions on health grounds.[90] However, in some cases this

[88] *Reg. Woodlock*, vol. 2, pp. 706–7.
[89] *CCR, 1307–1313*, p. 568; *Registrum Palatinum Dunelmense: The Register of Richard de Kellawe, Lord Palatine and Bishop of Durham 1311–1316*, ed. Sir Thomas Duffus Hardy, 4 vols., RS 62 (London, 1873–8), vol. 2, p. 912.
[90] There is a list of these exemptions in J. S. Roskell, 'The Problem of the Attendance of the Lords in Medieval Parliaments', *Bulletin of the Institute of Historical Research* 29 (1956), 153–204; reprinted in J. S. Roskell, *Parliament and Politics in Late Medieval England*, 3 vols.

may have been a recognition of reality rather than an act of generosity by the king. One of those granted such a life exemption was Wulstan of Bransford, bishop of Worcester, in 1340. Bransford had only become bishop the previous year, but had been prior of Worcester Cathedral since 1317 and as SC 10 and cathedral records show, had frequently sent proctors to represent him in parliament. The exemption granted Bransford in 1340, renewed in 1342 and lasting until his death in 1349, may have been less to do with his health than a realisation by the king that the new bishop of Worcester was not about to change his habits.

Bishops generally amenable to their parliamentary duties probably had various motives for sending proctors on some occasions. Finance was possibly one. It has plausibly been suggested that since 'a bishop necessarily travelled in state and had to take many of his household with him for the upkeep of his establishment', it would 'cost a bishop very little by comparison' to send proctors.[91] For example, the *Historia Roffensis* records that in May 1322, the bishop of Rochester's five weeks away from his diocese to attend parliament at York cost him £33,[92] not an insignificant sum. Politics may have played a part; that eleven bishops missed the March 1330 parliament at Winchester, at which the earl of Kent was condemned, may have reflected a desire not to become too closely involved in the increasingly violent tensions between the king on the one hand and his mother and Mortimer on the other.

The ten bishops from Canterbury province who appointed proxies for the Carlisle parliament in January 1307 simply may not have relished the trek to the far north-west in the middle of winter. There were also ten southern province bishops who sent apologies to York in January 1333. Travelling north in winter may not have been especially appealing for many bishops. However, the dispute between the two archbishops may also have played a part. After a particularly poor turn-out from the southern clergy at York in 1322, Archbishop Reynolds informed the king that his clergy were not obliged to attend meetings in the northern province, although admittedly letters from just four bishops survive in SC 10.[93] Naturally, the kings tried to compel their bishops and other senior clergy to attend their parliaments. From 1305, it was standard practice to include a line in the writs urging personal attendance; this was changed in 1334 to a more severe wording forbidding non-attendance.[94] However, the king was occasionally irritated by the bishops' habit of sending proctors to represent them, and some writs contain direct orders to the prelates to attend in person and not to send proxies on any account.[95] This

---

(London, 1981–3), vol. I, article II.

[91]   Dorothy Bruce Weske, *Convocation of the Clergy: A Study of its Antecedents and its Rise with Special Emphasis upon its Growth and Activities in the Thirteenth and Fourteenth Centuries* (London, 1937), p. 82.

[92]   *Anglia Sacra, sive Collectio Historiarum, Patrim Antiquitus, partim recenter Scriptarum, de Archiepiscopus et Episcopis Angliae, a Prima Fidei Christianae susceptione ad Annum MDXL*, ed. Henry Wharton, 2 vols. (London, 1691), vol. I, p. 362.

[93]   *PW*, II.ii, 259; *The Registers of Roger Martival, Bishop of Salisbury 1315–1330*, ed. C. R. Elrington, K. Edwards, D. M. Owen and S. Reynolds, 4 vols. in 5 parts, C&Y 55, 57–9, and 681 (1959–75), vol. 2, pp. 394–8; Clarke, *Medieval Representation and Consent*, p. 144; Denton and Dooley, *Representatives of the Lower Clergy*, p. 51.

[94]   Roskell, 'Problem of the Lords', p. 156.

[95]   For example, the parliaments of April 1328, October 1328, March 1332 and February

command was interpreted somewhat liberally by those bishops who decided to send proctors anyway. Sometimes the excuses must have been received particularly badly by the monarch; it would be interesting to know, for example, what Edward II made of John Dalderby missing the parliament in his own cathedral city in 1316, an assembly which was already meeting in a tense atmosphere.

The majority of individual bishops for which large numbers of documents survive in SC 10 were active in the reigns of Edward II and Edward III. This is to be expected, given that the majority of the collection dates from this period. The total number of letters for the fifteenth century, as already noted, is considerably smaller than for the fourteenth century, and the proportion of them coming from bishops falls from the reign of Henry IV onwards. Robert Lancaster of St Asaph is the only one of the fifteenth century bishops to have a significant number of his proxy appointments surviving in SC 10.

In the gap between the 1440s and the 1520s, for which no documents survive in SC 10, the political and ecclesiastical scene changed dramatically. Aside from two letters from 1523, all the sixteenth-century appointments in SC 10 relate to sessions of the Reformation Parliament (1529–36). The status of the church (and therefore its leaders, the bishops), was in question, and after Thomas Wolsey's fall from favour in 1530 and the move towards the break with Rome, it would be expected that the bishops would want to defend their position and dignity. What is surprising is that in reality the bishops, apart from men like John Clerk of Bath and Wells (who received several proxy appointments for the Reformation Parliament), had little interest in being present in parliament at a time of such major tension and change. If, as has been suggested, many of the bishops were 'conservatives' who 'found parliamentary business distasteful',[96] it is hard to see why they would have made the effort to have themselves represented by proxy. Episcopacy as a concept was never a matter of debate for Henry VIII, so unlike the heads of religious houses, the bishops as a group were not under threat from the Reformation, even if individuals among their number incurred the king's displeasure. As a consequence, it may have suited the bishops to avoid any distasteful involvement with the king's 'great matter' while continuing to have representatives in parliament to keep them informed. Careful political consideration may well explain the final set of appointments in this series.

Across the entire period covered by SC 10, most of the excuses given in the bishops' letters of appointment are routine and formulaic. Some cited royal business as a reason for being absent, usually when the king had sent them on a foreign mission or required them to organise defence in their sees. Others gave as their excuse the fact that urgent business in their diocese was detaining them, although this excuse was used far less frequently by bishops than by abbots. Commonly, bishops excused themselves on the grounds of illness, occasionally a grave illness or being at death's door. Sometimes this rings true, since the bishop died not long after parliament.[97] On other occasions, bishops spent years or even decades sending

1339: *RDP*, IV, pp. 381, 386; Roskell, 'Problem of the Lords', pp. 156–7.

[96]   Stanford E. Lehmberg, *The Reformation Parliament 1529–1536* (Cambridge, 1970), p. 39.

[97]   To take some examples from the early fourteenth century, Geoffrey Fromond of Glastonbury appointed proctors on 4 November 1322 (9/417) for the parliament due to open at York on the 14th and died on the first or second day of the assembly. William of Odiham, abbot of Hyde near Winchester, missed both parliaments held during his brief

apologies on health grounds. Only rarely are the excuses given in any detail, such as that from Roger Martival (which comes from his register rather than SC 10) for the assembly at Lincoln in July 1316, from which the bishop of Salisbury absented himself on the grounds of an illness he had caught at convocation in London.[98] For the most part, however, the excuses lack such detail, and can on occasion be presumed to cover other reasons. Even allowing for this, it is worth noting that compared with the other section of the higher clergy, the abbots, the bishops were extremely conscientious in their parliamentary duties.

The Heads of Religious Houses

For the most part, SC 10 demonstrates that the attendance record of the heads of religious houses at parliaments was extremely poor. That over half of the proxy appointments come from this source is an indication of how unimportant the abbots generally regarded their personal presence in parliament to be. Admittedly, the heads of religious houses formed the largest group of clergy summoned in the early years of parliament, with over a hundred being summoned on occasion, such as in 1265. Large numbers of abbots and priors continued to be summoned, when they were invited to parliament, into the early years of the fourteenth century. Seventy-nine abbots and three heads of religious orders (but no priors) were summoned to Lincoln for the 1301 assembly. There is little discernible pattern to the lists of summons in the reigns of Henry III and Edward I, with those representing large, wealthy foundations accompanied by the heads of tiny, fairly insignificant foundations. During the reign of Edward II, the list of parliamentary abbots and priors was significantly reduced as parliament assumed a more stable format. Although there were often meetings without heads of religious houses (or representatives of shires and boroughs) in the first decades of parliament, the assembly of January 1327, which deposed Edward II and was atypical in many respects, was the last one to which no heads of religious houses were summoned.

Early in the reign of Edward III, the list began to stabilise and it seemed as though the twenty-nine heads of religious houses summoned in 1339 would be a permanent list. However, some abbots saw their parliamentary summonses as a burden and pressed for removal from the list. The abbot of Beaulieu was exempted from parliamentary attendance in 1341, and after him the abbot of St Augustine's, Bristol (1343), the abbot of Thornton (1343), the prior of Spalding (1343), the master of Sempringham (1343), the abbot of Osney (1346), the abbot of Leicester (1352) and the prior of Lewes (1365) all disappeared permanently from the lists of summons. The abbots of Battle and Shrewsbury disappeared from the lists of summons for a while under Edward III but reappeared later in the century. Despite some fluctuations, from the reign of Richard II the list of summons usually

---

abbacy (1317–19). Peterborough's Godfrey of Crowland died less than two months after sending proctors to the 1321 parliament, although he had also missed he previous five meetings; his successor, Adam of Boothby, died a little over a fortnight after the opening of the November 1338 great council, but as his attendance record was arguably the worst of any individual in SC 10, illness probably made little difference.

[98]   'Verum quia ab infirmitate que in novissimo tractatu ante festum nativitatis sancti Johannis Baptiste London' habito nos arripuit nondum curamur ad plenum cujus pretextu hac vice dicto tractatui nequimus absque corporis nostri periculo medicorum judicio et prout nos ipsi sentimus personaliter interesse.' *Registers of Martival*, vol. 2, pp. 112–13.

included twenty-five abbots (two Augustinian and twenty-three Benedictine) and the prior of St John of Jerusalem in England.[99]

Seventy-one houses are represented in SC 10, roughly divided into four groups. There are also some surprising omissions, such as the fact that there are no extant letters from Osney Abbey, despite the fact that its abbot was regularly summoned until 1346. Twenty-six make only a single appearance,[100] of which fifteen are found together in a single parliament, that of March 1332, which will be discussed shortly. Of the other ten, the abbot of Abbotsbury appears in Henry III's reign, with the abbots of Buckland, Byland, Faversham, Jervaulx, Northampton (if the identification of a damaged letter is correct), Sherborne and Welbeck, and the priors of Lewes and St Frideswide's all found during the reign of Edward II. A further nineteen houses account for between two and eight letters each.[101] The most interesting of these is Waltham, which was a fixture on the list of summons across the period yet accounts for just four letters in SC 10. The heads of five abbeys sent between sixteen and twenty-one letters apiece which have survived in SC 10.[102] Most notable in this group are the abbots of Westminster. Westminster Abbey was one of the major foundations, but unlike the heads of other major houses, the abbots rarely seem to have sent excuses for parliament, probably because it was so frequently held in their abbey, and the abbot of Westminster occasionally appears on the list of triers of petitions in the parliament rolls. In total, these forty-nine houses, more than two-thirds of the number represented in SC 10, account for 191 identifiable letters. The final group, consisting of twenty-one houses, accounts for more than six times as many documents as these other groups combined, with 1,284 identifiable documents. In general, then, the trend in SC 10 reflects that in the lists of summons, of a move from a large, disparate group of 'parliamentary' abbots and priors to a smaller, more obvious elite. It is worth noting that there is an added

---

[99]   Augustinian abbots: Cirencester and Waltham. Benedictine abbots: Abingdon, Bardney, Battle, Bury St Edmunds, St John's Colchester, Crowland, Evesham, Glastonbury, Hyde near Winchester, Malmesbury, Peterborough, Ramsey, Reading, Selby, Shrewsbury, St Albans, St Augustine's Canterbury, St Benet of Hulme, St Mary's York, St Peter's Gloucester, Thorney, Westminster and Winchcombe. In the early Tudor period, Tewkesbury, Tavistock and Burton-upon-Trent were also on the list.

[100]   The abbots of Abbotsbury, Bordesley, Buckland, Byland, Faversham, Jervaulx, Sherborne, Tewkesbury, Welbeck and Wellow, and the priors of Bodmin, Coxford, Lancaster, Launceston, Lewes, Nostell, Repton, St Frideswide's Oxford, St German's, St Michael's Mount, Thurgarton, Torre, Tutbury, Westacre and Wilmington. The twenty-sixth is 8/372, which is damaged but from the abbot of a house dedicated to St James. This is probably Northampton Abbey, but as the place name has been lost and it is simply dated 'in the aforementioned monastery', this cannot be stated with certainty. Taking into account the *Vetus Codex* would add the names of twelve abbots (Alnwick, Chertsey, Coombe, Netley, Newhouse, Quarr, St Agatha, St Radegund, Swineshead, Tupholme, Vaudey and Waverley) and the master of the Order of the Temple. The abbot of Torre is an interesting case as his only appearance in SC 10 (in 1404) is extremely late.

[101]   Bourne (2) Bridlington (2), Burton-upon-Trent (2), Lessness (2), Meaux (2), Croxton Kerrial (3), Fountains (3), Furness (3), St Augustine's Bristol (3), Stanley (3), Sempringham (4), Waltham (4), Beaulieu (5), Order of St John of Jerusalem in England (5), Rievaulx (5), Spalding (6), Hailes (7), Pershore (7) and Barlings (8). The abbots of Barlings, Croxton Kerrial, Furness and Jervaulx also sent proxies which are enrolled in the *Vetus Codex*.

[102]   Battle (16), Leicester (16), Westminster (18), Thornton (19) and Shrewsbury (21).

complication in reviewing the evidence of the proxy appointments of the abbots, since heads of religious houses or orders occasionally sent proctors even when they were not included on the list of summons. The two most notable cases saw twelve and thirteen uninvited abbots send proctors to parliament in January 1307 and March 1332 respectively.[103]

On occasion, the information about the abbots in SC 10 can also provide details about politics not necessarily found in other sources. A good example of this is the parliament of March 1332. This was a highly unusual assembly, with two lists of abbots on the enrolled summons.[104] The second explicitly states that the summons was being issued to abbots and priors not usually summoned to other parliaments, going on to name twenty-eight heads of religious houses (although the abbot of Bardney was somehow placed on both lists). Several of these had certainly been summoned under Edward II and sent proxies on previous occasions which survive in SC 10. Others make a sudden and puzzling appearance on the list of summons, having not been invited to parliament since the reign of Edward I (if at all), with no trace of them anywhere in SC 10. More confusing is the fact that thirteen of the fifteen abbots and priors whose only appearance in SC 10 is for this parliament do not actually appear to have been summoned; only the names of the abbots of Byland and Tewkesbury can be found on the enrolled list. It is notable that there is a distinct south-western bias in these fourteen uninvited abbots, including several minor Cornish houses, whereas the additional heads summoned had a fairly broad geographical spread across England.

The writ of summons for March 1332 made specific reference to the crusade Edward III was planning with Philip VI of France 'and other Catholic kings and princes', a theme developed by the archbishop of Canterbury and the bishop of Winchester in the opening sermons and an intention apparently approved by the assembly.[105] It is possible that with war in the Holy Land and on behalf of Christendom under consideration, the king wanted to consult as widely as possible with representatives of the church. However, while this might explain the additional heads who were actually summoned, it does not satisfactorily explain the presence of so many uninvited proctors representing priors from the diocese of Exeter. An alternative explanation is that Edward III was preparing for the marriage of his sister Eleanor to the count of Flanders. To finance the royal wedding, the king sent 295 letters on 26 June, seeking aid from all bishops, deans and chapters, and a large number of heads of religious houses.[106] Those on both lists of summons and the uninvited contingent were amongst those asked for money, but so were many more heads not invited to or represented in parliament that March. Again, although the parliament roll is silent on the matter, it is plausible that Edward was preparing the ground for begging financial assistance by inviting some of the medium-sized houses to parliament, but this still does not explain

---

[103] In 1307, found in the *Vetus Codex* rather than SC 10, these were the abbots of Abingdon, Bindon, Chertsey, Crowland, Easby, Hyde near Winchester, Netley, Quarr, Stoneleigh, Swineshead, Warden and Waverley. The March 1332 case is discussed below.

[104] *RDP*, IV, 865.

[105] *PROME*, iv, 166. For discussion of this, see Ormrod, *Edward III*, pp. 181–3.

[106] *CCR, 1330–1333*, pp. 587–93; A. K. McHardy, 'Paying for the Wedding: Edward III as Fundraiser 1332–3', in *Fourteenth Century England IV*, ed. J. S. Hamilton (Woodbridge, 2006), pp. 43–60.

why so many heads of foundations in Devon and Cornwall would take it upon themselves to send proctors.

Far more likely to explain the SC 10 evidence is something specific to the diocese of Exeter. Bishop John Grandisson was in dispute with the crown (as had been his predecessor Walter Stapeldon) about the status of the church at St Buryan's, a small collegiate church in south-west Cornwall. At issue was the question of whether St Buryan's was a royal free chapel or subject to the ordinary jurisdiction of the bishop of Exeter.[107] There was some heat in the argument between crown and bishop, but it seems strange that Grandisson would chose to mobilise the support of some of the foundations in his diocese on this one occasion, especially when the main subject of the parliament was a potential crusade. A more likely explanation lies in another dispute Grandisson was engaged in, this one with the archbishop of Canterbury, Simon Meopham. Meopham was one of the more tactless and less skilled occupants of the throne of St Augustine, his relatively brief tenure marked by disputes with his suffragan bishops, the archbishop of York and the pope. One of the policies which made him unpopular with the other bishops was his zealous habit of undertaking visitations of the dioceses in his province. His plan was for a visitation of Exeter during 1332, an intention against which Grandisson reacted with fury and which very nearly led the archbishop to be involved in a pitched battle outside Exeter in June.[108] Given Meopham's unpopularity with his fellow-bishops (who would later back Grandisson when the question of the Exeter visitation came before a provincial council), the bishop may well have thought that parliament was an ideal place to push his case against the archbishop and requested several of the priories in his diocese to send proctors to give him numerical support. It may not have been entirely displeasing that such a move would probably have also aggravated the king. The objection to this theory could be that not all of the thirteen houses appointing proctors were in Exeter diocese or in the dioceses Meopham had already irritated by undertaking visitations. We cannot be certain why proctors for thirteen uninvited heads of religious houses turned up in March 1332, but without SC 10, we would know nothing about this incident, a reminder that the series contains evidence not found elsewhere.

For the most part, though, the evidence in SC 10 relating to heads of religious houses derives from the most obvious source, the group which became the parliamentary abbots. Eighty-five letters come from the abbots of Peterborough, more than 3 per cent of the identifiable documents in the whole of SC 10. Peterborough was well placed for parliaments in Westminster, York and the East Midlands, so it is reasonable to assume that the abbots of this house did not see their participation in parliament as a priority. Seventy-nine documents from Evesham indicate a lack of inclination on the part of the abbots of the Worcestershire house to journey to parliament. The abbots of St Benet of Hulme clearly felt a similar disinclination to leave the peace of the Norfolk Broads for sessions of parliament, with seventy-six of the letters in SC 10 coming from them. There are seventy-two survivals

[107]   The case is discussed fully in Buck, *Politics, Finance and the Church*, pp. 90–6.

[108]   'Annales Paulini', in *Chronicles of the Reigns of Edward I and Edward II*, ed. William Stubbs, 2 vols., RS 76 (London, 1882–3), vol. I, pp. 356–7; *Adae Murimuth Continuatio Chronicarum, Robert de Avesbury de Gestis Mirabilibus Regis Edwardi Tertii*, ed. E. M. Thompson, RS 93 (London, 1889), p. 65.

from Hyde Abbey near Winchester and seventy-one from Ramsey.[109] The other major sources are: Malmesbury (sixty-eight); Selby (sixty-six); Glastonbury and Thorney (sixty-four apiece); Cirencester and St Mary's York (sixty-two each); Bury St Edmunds (fifty-nine); St Peter's Gloucester (fifty-eight); Reading (fifty-seven); Abingdon (fifty-five); Bardney, Crowland and Winchcombe (all fifty-one); St Albans (forty-seven); St Augustine's Canterbury (forty-six); and St John's Colchester (forty). In most cases, there is a reasonable spread across the period, although with most documents from the fourteenth century. The exception is Bardney, for which there are no surviving letters before 1332.[110]

As noted earlier, particular abbots count for a disproportionate number of the letters in SC 10. For the most part, the excuses of the heads of religious houses were formulaic and mundane, a trend demonstrated by examination of some of the serial non-attenders. Peterborough's Adam of Boothby missed his first parliament in May 1322 on the singularly uninformative grounds that he was hindered by a 'legitimate reason' (7/342). By November, his excuse for not travelling to York was ill-health (9/418). In June 1325, he cited 'various reasons touching us and our monastery' (10/460), which by the November parliament had become 'various and urgent reasons' (11/504). The urgency seems to have vanished by July 1328, which still did not prevent Boothby from missing parliament (12/560). In March 1330, he claimed 'various difficult reasons and business' (13/618), which by October had become 'difficult and unexpected business' (13/641), although by the time he sent a supplementary letter appointing more proctors three days before the latter parliament began it was back to 'various difficult reasons and business' (14/660). Thereafter, nearly all of his frequent excuses until his death in 1338 related to ill-health, explained with varying degrees of extravagance, with the exception of an instance in February 1337 when he seems briefly to have recovered his health sufficiently to miss parliament on the grounds of difficult business once again. It was a brief respite, the ill-health returning for the next parliament and keeping him from parliament for the remaining months of his life. It is hard to miss Boothby's determined lack of interest in travelling to parliament. A similar sentiment can be detected in Walter Fifehead, the individual responsible for the greatest number of letters in SC 10. As he was abbot of Hyde near Winchester for forty-three years (1319–62), it is perhaps unsurprising that so many documents survive from him, but the veracity of his excuses is open to question. For the final six parliaments of Edward II's reign, Fifehead – at that stage a new abbot – claimed ill-health, although on both occasions in 1325 he additionally cited 'unexpectedly serious infirmity' (7/316, 8/391, 9/406, 9/428, 10/464 and 10/497). Given that he had another thirty-seven years of life left in him, his condition cannot have been too serious. He briefly toyed with a 'necessary reason' in 1328 (12/573), before returning to illness of varying degrees of severity, then simply sending letters patent in which he avoided naming the reason for his absence (although it is plausible that these were included in letters close to the king, since lost). Unless Fifehead was both particularly sickly and particularly lucky to survive his poor health for so long, it is hard to avoid the conclusion that he had no desire to attend the king's parliaments and councils.

---

[109]   The Ramsey figure is seventy-two if the damaged 1/7 derives from that house.
[110]   This is perhaps explained by the turbulent opening to the century experienced by the Lincolnshire house: Alison K. McHardy, 'The Great Bardney Abbey Scandal, 1303–18', in *Fourteenth Century England VII*, ed. W. Mark Ormrod (Woodbridge, 2012), pp. 31–45.

These examples are not atypical. The overwhelming majority of the abbots' proxy appointments cite unspecified ill-health or infirmity, if not being on the brink of death, or else some undefined kind of essential and urgent business, as the reason that personal attendance at parliament is simply not possible. For good measure, an abbot exceptionally combines all these reasons in an onslaught of justification. Sometimes the excuses are credible, especially where an abbot died not long afterwards. However, for the most part it appears that the heads of religious houses hid behind standard, intentionally vague reasons to evade parliamentary duty. For that reason, the occasional deviation from the normal form of excuse stands out. Selby Abbey seemed to suffer from problems with finance and fabric, or at least claimed to do so. In 1354, the abbot, Geoffrey Gaddesby, referred to problems caused by the flooding of their most important lands by the River Ouse (26/1280). In 1391, Abbot John of Sherburn combined the standard claims about ill-health with a reference to the state of need in which his house found itself, meaning that he could not personally attend without subjecting the house to great expense (37/1847).[111] He made a similar claim with slight changes of wording in 1404 (41/2049), as did his successor William Pigot in 1410 (43/2145). Interestingly, this did not prevent them appointing two proctors in 1391 and four in both 1404 and 1410, although it is possible that all would have been at parliament anyway and therefore would not require payment from Selby. Sherburn had been named as a proctor for Archbishop Alexander Neville of York in 1382 and 1383 (34/1690 and 34/1684), parliaments for which no letters of appointment survive from him, so he was presumably not averse to parliamentary attendance, at least in his early days. Like so many heads of religious houses, however, he soon preferred to be represented by others rather than travel in person. For the abbots, participating in parliament rarely seems to have been important.

Even in the sixteenth century, in the turbulent days of the early Reformation, very few abbots felt the need to be present in the House of Lords to discuss matters which were so critical to the church and to their own positions. By this stage, not only was the time of parliamentary abbots drawing to a close, but the religious houses themselves were in their final years (although this is clear only in hindsight). For the most part, it seems that the major abbots either supported or at least did not obstruct royal policy in Henry VIII's divorce from Katherine of Aragon and then the dissolution of the monasteries, and in consequence their personal attendance in the House of Lords remained rare. Just three abbots opposed the king, none strongly or especially vocally.[112] Thomas Marshall or Beche of St John's, Colchester, had served as the proctor of the abbot of St Peter's, Gloucester in 1529, when he was the abbot of Chester. Both he and Hugh Cook, abbot of Reading, may well have attended sessions of the Reformation parliament (there are no proxy appointments for them in SC 10), with their dissident views leading to them being executed late in the decade. Richard Whiting of Glastonbury seems to have evaded parliament and sent proctors in his stead, but he would become the most graphic victim of the dissolution of the monasteries, hanged on Glastonbury Tor in 1539. Otherwise, this element of the House of Lords simply resigned meekly

---

111   'Quia domus nostra in tanta penuria casualiter est collapsa nosque tam grandi corporis infirmitate sumus continue lacessit quod in instanti parliamento vestro […] quam dispendio domus nostre predicte et corporis nostri periculo personaliter esse non valemus.'

112   Lehmberg, *Reformation Parliament*, pp. 43–4.

into the history books. There is little evidence that the abbots had any collective policy or used parliament as a forum to fight against their demise; they had as little interest in their parliamentary end as they had had in their parliamentary beginning.

THE LOWER CLERGY IN SC 10

It is ironic that the proctors of the lower clergy, whose inclusion in church and royal councils of the early and middle thirteenth century contributed largely to the growth of parliament as a national representative body, should have been almost entirely overlooked by most parliamentary historians.[113] Only the fortuitous discoveries, in monastic accounts, of sums of money to pay diocesan proctors rescued this element of parliament from complete oblivion in twentieth century historiography.[114] Yet, ironically again, it is this aspect of the clergy in parliament which alone has been subject of detailed scholarly scrutiny.[115]

Historians of parliament have identified a number of occasions in the later thirteenth century when the lower clergy were present in national assemblies: 1247, 1253, 1254 and 1269.[116] In 1295 the so-called 'Model Parliament' saw the whole range of lower clergy summoned for the first time: cathedral deans (and the priors of monastic cathedrals) and archdeacons who were to attend in person; cathedral chapters to be represented by one man; and the diocesan clergy – whatever the size of the diocese – to send two representatives. From 1295, when the lower clergy were summoned to parliament, they were warned to attend. This warning was a subsidiary clause in the writ of summons of the bishop himself, the *praemunientes* clause.

From 1311 to the March parliament of 1340 the clergy were summoned in this way on twenty-four occasions out of the forty-two meetings described as 'parliaments' in this period.[117] But during these years the procedure for calling the clergy and ensuring their attendance underwent several changes; sometimes the lower clergy were only warned to attend, but on other times they were ordered to do so, by writs of *venire faciatis* sent to the archbishops, making them responsible for ensuring that their bishops obeyed the king's summons. On those occasions the crown mandate was sent to the two archbishops for execution; the archbishop of Canterbury then forwarded this to the bishops of the southern province through the bishop of London.[118] In theory the conscientious bishop then reported to his metropolitan that he had obeyed the order, and recorded this in his register.

---

[113]   See n. 16 above.

[114]   See nn. 17–20 above.

[115]   Denton and Dooley, *Representatives of the Lower Clergy*; see also now *The Records of Convocation III: Canterbury 1313–1377*, ed. Gerald Bray (Woodbridge in association with the Church of England Record Society, 2005), pp. 351–98, though this is not error-free.

[116]   Maddicott, *Origins of Parliament*, pp. 159, 202, 214–5, 268–9.

[117]   The occasions were Dec. 1311, Sept. 1314, Jan. 1315, Jan. 1316, July 1321, May 1322, Feb. 1324, Jan. 1327, Sept. 1327, Feb. 1328, July 1328, Oct. 1328, March 1330, March 1332, Feb. 1334, Sept. 1334, May 1335, March 1336, Sept. 1336, March 1337, Feb. 1339, Oct. 1339, Jan. 1340 and March 1340. Further details and references are in Denton and Dooley, *Representatives of the Lower Clergy*, pp. 19–20. For the complete list of parliaments see the list in *Handbook of British Chronology*, ed. E. B. Fryde, D. E. Greenway, S. Porter and I. Roy, 3rd. edn (London, Royal Historical Society Guides and Handbooks, No. 2, 1986), pp. 552–9.

[118]   Denton and Dooley, *Representatives of the Lower Clergy*, p. 21.

These warnings and commands were indeed heeded. Evidence was gathered by Denton and Dooley from every diocese in which registers survive,[119] and although it was in most sees incomplete and scrappy this fact probably owed more to variations in local chancery practice and record-keeping traditions than to reluctance to answer the summons.[120] Particularly rich and rewarding are the register of John Dalderby of Lincoln (1300–20), which remains unpublished,[121] and the edited registers of Roger Martival of Salisbury (1315–30), who before his elevation had been a residential canon at Lincoln, and whose register is unusually full and well organised.[122] Further evidence is found in registers published more recently. Thus we find William Melton, archbishop of York, exercising his provincial authority by forwarding the writ of summons to the bishops of Durham and Carlisle in 1336, and ensuring that this command was obeyed within his own diocese by ordering the official of the court of York to see that it was carried out, in both 1328 and 1336.[123] Similarly, the register of Bishop John Stratford of Winchester has Stratford reporting in 1327 on his execution of the order. He concluded, 'the archdeacon of Winchester, however, is well known to be abroad and could not be cited.'[124] In the following year the registrar carefully recorded the summons to the parliament at York, but made the return that the writ arrived too late for it to be executed.[125] Twice, however, in 1324 and 1327, Stratford reported that he had executed the writ to the best of his ability, and the names of those cited were on the annexed schedule; but these were not copied into the register.[126] The next big change came after the parliament of March 1340. From that date execution of the *praemunientes* clause in the writ of summons to bishops was not enforced.

In considering these forty-five years some comments may be made. Both 1295 and 1340 were occasions when relations between crown and church were severely strained, as exemplified by tensions between the kings and the archbishops of Canterbury (Edward I and Robert Winchelsey, and Edward III and John Stratford), and had become so against a background of foreign warfare and the domestic problems caused by the imposition of high taxes.[127] The contest between Edward I

---

[119]   Chichester and the Welsh dioceses have no surviving registers from this time.

[120]   Denton and Dooley, *Representatives of the Lower Clergy*, pp. 18–39. Three registers noted there have since been printed: *Calendar of the Register of Simon de Montacute Bishop of Worcester, 1334–1337*, ed. Roy Martin Haines, Worcester Historical Society, New Series 15 (1996); and *The Register of John Kirkby Bishop of Carlisle 1332–1352, and the Register of John Ross Bishop of Carlisle, 1325–32*, ed. R. G. Story, C&Y 79 and 81 (1993 and 1995).

[121]   Lincolnshire Archives Office, Lincoln Register 3, Dalderby (Memoranda).

[122]   Martival's registers have been published; see n. 81 above. Martival was dean of Lincoln 1310–15, and during this time he kept canonical residence at the cathedral: Kathleen Edwards, *The English Secular Cathedrals in the Middle Ages* (Manchester, 1967), pp. 332–3.

[123]   *The Register of William Melton archbishop of York 1317–1340, vol. III: Diverse Littere*, ed. Rosalind M. T. Hill, C&Y 76 (1988), nos. 161, 268–70.

[124]   *The Register of John de Stratford, Bishop of Winchester, 1323–1333*, ed. Roy Martin Haines, Surrey Record Society 42 (2010) and 43 (2011), vol. 1, no. 294, 4(?) Nov. 1327. Philip Sapiti, archdeacon from 1325, was dead by 6 Jan. 1328: Le Neve, *Fasti: Monastic Cathedrals*, p. 50.

[125]   *Reg. Stratford*, vol. 1, nos. 391–2.

[126]   *Ibid.*, nos. 1, 294.

[127]   J. H. Denton, *Robert Winchelsey and the Crown 1294–1313: A Study in the Defence of Ecclesiastical Liberty* (Cambridge, 1980), especially pp. 55–176; Prestwich, *Edward I*, pp. 401–35; Roy Martin Haines, *Archbishop John Stratford: Political Revolutionary and Champion of the Liberties of*

and Winchelsey was the worst between king and primate since Henry II's contest with Becket, leading to the crisis of 1297, while in 1340–1 Stratford consciously took Becket as his model when challenged by Edward III. The development, in these intervening years, of the two provincial convocations, at whose meetings the clergy voted their direct taxation to the crown, may explain the monarchs' lack of interest in compelling the lower clergy to attend. Alongside this was the development of the mechanism by which the clergy became responsible for collecting the taxes they granted to the crown.[128] Nor must we forget that during these years the crown derived large sums by creaming off a considerable percentage of the taxes levied by the papacy upon the English church.[129] The convocation of Canterbury province, which carried the overwhelming majority of the clergy's taxable value, was very often held immediately before, but more usually after, or even coincidently with, meetings of parliament. Perhaps posterity has tended to contrast the two bodies to a greater degree than contemporaries would have done; in practice there was considerable overlap between them. Some appointments of proctors for convocation have strayed into SC 10,[130] while in 1419 the archdeacon of Leicester used a single letter to name his three proctors both for the parliament called for 16 October at Westminster, and for the convocation called for 30 October in St Paul's (46/2299).

Parliament, meanwhile, was developing judicial powers in the years before 1340, and it has been speculated that the clergy were unwilling to attend a lay court.[131] Even had the lower clergy been able to pick which of the crown's demands they chose to obey, there was every incentive for them to continue to maintain close connections with parliament. The years 1295–1340 were, as can be seen in retrospect, the golden age of the private petition, when clergy of every rank presented petitions to the king in parliament requesting the removal of grievances and the exercise of mercy and grace.[132] What is certain is that these years witnessed a rise in the size of the crown's bureaucracy, and it would be unsurprising if king's clerks wished to unload some of its functions on to bishops, making them responsible for calling the clergy of their dioceses to parliament.

Contrary to what was once believed,[133] the year 1340 did not mark the end of

---

the English Church, ca. 1275/80–1348 (Toronto, 1986), pp. 214–327; Ormrod, *Edward III*, pp. 212–46. A discussion of these taxes can be found in W. M. Ormrod, 'The Crown and the English Economy, 1290–1348', in Bruce M. Campbell (ed.), *Before the Black Death: Studies in the 'Crisis' of the Early Fourteenth Century* (Manchester, 1991), pp. 149–83.

[128] W. E. Lunt, 'The Collectors of Clerical Subsidies', in *The English Government at Work 1327–1337*, 3 vols. (Cambridge, MA, 1940–50), vol. II, pp. 227–80.

[129] Lunt, *Financial Relations of the Papacy to 1327*, pp. 366–418; W. E. Lunt., *Financial Relations of the Papacy with England 1327–1534* (Cambridge, MA, 1962), pp. 75–94.

[130] For example, two letters of appointment from Hereford diocese, the president and chapter, and the archdeacon of Salop, in 1413: 44/2185 and 44/2186.

[131] See the discussion in Pollard, *Evolution of Parliament*, pp. 187–215.

[132] Dodd, *Justice and Grace*, pp. 49–88. The series is TNA SC 8 (Ancient Petitions), whose images may be freely downloaded. See also *Petitions to the Crown*, ed. Dodd and McHardy; and M. Phillips, 'Church, Crown and Complaint: Petitions from Bishops to the English Crown in the Fourteenth Century', University of Nottingham Ph.D. thesis (2013).

[133] Clarke, *Medieval Representation and Consent*, pp. 140, 150; Reich, *Parliamentary Abbots*, p. 361; Miller, *Historical Studies*, vol. I, p. 17. None of these scholars, apparently, knew of the existence of the series SC 10.

the lower clergy's attendance in parliament.[134] Only one instance has been found of lower clergy who were reluctant to comply with the new model of summons. When summoned to an archidiaconal meeting in connection with a call to parliament in 1362, the clergy of Worcester archdeaconry 'with one voice replied and alleged that they were neither bound nor accustomed, from time immemorial, to choose any proctor to attend the king's parliament nor any other council of proctors or magnates, save at the command of the lord archbishop of Canterbury'.[135] They therefore humbly begged to be excused. This response was exceptional, for between 1340 and the end of the century fifty-one parliaments were held, and the files of SC 10 show that the lower clergy appointed proctors to represent them for at least thirty-six of these. Between 1340 and 1400 the *praemunientes* clause was executed on a considerable scale in the dioceses of Carlisle, Durham, Lincoln and York. Less activity is observable in Bangor, London and Worcester, while sporadic examples of such compliance can be seen in Chichester, Ely and Exeter. Every element of the lower clergy can be observed obeying this summons: deans of secular cathedrals, priors of monastic cathedrals (in much greater numbers), cathedral chapters, archdeacons, and diocesan clergy. While it is true that the number of letters never reaches double figures for any parliament, the years for which there is no evidence are interspersed randomly over the period, and there is no falling off towards 1400.

This evidence comes from files 23 to 40 of SC 10. Supporting material is found in bishops' registers and chapter act books and, since this rarely coincides with the SC 10 letters, it adds to the argument that the later fourteenth century saw no cessation of parliamentary activity by the lower clergy. Appointing representatives was a greater effort for the diocesan clergy than for any other group. In dioceses with one or two archdeaconries the choice of proctors was quite straightforward, but in larger sees more layers of organisation were required. In some dioceses it looks as though only part of the see was represented, as happened in London where the clergy of Colchester, one of its four archdeaconries, sent their own proctors three times in Richard II's reign.[136] Similarly, the clergy of the archdeaconry of Cleveland, in the diocese of York, sent proctors to parliament in February 1388 (37/1808).

The diocese of Lincoln provides evidence for the execution of the *praemunientes* clause during the later fourteenth century and beyond. John Buckingham, newly arrived in his diocese in September 1363, sent three proctors to represent him. The original appointment survives in SC 10 (29/1411), and the appointment was registered among his memoranda.[137] Twice more in his episcopate both the original and 'file' copies of his appointments survive.[138] In 1369 both the writ of summons and an unaddressed mandate to execute were recorded in the memoranda.[139] Most informative is a commission dated 15 October 1381. Addressed to the abbot of St

---

[134]   The following paragraph is drawn from McHardy, 'Representation of English Lower Clergy', pp. 97–107, where more detailed references may be found.

[135]   Worcestershire Archive and Archaeology Service, Register of John Barnet (Worcester), f. 11.

[136]   Nov. 1384, 1385 and 1393: see 35/1735, 36/1767 and 38/1894.

[137]   Lincolnshire Archives Office, Register 12 (John Buckingham, Memoranda) f. 10v.

[138]   Feb. 1383: 35/1709 and Reg. 12, f. 260; 1385: 36/1757 and Reg. 12, f. 312.

[139]   Writ of summons 6 April 1369; mandate to execute 4 May 1369: Lincolnshire Archives Office, Reg. 12 (Buckingham, Memoranda), f. 69v.

James', Northampton and Thomas Boyvill, rector of Seaton (Rutland), it commanded their presence on the following Monday in All Saints church, Northampton. The commissaries' duties were to receive the certificates about the preliminary elections which had been held in each archdeaconry, to ensure that parliamentary proctors were duly elected, and to report back to the bishop.[140]

In a thirty-five year episcopate (1363–98) this is meagre evidence, even allowing for the bishop's lifetime exemption from attending parliament which was granted on 3 December 1384.[141] But, in addition to the memoranda evidence, the collection of writs addressed to Buckingham contains twenty-three summonses to parliament, and fourteen of these are followed by notes of execution of the *praemunientes* clause. From these we learn that although All Saints, Northampton, was the usual place for the diocesan meeting to elect parliamentary proctors, twice, in 1373 and 1380, the election took place in St Mary *ad Pontem*, Stamford.[142] We also learn, on occasion, the names of those presiding at these elections.[143] What were never recorded, in either register, were the diocesan proctors' names.

Among the commissaries' duties was arranging for the proctors to be paid their expenses,[144] and entries about this cost (found in manorial accounts) provide the third source of evidence that the diocesan clergy continued to attend parliament after 1340. We have already noted that evidence stretching up to 1400 was found in the archives of Crowland Abbey and of Merton College, Oxford.[145] Another example has since been discovered; in 1393 the rector of Longbridge Deverill (Wiltshire) paid 15*d* towards the expenses of the clerical proctor attending the parliament at Winchester that year.[146] This is noteworthy as there is otherwise no evidence of Salisbury diocesan proctors in parliament. It seems likely that similar evidence from financial records will come to light.

Finally, at the end of the fourteenth century comes vivid confirmation of the importance of the lower clergy as an essential element in the 'community of the realm'. In late September 1399, when Henry Bolingbroke was pressing his cousin Richard II to resign the throne, he was careful to ensure that representatives of every element of the political community were present to witness King Richard's renunciation. The witnesses were the archbishop of York and the bishop of Hereford, two earls, two barons, the prior of Canterbury and the abbot of Westminster, two knights, and 'Master Thomas Stow and Master John Burbach, doctors'.[147]

---

[140] *Ibid.*, f. 229.

[141] *CPR, 1381–1385*, p. 484.

[142] *Royal Writs Addressed to John Buckingham Bishop of Lincoln, 1363–1398*, ed. A. K. McHardy, C&Y 86 and Lincoln Record Society 86 (1997), nos. 157, 213.

[143] *Ibid.*, nos. 157, 267, 274, 293, 341, 496.

[144] The note of execution after the writ of summons to what would be called Richard II's 'Revenge' parliament of September 1397 is especially full: *ibid.*, no. 496.

[145] Lowry, 'Clerical Proctors', pp. 224–55; Page, *Estates of Crowland Abbey*, p. 63.

[146] Longleat House Ms. 10699, m. 4. Thanks are due to T. C. B. Timmins for this reference.

[147] G. O. Sayles, 'The Deposition of Richard II: Three Lancastrian Narratives', *Bulletin of the Institute of Historical Research* 54 (1981), pp. 257–70. This may be conveniently consulted in translation in *Chronicles of the Revolution 1397–1400*, ed. and trans. Chris Given-Wilson (Manchester, 1993), pp. 162–3. In addition to the two doctors, the recording notaries, Master Denis Lopham and Master John Ferriby, were also clerics.

The new century and new dynasty saw no lessening of the lower clergy's attendance in parliament. The Lincoln tradition of executing the *praemunientes* clause was continued by Buckingham's successor but one, Philip Repingdon (bishop 1405–19). On 26 January 1414 he ordered the sequestrator in the archdeaconry of Leicester to cite the archdeacon's official for his contempt in failing to execute the king's writ of summons to the forthcoming parliament at Leicester; he had failed to cite the clergy of that archdeaconry to attend a meeting to elect two 'suitable and sufficient proctors', in conjunction with representatives of the other archdeaconries.[148] Repingdon's concern that the *praemunientes* clause be executed is supported by contemporary evidence from SC 10. From Henry IV's reign forty-five appointments of proctors survive, mostly from cathedral chapters (thirty-six), followed by archdeacons (six), diocesan clergy (two), and one dean acting alone; most acted in concert with their chapters. From Carlisle the evidence of diocesan proctors persists longest; diocesan proctors were sent to the autumn parliament of 1404, and again to the 1410 parliament (42/2084 and 44/2158). The pattern scarcely changed under Henry V; there are eighteen appointments by chapters, or deans (including priors and sub-deans) and chapters acting together, twelve appointments by archdeacons, and three by the clergy, in each case of Carlisle diocese. Only under Henry VI is there a tailing off, but this parallels the dropping off of the evidence for bishops and abbots. Thus between 1423 and 1447 there are thirteen chapter appointments, and one each by an archdeacon and by diocesan clergy, once more from Carlisle.

Even had the *praemunientes* clause never been obeyed there was no danger that the lower clergy would be unrepresented in parliament. It was they, after all, who administered parliament, and were thus essential to its meetings and functioning. Those prominent in parliamentary business, notably the receivers of petitions, were the most popular proctors for the ecclesiastical peers, and in the Yorkist period, a complete blank in the SC 10 series, there is considerable evidence for the presence of members of the lower clergy, albeit higher members of the lower clergy, namely archdeacons, in parliament.[149] A new century and dynasty did not end the attendance of the lower clergy after 1500, for the chapter of Wells elected proctors for parliament, as did the chapter of Lincoln in 1536.[150]

Why, then, is there so little evidence for the attendance in parliament of the lower clergy? Even their best publicist has called them 'parliament's invisible men'.[151] Lower clergy are notably absent from the official record, the rolls of parliament. The main evidence of their presence comes from clerical *gravamina* and related responses to this particular form of common petition, including statutes.[152] Otherwise, we have very little to demonstrate the presence of the lower clergy in parliament. The evidence from ecclesiastical records is little more substantial.

[148]   *The Register of Bishop Philip Repingdon 1405–1419*, ed. Margaret Archer, vol. II, Lincoln Record Society 58 (1963), pp. 377–9.

[149]   Hannes Kleineke's forthcoming book on the Yorkist parliament will include a chapter on the clergy.

[150]   Eric Kemp, 'The Origins of the Canterbury Convocation', *Journal of Ecclesiastical History* 3 (1952), p. 142; Lincoln Archives Office, Lincoln Dean and Chapter Wills, II, f. 44.

[151]   Maddicott, *Origins of the English Parliament*, p. 367.

[152]   W. R. Jones, 'Bishops, Politics and the Two Laws: The *Gravamina* of the English Clergy, 1237–1399', *Speculum* 41 (1966), 209–45.

Bishops' registrars did not systematically record the receipt of summonses to parliament, or, if they did, rarely bothered to indicate that the *praemunientes* clause had been executed.[153] The recording of the receipt of writs of every kind, and the noting of any resulting action, was the object of a rise and fall, from the late thirteenth century until the first third of the fifteenth century.[154] It would be unkind to call this a fashion, for the changes reflected not only the pressures upon bishops' chanceries, but wider social forces too. Much more important, for registrars, was to record the appointment of their bishops' proctors, whether for parliament, or for any other matter, such as legal proceedings. Even then, their responses were no better than sporadic.

By the time meetings of parliament were becoming a permanent place in the nation's public life, bishops' record-keeping was well established, with certain classes of acts regarded as worthy of systematic record. By contrast, parliament was a recent innovation. Similarly, both parliament and convocation were well established before the regular keeping of their proceedings' records began. In the course of the fourteenth century parliament's importance was recognised by bishops and their staff, but the way that information about calling and attendance might be registered in more than one place – among the writs or with the memoranda – suggests that registrars were not entirely sure how to classify, record and file this material. Above all, perhaps, it was the temporary nature of the parliamentary proctors' powers (however wide these were) which prevented their records being thought worthy of inclusion among the subjects for permanent preservation at the end of an episcopate.

Another question concerns the meagre evidence about the lower clergy within the files of SC 10. We could argue that the comparative abundance of material from the northern province is explained by the fact that the York convocation, unlike Canterbury's, did not happen very close (in either time or place) to parliament, so there was a greater incentive to ensure representation. Moreover, Carlisle and Durham dioceses did not have the links to those in crown service which made informal and regular contact more likely.[155] This does not explain, though, the large amount of material from the diocese of Worcester.

A certain amount of what can only be called 'clumping' of evidence hints at how much of such material we have lost. For example, from the large diocese of Lincoln, with its eight archdeaconries, there survive only thirteen appointments of proctors by archdeacons, but eleven of these date from after 1400. More remarkable, of the six appointments by archdeacons in Lincolnshire (1404–17), five were by one man. Was Hugh Hanworth, archdeacon of Stow from 1402 to 1419, uniquely conscientious in fulfilling his parliamentary obligations?[156] And why should the diocese of Wells, conspicuous by its low presence in this series, give

[153]   An exception can be found in the register of Edmund Lacy, bishop of Exeter (1420–55), where the execution of the *praemunientes* clause was recorded up to 1450.

[154]   Collections, or even complete registers of writs, can be identified in Smith, *Guide to Bishops' Registers*; see also *Royal Writs addressed to John Buckingham*, ed. McHardy, pp. xii–xvi.

[155]   The contributions made by their non-resident canons are discussed by Edwards, *English Secular Cathedrals*, pp. 83–101.

[156]   1414 2: 44/2187 and 45/2223; 1416 (2): 45/2243 and 46/2251; 1417 (1): 46/2276. Stow, a small archdeaconry in north-west Lincolnshire, was traditionally held by a member of the bishop's household.

us four appointments for one parliament, in 1439?[157] Since we are always told to assume that stray examples of any object are typical, and in no way exceptional, we can only assume that these represent random survivals of once considerable material. This still leaves the question: why were the letters of bishops and abbots preserved in considerably greater numbers than those of the lower clergy? It is not inconceivable that the letters of the higher clergy were simply considered more important.

There is an interesting footnote to the theoretical place of the lower clergy in the medieval parliament. It is worth noting that although not acted upon for some centuries, the *praemunientes* clause remained in the writs of summons to the bishops well into the twentieth century.[158] In one of those strange quirks of the British constitution, the presence of proctors continued to be explicitly requested a century after the abolition of proxy voting, even though it is highly unlikely anyone would have known what to do had a dean, archdeacon or clerical proctor turned up in the Palace of Westminster to attend a session of parliament. The connection between the summoning of parliament and convocation had presumably been the reason for retaining the *praemunientes* clause, but changes to convocation now made it entirely redundant. The clause was finally dropped by means of the Crown Office (Writs of Summons) Rules 1969. This was part of a wider reform of the governance of the Church of England, which included the passing of the Church of England Convocations Act 1966 and the Synodical Government Measure 1969, which saw General Synod come into being in 1970. Announcing the change to the House of Lords, the lord chancellor, Lord Gardiner, noted that he wished to avoid the fate of Richard Cammell, dispatched to the Fleet Prison by the Lords in February 1621 for issuing writs of summons 'in other Form than heretofore had been accustomed, and therein, contrary to the Honour of this House, omitting certain Words accustomed and fit to be inserted in such Writs'.[159] In an explanation welcomed by the bishop of Coventry on behalf of the lords spiritual, Lord Gardiner treated the peers of 1969 to a brief explanation of the historical roots of the *praemunientes* clause, noting that it had long been obsolete and was thus a very minor change.[160] It is perhaps a fitting comment on a clause so little heeded even by medieval historians that something devised under Edward I should survive, practically unnoticed, until the days of Harold Wilson.

---

[157]   The archdeacon of Wells, the chapter of Bath Cathedral [Abbey], the dean of Wells, and the chapter of Wells cathedral: 49/2440, 49/2442, 49/2448 and 49/2450.

[158]   See, for example, the template for a writ of summons from early in Elizabeth II's reign printed in 'Appendix III: Archbishop's or Bishop's Writ of Summons to a New Parliament', *Parliamentary Affairs* 7 (1953), 138–9. The writ includes among the (arch)bishop's duties: 'Forewarning the Dean and Chapter of your Church of [ ] and the Archdeacons and all the Clergy of your Diocese that the said Dean and Archdeacon in their proper persons and the said Chapter by one and the said clergy by two meet Proctors severally having full and sufficient authority from them the said Chapter and Clergy at the said day and place be personally present to consent to those things which then and there by the Common Council of Our said Kingdom (by the favour of the Divine Clemency) shall happen to be ordained.'

[159]   *Journal of the House of Lords*, vol. 3, pp. 11, 13–15.

[160]   *Hansard: House of Lords Debates*, 11 November 1969, vol. 305, cc. 523–6.

EDITORIAL PRACTICE

The documents in SC 10 have been calendared in tables arranged chronologically by parliament, and within parliaments the numerical sequence of SC 10 is followed. Documents drawn from other series in TNA are placed at the end of each parliament, with full reference given. This volume contains the appointments from 1248 to Edward III's death in 1377; the second volume will calendar those and other material from the accession of Richard II until the end of monastic representation. All editorial additions are given in square brackets.

LANGUAGE AND LETTER TYPE

All documents are letters close and in Latin unless otherwise noted in the text.

PLACE-NAMES

Names of dioceses, cathedrals, archdeaconries, priories and abbeys have been given in the modern English form. Other place-names (for example, in dating clauses) have been identified, when possible, with their modern spelling following the form given in Eilart Eckwall, ed., *The Concise Oxford Dictionary of English Place-Names* (4th edition: Oxford, 1960). The historic English and Welsh counties have been used for identification. Unidentified places are indicated between single quotation marks.

PERSONAL NAMES

Bishops' names follow the spelling in E. B. Fryde, D. E. Greenway, S. Porter and I. Roy, eds., *Handbook of British Chronology* (3rd edition: London, 1986). Surnames of heads of religious houses are supplied, where possible, from David M. Smith and Vera C. M. London, eds., *Heads of Religious Houses: England and Wales II: 1216–1377* (Cambridge, 2001); conflicts between this volume and SC 10 are noted in the text. In the few instances where the full name of the sender of a document is found in the text, a standardised form of the name is found in square brackets. Christian names are given in their modern English form, if one exists, but some Welsh names are left unmodernised. The spelling of surnames is highly inconsistent. All are given as in the documents, with square brackets providing a consistent form where the name is obviously a toponym or known from other sources, to provide for ease of cross-referencing. Major variants are noted in Appendix 4 of this volume. For the proctors, the title provided in the letters – M. (*Magister*), D. (*Dominus*) and F. (*Frater*) – have been retained, although it should be noted that these are not always consistent.

IDENTIFICATION

An asterisk after a proctor's name identifies those proctors for whom further details are provided in Appendix 4 of this volume.

DATES

Multiple styles of dating were used by the senders of letters in SC 10. Where the date relates to a feast day or a saint's day, this style has been retained with the equivalent date given in square brackets. Dates given in Roman style (kalends, ides and nones) and regnal years have been translated silently into a modern style, and all Roman numerals and written numbers have been rendered in Arabic numerals, unless the dating clause is insufficiently complete to permit translation or its reliability is uncertain. All dates from 1 January to 24 March are given in new style.

ABBREVIATIONS USED IN THE CALENDAR

CoP	The proctor was the clerk of parliament for the parliament concerned.
F	The document is in French.
LP	The document is a letter patent.
MP	Member of Parliament for the parliament in question, with the constituency noted. Where a proctor was an MP in a parliament other than the one for which he was a proctor, this is noted in Appendix 4.
RoP	The proctor is named in the parliament roll as one of the receivers of petitions for the parliament concerned.
*	Denotes a proctor about whom further details are provided in Appendix 4.

SC 10/1/1. Undated letter close from the abbot of St Benet of Hulme excusing his absence from parliament. It is likely that this is one of three letters for the assembly of February 1248, the earliest documents in SC 10 and amongst the earliest parliamentary records to survive.

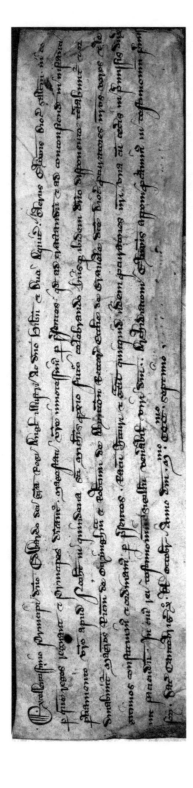

SC 10/1/33. Letter close from the clergy of Ely diocese appointing Richard de Ottringham and Robert de Abington to represent them in the Northampton parliament of October 1307. The clergy of each diocese were meant to appoint two representatives when summoned under the praemunientes clause; this letter is in many ways a standard example of the period.

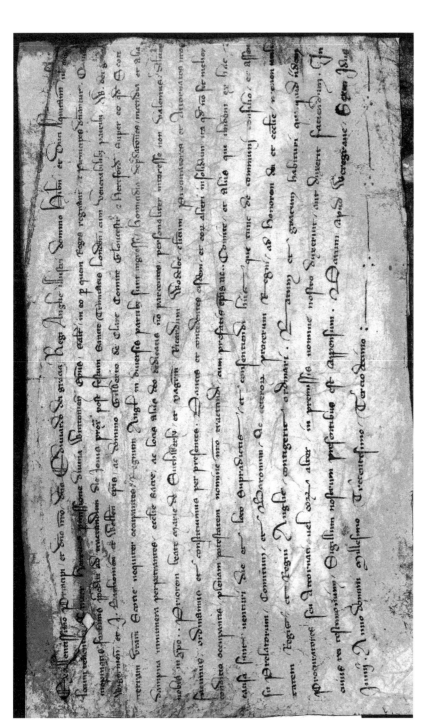

SC 10/3/112. Letter close from Henry [Woodlock], bishop of Winchester, naming the prior of Southwark and Richard Woodlock as his parliamentary proctors for the June 1313 assembly at Westminster. The hand is unusually elegant.

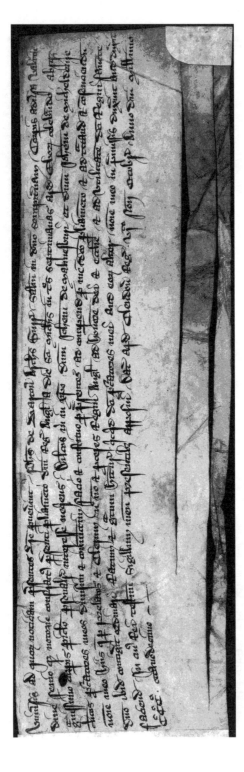

SC 10/6/251. Letter close from Philip de Barton, archdeacon of Surrey (Winchester diocese), appointing John de Malmesbury and John de Micheldever as his proxies for the October 1318 parliament at York. Although archdeacons were meant to attend parliament in person when summoned through the bishop, this is one of several examples of them appointing proxies to be found in SC 10.

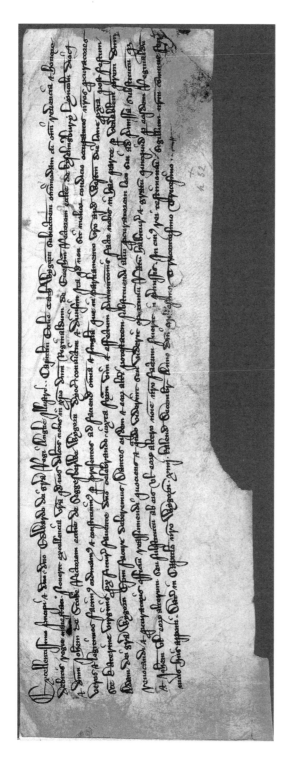

SC 10/14/693. Letter close from the Chapter of Worcester Cathedral naming Reginald de Evesham and John de Stoke to represent them in the Westminster parliament of November 1330. Under the praemunientes clause, cathedral chapters were only meant to appoint one proctor, although this stipulation was rarely observed.

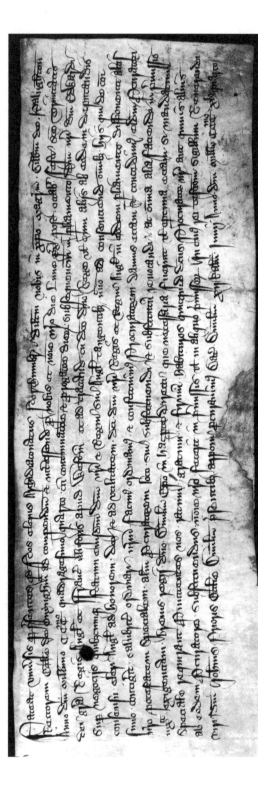

SC 10/24/1176. Letter patent from the clergy of Northumberland archdeaconry (Durham diocese) appointing Gilbert de Halghton as their proctor in the June 1344 parliament at Westminster. Many of the surviving letters patent are clergy appointments. Clergy often appointed their representatives by archdeaconry rather than as a whole diocese.

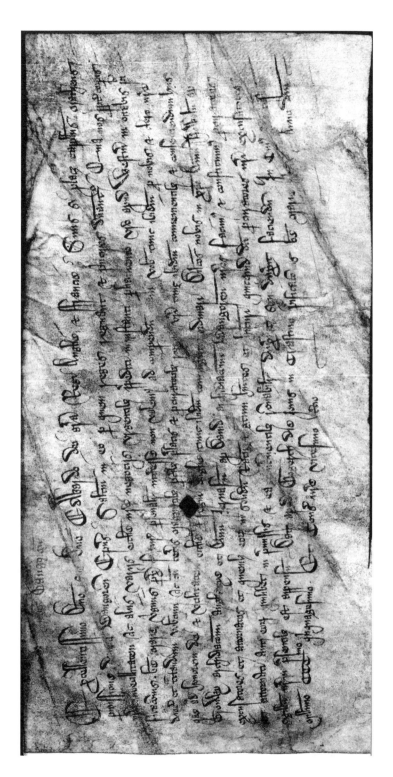

SC 10/25/1224. Letter close from Matthew [of Englefield], bishop of Bangor, with the appointment of Hywel ap Gronow and Gervase ap David as proctors for the Westminster parliament of February 1351. A considerable amount of Welsh evidence survives in SC 10 which supplements other sources.

SC 10/29/1405. Letter close from Geoffrey [de Gaddesby], abbot of Selby, naming John de Goldale and William de Mirfield as proctors for the parliament at Westminster in October 1363. Letters from abbots represent the largest single group in SC 10.

THE CALENDAR

PARLIAMENTS OF THE REIGN OF HENRY III (1216–72)

The first six letters in SC 10 all date from the reign of Henry III. Of these, only one is dated. It is probable that 1/7 is also a proxy for one of Henry III's parliaments, but the letter is a fragment and cannot be dated with certainty.

PARLIAMENT AT LONDON, 9 SEPTEMBER 1263

1/5	[William of Bitton I], bishop of Bath and Wells	*No proctors named*	Wok [Wookey], 1 Sept. 1263

UNDATED LETTERS FROM HENRY III'S PARLIAMENTS

Five of the letters from Henry III's reign lack dates. Although they are all addressed to King Henry [III] and in handwriting consistent with thirteenth-century style, none can be dated with complete certainty. Letters 1/1, 1/2 and 1/3 contain apologies for absence from a parliament taking place at London or Westminster on the octave of the Purification of the Blessed Virgin Mary (9 February). As suggested in the Handbook of British Chronology *(p. 538[1], this is possibly the parliament of February 1248.*

1/1	R, abbot of St Benet of Hulme [*if parliament is that of Feb. 1248, Robert of Torksey*]	*No proctors named*	[*Undated (Feb. 1248?)*]
1/2	H., abbot of Cirencester [*if parliament is that of Feb. 1248, Hugh of Bampton*]	F. Philip, monk of abbey	[*Undated (Feb. 1248?)*]
1/3	H, abbot of Leicester [*if parliament is that of Feb. 1248, Henry of Rothley*]	*No proctors named*	[*Undated (Feb. 1248?)*]

1 / 4 is for a parliament to be held in London on the quindene of St John. If the feast referred to is the Nativity of St John the Baptist, then this could be the parliament of 8 July 1260.

1/4	Abbot of Abbotsbury [*if parliament is that of July 1260, John of Hilton*]	*No proctors named*	[*Undated (July 1260?)*]

1/6 is for a parliament in London on the octave of St Hilary (20 January), possibly the parliament of January 1265.

1/6	H, Abbot of Ramsey [*if parliament is that of Jan. 1265, Hugh of Sulgrave*]	F. William de Gumecestre [Godmanchester], monk of abbey D. William de Camberlanu [Chamberlain], clerk	[*Undated (Jan. 1265?)*]

4

PARLIAMENTS OF THE REIGN OF EDWARD I (1272–1307)

PARLIAMENT AT LONDON, 25 APRIL 1275

1/8	Henry [de Caldewelle], abbot of Pershore	Alan de Opton, monk of abbey	Pershore, 17 April 1275

PARLIAMENT AT WESTMINSTER, 13 OCTOBER 1275

1/9	W[alter Giffard], archbishop of York	M. William, 'our official'	Boulton in Craven [Bolton in Craven], 7 Oct. 1275

GREAT COUNCIL AT WESTMINSTER, 4 MAY 1287

1/10	John [le Romeyn], archbishop of York *(to E[dmund], earl of Cornwall, holding the place of the king)*	John de Lythegreyns, 'our steward'	Hemingford [Hemingford Abbots], 23 March 1287

CONVOCATION AT LONDON, 13 JANUARY 1297

1/11A	[Roger of Driffield], abbot of Meaux *[LP]*	F. Robert, monk of abbey	Meaux, feast of the Epiphany [6 Jan.] 1297

1/11B	Thomas [Corbridge], archbishop of York	[M.] William de Pikering [Pickering]*, archdeacon of Nottingham	Hornsee [Hornsea], 22 Sept. 1302
1/12	Thomas [Corbridge], archbishop of York	[M.] William de Pikering [Pickering]*, archdeacon of Nottingham	Langeton [Langton], 7 Oct. 1302
1/13	G[ilbert of St Leofard], bishop of Chichester	Henry de Garland*, 'our official'	Druyngewy [Drungewick], 5 Oct. 1302
1/14	William [of Aslackby II], abbot of Selby	F. Robert de Alkebari [Alkborough], monk of abbey	Selby, 7 Oct. 1302
1/14A	Godfrey [of Crowland], abbot of Peterborough	F. William Saleman, sacristan of abbey M. Geoffrey de Makeseye [Maxey]	Peterborough, 12 Oct. 1302

1/15	John [Dalderby], bishop of Lincoln	D. Hugh de Normanton*, canon of Lincoln Simon de Asewarby [Aswarby]	Newark, 24 May 1306

6

PARLIAMENTS OF THE REIGN OF EDWARD II (1307–27)

PARLIAMENT AT NORTHAMPTON, 13 OCTOBER 1307

1/17	John [of Fressingfield], prior of Ely	F. Robert de Swafham [Swaffham], monk of priory	Ely, 12 Oct. 1307
1/18	Adam [illegible]	[Illegible]	Hereford, 19 Sept. 1307
1/19	Richard [Swinfield], bishop of Hereford	D. William de Mortuomari [Mortimer]*, canon of Hereford D. Adam de Osegotby [Osgodby]*, rector of Bureford [Burford] D. Walter de Lugwardine, rector of Monesleye [Munsley], Hereford diocese	Sugwas near Hereford [Stretton Sugwas], 7 Oct. 1307
1/20	Clergy of Bath and Wells diocese [LP]	M. Hugh de Pencryz [Penkridge], clerk M. Robert Fayrmay [Fairmay], clerk	Wells, Monday after feast of St Michael [2 Oct.] 1307
1/21	Thomas [Wouldham], bishop of Rochester [LP]	M. John Buss [Bush]*, canon of York John de Colonia [Cologne]*, clerk	Waltham, 10 Oct. 1307
1/22	John, abbot of Byland	F. Peter de Wyluby [Willoughby], monk of abbey	Byland, feast cf St Dionysius [9 Oct.] 1307
1/23	Richard [of Bishops Cleeve], abbot of Abingdon	Robert de Upton, clerk	Abingdon, 8 Oct. 1307

7

1/24	Roger de Wesenham, archdeacon of Rochester	M. John Bussh [Bush]*, canon of York John de Colonia [Cologne]*, clerk	Langefeld [Longfield], day of St Fides, virgin and martyr [6 Oct.] 1307
1/26	R[alph Baldock], bishop of London [LP]	M. Richard de Neuport [Newport]*, archdeacon of Middlesex	Hereford, 10 Oct. 1307
1/27	Prior [John of Fressingfield] and Chapter of Ely	F. Robert de Swafham [Swaffham], monk of abbey	Ely, 12 Oct. 1307
1/28	Clergy of Salop archdeaconry, Hereford diocese [LP]	D. Walter, vicar of Cleobury Mortimer M. John de Brunsope [Brunshope], rector of Oldebur' [Oldbury]	Lydebur [Lydbury], Friday before feast of St Dionysius [6 Oct.] 1307
1/29	Clergy of Carlisle diocese [LP]	M. William de Brampton M. Adam de Appelby [Appleby]* D. Hugh de Burgo [Burgh]*	Carlisle, Monday after feast of St Michael [2 Oct.] 1307
1/30	Clergy of York diocese [LP]	M. John de Snaynton [Snainton]*, rector of Ruddestan [Ruddston] D. William de Pykering [Pickering]*, rector of Haukewsorth [Hawksworth]	York, 5 Oct. 1307
1/31	Robert [Orford], bishop of Ely	M. Richard de Deneford [Denford], 'our clerk'	Waltham, 10 Oct. 1307
1/32	John [of Babraham], abbot of Waltham	F. Gilbert de Cokham [Cookham], monk of abbey Robert de Jarpenvill [Jarpenville], clerk	Waltham, 11 Oct. 1307

8

1/33	Clergy of Ely diocese	M. Richard de Otryngham [Ottringham]* M. Robert de Abynton [Abington], rector of Graveley	Cambridge, 22 Sept. 1307
1/34	Robert [Bishopton], abbot of Fountains	F. William de Ayrton [Airton], monk of abbey	Fountains, day of St Dionysius [9 Oct.] 1307
1/35	Chapter of Hereford	D. Walter de Logwardyn [Lugwardine]	Hereford, 10 Oct. 1307
1/36	Walter [Haselshaw], bishop of Bath and Wells	No proctors named	Tettebur [Tetbury], 10 Oct. 1307
1/37	[Henry de Shorne], archdeacon of Hereford	D. Walter de Lugwardyn [Lugwardine], rector of Muneslee [Munsley]	Hereford, morrow of St Dionysius [10 Oct.] 1307
1/38	Clergy of Durham diocese [LP]	D. Roger Bertram, rector of Bothall [Bothal] M. Reginald de Stepilton [Stapleton], rector of Wolsingham	Durham, 2 Oct. 1307
1/39	Chapter of St Paul's, London	M. John de Dutone [Dutton], canon of London	St Paul's, 8 Oct. 1307
1/41	Thomas [Wouldham], bishop of Rochester (to John, bishop of Chichester and chancellor)	No proctors named	Waltham, 9 Oct. 1307
1/42	Chapter of Wells [LP]	D. William de Bourn*, canon of Wells	Wells Chapter House, 30 Sept. 1307
4/168	Chapter of York [LP]	D. Adam de Osgoteby [Osgodby]*, canon of York D. John de Merkenfeld [Markenfield]*, canon of York D. Robert de Bardelby*, canon of York	York, 26 Sept. 1307

PARLIAMENT AT WESTMINSTER, 28 APRIL 1308

1/43	L[lywelyn de Bromfield], bishop of St Asaph	M. Henry de Oswaldestr [Oswestry], 'our clerk'	St Asaph, 18 April 1308
1/45A	[Gruffydd ap Iorwerth], bishop of Bangor	M. Adam Goch, clerk	Gogerth [Gogarth], 16 April 1308

PARLIAMENT AT WESTMINSTER, 20 OCTOBER 1308

1/44	Richard [Swinfield], bishop of Hereford	D. William de Mortuomari [Mortimer]*, canon of Hereford; D. Adam de Herwynton [Harvington]*, rector of Aure [Awre], Hereford diocese	Bosebur [Bosbury], 3 Oct. 1308
1/45	J[ohn of Gilling], abbot of St Mary's, York	M. J. de Mueynton	York, day of St Edward, king [13 Oct.] 1308

PARLIAMENT AT WESTMINSTER, 27 APRIL 1309

1/46	Henry [de Shorne], archdeacon of Hereford	D. William de Mortuo Mari [Mortimer]*, canon of Hereford; M. Thomas de Orlintone [Orleton]*	Hereford, 13 April 1309
1/46A	L[lywelyn de Bromfield], bishop of St Asaph	M. Howel [Hywel] ap Ithel, clerk; M. Richard de Oswaldestre [Oswestry]*, clerk	Alltmedlyn [Meliden], 17 April 1309

1/47	Thomas [of Tottington], abbot of Bury St Edmunds	F. John de Everesdon [Eversden], monk of abbey; M. Ralph Thorny, clerk	Cheventon [Chevington], 23 April 1309
1/48	Chapter of Rochester	F. Geoffrey de Mepham [Meopham], monk of abbey; F. Hamo Hethe*, monk of abbey	Rochester, 24 April 1309
1/49	John, abbot of Jervaulx	F. Thomas de Gristwayt [Gristhwaite], monk of abbey	Jervaulx, 18 April 1309
1/49A	Clergy of Winchester archdeaconry	[D.] John de Malmesbury, rector of Blessed Mary of Wath near Winchester	Winchester, 23 April 1309
1/50	John [of Brockhampton], abbot of Evesham	Thomas de Grenshull	Evesham, Wednesday before feast of St Mark, evangelist [23 April] 1309
2/51	Clergy of St Asaph diocese [LP]	M. Howel ap Ithal [Hywel ap Ithel]; M. Richard de Albo Monasterio [Whitchurch]	St Asaph, 16 April 1309
2/53	Nicholas [of Whaplode], abbot of Reading	F. Henry de Lynton	Reading, Saturday, morrow of feast of St Mark, evangelist [26 April] 1309
2/54	Chapter of Lincoln [LP]	D. Hugh de Normanton*; M. Thomas de Langetoft [Langtoft]*	Lincoln, 21 April 1309
2/55	Clergy of Lewes archdeaconry, Chichester diocese [LP]	D. William de Loppedel, vicar of Preston	Sefford [Seaford], 25 April 1309
2/56	Clergy of York diocese	[Damaged – at least one name illegible] John de Fraunceys*, rector of Wheldrake	York, 15 April 1309

2/57	Chapter of Hereford [LP]	D. William de Mortuo Mari [Mortimer] M. [Damaged – Thomas] de Orletone [Orleton]*	Hereford Chapter House, Id. [damaged] 1309
2/58	Thomas [de Fyndon], abbot of St Augustine's, Canterbury (to the bishop of Chichester, chancellor)	No proctors named	Canterbury, Sunday after feast of St Mark, evangelist [27 April] 1309
2/58A	Henry [de Shorne], archdeacon of Hereford [LP]	D. William de Mortuo Mari [Mortimer]*, canon	Hereford, 13 April 1309
2/59	Thomas [de Fyndon], abbot of St Augustine's, Canterbury	F. Richard de Cantuar [Canterbury], monk of abbey [D.] William de Ayreminne [Airmyn]*, clerk	Canterbury, 26 April 1309
2/60A	Richard [Swinfield], bishop of Hereford	D. William de Mortuomari [Mortimer]*, canon of Hereford D. Adam de Herwynton [Harvington]*, rector of Aure [Awre], Hereford diocese M. Thomas de Orleton*, clerk	Bosebury [Bosbury], 23 April 1309
2/61	Clergy of Stafford archdeaconry [LP]	M. Geoffrey de Blasten [Blaston]*, canon of Lichfield D. Robert, rector of Wolfhampcote	Stafford, Saturday in Easter week [5 April] 1309
2/62	Clergy of Hereford	M. Thomas de Olreton [sic, recte Orleton]* M. Simon de Radnore [Radnor]	Bosebury [Bosbury], 22 March 1309
2/63	[John of Cockerham], abbot of Furness	F. Michael, prior of Furness	Furness, 12 April 1309
2/64	J[ohn of Gilling], abbot of St Mary's, York [LP]	M. John de Snaynton [Snainton]*, clerk	York, 18 April 1309

12

2/65	John [Thoky], abbot of St Peter's, Gloucester [LP]	F. William Irebi, monk	Gloucester, 17 April 1309
2/69A	Clergy of Bangor diocese	M. A[nian Sais]*, archdeacon of Anglesey M. Llywelyn	Bangor, Wednesday the feast of the Blessed Calixtus 1309 [sic][1]
C 270/35/17	Clergy of Salop archdeaconry [LP]	G. [Gap left for additional initial]	Shrewsbury, Thursday after the second Sunday after Easter [17 April] 1309

PARLIAMENT AT STAMFORD, 27 JULY 1309

2/66	Richard [Swinfield], bishop of Hereford	D. James de Henlee [Henley]*, rector of Ross[-on-Wye], Hereford diocese	Bosebury [Bosbury], 22 July 1309
2/67	Robert [Orford], bishop of Ely	M. Richard de Deneford	Aumham, 20 July 1309
2/68	[Simon of Ghent], bishop of Salisbury	M. Gilbert Lovel*, canon of Salisbury M. Thomas Chaumpeneys, clerk	Banneby [Banbury], 26 July 1309
2/69	D[avid Martin], bishop of St Davids	M. Philip le Lung, canon of St Davids	Reading, feast of Blessed Mary Magdalene [22 July] 1309

1 The feast of Calixtus falls on 14 October, which was in any case a Tuesday in 1309. The parliament referred to in the letter is clearly that of April 1309, which means that the date is presumably a scribal error, or perhaps some other feast of Calixtus was celebrated in Bangor diocese.

PARLIAMENT AT WESTMINSTER, 8 FEBRUARY 1310

2/70	Richard [Swinfield], bishop of Hereford	D. Adam de Herwynton [Harvington]*, rector of Aur [Awre] D. Hugh de Leoministra [Leominster]*, canon of Hereford	Sugwas near Hereford [Stretton Sugwas], 24 Jan. 1310
2/71	L[lywelyn de Bromfield], bishop of St Asaph	M. Richard de Albo Monasterio [Whitchurch]	St Asaph, feast of the Purification of the Blessed Virgin Mary [2 Feb.] 1310
2/72	John [de Monmouth], bishop of Llandaff	*No proctors named*	Lank, 3 Feb. 1310

PARLIAMENT AT LONDON, 8 AUGUST 1311

2/73	John [of Brockhampton], abbot of Evesham *[LP]*	F. William de Chyrinton [Chiriton]*, monk and cellarer of Evesham	Evesham, 4 Aug. 1311
2/74	[Richard of Sutton], abbot of Barlings	F. John de Hornley, monk of abbey	Barlings, 27 July 1311
2/75	William [of Badminton], abbot of Malmesbury	F. Philip de Daunteseye, monk of abbey Guichard de Pardinis*	Malmesbury, Thursday after feast of St Peter [1 July] 1311
15/725	Adam [of Brokenborough], abbot of Cirencester	F. Adam de Whitele [Whitley], monk of abbey D. Richard de Ayremyn [Airmyn]*, clerk	Shryuenham [Shrivenham], 4 Aug. 1311

14

Ref			
2/80	[Llywelyn de Bromfield], bishop of St Asaph	M. Richard de Albo Monasterio [Whitchurch]	St Asaph, 13 Aug. 1312
2/81	[John of Gilling], abbot of St Mary's, York	M. John de Snaynton [Snainton]* M. William de Brampton	York, 12 Aug. 1312
3/150B	[William of Aslackby II], abbot of Selby	F. William de Goldale, monk of abbey	Selby, 15 Aug. 1312
16/790	Thomas [of Tottington], abbot of Bury St Edmunds	F. Reginald de Ufford, monk of abbey John Clement de St Edmundo [Bury St Edmunds], clerk	London, 29 Aug. 1312

Ref			
2/77	[John of Sawtry], abbot of Ramsey	F. Simon Burgo Sancti Petri [Peterborough], monk of abbey D. William de Corton, clerk	Ramsey, Thursday after feast of St Gregory, pope [15 March] 1313
2/78	John [of Gloucester], abbot of Hailes	F. Roger de Novo Castro [Newcastle], monk of abbey [D.] Thomas de Evesham*, clerk	Hailes, first Sunday of Lent [4 March] 1313
2/79	Simon [of Luffenham], abbot of Crowland	M. Robert Russeal	Crowland, 22 March 1313
2/84	[Nicholas of Whaplode], abbot of Reading	M. Hubert Constable	Reading, third Sunday of Lent [18 March] 1313

Ref.	Person	Proctors	Place and date
2/85	Richard [of Sutton], abbot of Barlings	F. Simon de Bamuburg [Bamburgh], monk of abbey M. John de Rodes, clerk	Barlings, day of St Gregory, pope [12 March] 1313
2/86	[Godfrey of Crowland], abbot of Peterborough	F. Robert de Thornton, monk of abbey Thomas de London* Godfrey de Ware	Peterborough, 21 April 1313
2/87	[John de Greenstreet], prior of Rochester [LP]	M. William de Fakenham, clerk	Rochester, 2 March 1313
2/88	[William of Brackley], abbot of Croxton [Kerrial]	D. Thomas de Nova Aya [Newhay]*	Croxden, Sexagesima Sunday [18 Feb.] 1313
2/89	John [of Brockhampton], abbot of Evesham	F. William de Chyrinton [Chiriton]*, monk and cellarer of Evesham [D.] John de Geyrgave [Gargrave], clerk	Evesham, 15 March 1313
2/90	P[eter of Chichester], abbot of Beaulieu	No proctors named	Beaulieu, 13 April 1313
2/91	William [Greenfield], archbishop of York	M. Robert de Pykering [Pickering]*, dean of York D. Stephen de Malo Lacu [Mauley]*, archdeacon of Cleveland D. Adam de Osegodeby [Osgodby]*, canon of York D. Robert de Bardelby*, canon of York M. John Fraunceys*, canon of York	Cawod [Cawood], 6 March 1313

16

2/92	Geoffrey [Fromond], abbot of Glastonbury	F. Thomas de la Nye, monk of abbey	Glastonbury, morrow of St Gregory, pope [13 March] 1313
2/93	Dean and Chapter of Bangor	[M.] David de Guelt [Guellt], clerk	Bangor, 9 March 1313
2/94	John [Thoky], abbot of St Peter's, Gloucester	F. Philip de Quedesleye [Quedgeley], monk of abbey M. Thomas de Portynton [Portington]*, clerk	Gloucester, 14 March 1313
2/95	A[dam of Brokenborough], abbot of Cirencester	F. Henry Bacun, monk of abbey D. Richard de Eyrminne [Airmyn]*, clerk	Cirencester, 15 March 1313
2/96	Henry [de Brok], abbot of St Benet of Hulme	F. Simon de Withingham, monk of abbey	St Benet of Hulme, 15 March 1313
2/97	Richard [Kellaw], bishop of Durham	D. William de Rasne D. William de Eyreminne [Airmyn]* D. Geoffrey de Edenham*	Stockton[-on-Tees], 6 March 1313
2/99	Roger de Wesenham, archdeacon of Rochester [LP]	M. William de Fakenham, clerk	Langfeld, 11 March 1313
2/100	Edmund, subprior of Rochester and the Chapter [LP]	F. Hamo Hethe*, monk of priory	Rochester, 6 March 1313
3/101	Chapter of St Asaph [LP]	Richard de Oswaldestre [Oswestry]*	St Asaph, 1 March 1313
3/102	J[ohn of Gilling], abbot of St Mary's, York	D. John de Ayremyn [Airmyn], clerk	York, 13 March 1313

3/103	Philip [ap Hywel], archdeacon of Brecon, St Davids diocese [LP]	M. Gilbert de Mosselwyk [Musselwick]*, archdeacon of Carmarthen	Hergast [Hergest], Thursday the morrow of St Valentine, martyr [15 Feb.] 1313
3/104	Richard [of Bishops Cleeve], abbot of Abingdon	[D.] John de Braye [Bray]*, clerk	Abingdon, 16 March 1313
3/105	William [of Aslackby II], abbot of Selby	D. Thomas de Nova Haya [Newhay]*, clerk D. John de Carleton [Carlton]*, clerk	Selby, 13 March 1313
3/106	L[lywelyn de Bromfield], bishop of St Asaph	M. Richard de Oswaldestre [Oswestry]*, clerk	St Asaph, 5 March 1313
3/107	Chapter of St Davids	M. Gilbert de Mosselwyk [Musselwick]*, archdeacon of Carmarthen D. Walter de Hyll	St Davids Chapter House, Wednesday before feast of St Peter in Cathedra [21 Feb.] 1313
3/108	A[nian Sais], bishop of Bangor	M. David de Buelt [Guellt], clerk	Bangor, 2 March 1313
15/745	William [of Badminton], abbot of Malmesbury	F. John de Tynterna [Tintern]*, monk of abbey D. John de Bray*, clerk	Malmesbury, Wednesday before feast of Gregory, pope [11 March] 1313

PARLIAMENT AT WESTMINSTER, 8 JULY 1313

3/109	John [Dalderby], bishop of Lincoln [LP]	D. Hugh de Normanton*, canon of Lincoln D. Walter de Thorp*, canon of Lincoln D. John de Buckeden [Buckden]	Lydington [Lyddington], 3 June 1313
3/110	John [Ketton], bishop of Ely	M. John de Rodes, clerk	Somerisham [Somersham], 12 June 1313
3/111	Simon [of Ghent], bishop of Salisbury	M. Hugh de Spineto*, canon of Salisbury [M.] John de Blebury [Blewbury]*, rector of Schalyngford [Shillingford], Salisbury diocese	Sonnyngg [Sonning], 12 June 1313
3/112	Henry [Woodlock], bishop of Winchester	[Peter of Cheam]*, prior of St Mary's, Suthwerk [Southwark] M. Richard Wodeloc [Woodlock]*, clerk	Weregrave [Wargrave], 8 June 1313
3/113	Thomas [Wouldham], bishop of Rochester [LP]	D. John de Dytton, rector of Kemesing [Kemsing]	Trottesclyve [Trottiscliffe], 11 June 1313
3/114	John [Salmon], bishop of Norwich (to W[alter Reynolds], bishop of Worcester, J[ohn Droxford], bishop of Bath and Wells, and Gilbert de Clare, earl of Gloucester and Hertford)	M. Ralph de Pagrave*, clerk	Hoxne, 10 June 1313

3/115	[Henry Woodlock], bishop of Winchester (to W[alter Reynolds], bishop of Worcester, J[ohn Droxford], bishop of Bath and Wells, and Gilbert de Clare, earl of Gloucester and Hertford)	No proctors named	Weregrave [Wargrave], 8 June 1313
3/116	Ralph Germeyn, precentor of Exeter, and Roger de Otery, chancellor of Exeter, vicars-general of Walter [Stapeldon], bishop of Exeter	No proctors named	Exeter, 1 July 1313
3/117	Richard [Swinfield], bishop of Hereford	D. Adam de Osegodeby [Osgodby]*, canon of Bureford [Burford collegiate church]; D. John de Geregrave [Gargrave], canon of Bureford [Burford collegiate church]; M. Stephen de Ledbury*, doctor of civil law	Bosebury [Bosbury], 22 June 1313
3/118	Richard [Swinfield], bishop of Hereford	No proctors named	Bosebury [Bosbury], 22 June 1313
3/126	Chapter of York [LP]	D. Adam de Osgotby [Osgodby]*; D. Robert de Bardelby*	York, 25 June 1313

3/120	[Richard Swinfield], bishop of Hereford	Bosebur [Bosbury], 1 Sept. 1314
	D. John de Gergrave [Gargrave], prebendary in [collegiate] church of Bureford [Burford]	
	M. Robert de Ikelesham [Icklesham]*, canon of Hereford	
3/121	Peter [of Chichester], abbot of Beaulieu	Beaulieu, day of St Bartholomew [24 Aug.] 1314
	Thomas de Ev[damaged – Evesham?]	
3/122	D[avid Martin], bishop of St Davids	Lando [Llandrindod Wells], 1 Sept. 1314
	D. Matthew de Shyreford [Sherford], rector of Upton Helyoun [Upton Hellions]	
3/123	[Geoffrey de Feringges], abbot of Hyde near Winchester	Hyde, 1 Sept. 1314
	Nicholas de Tarente, monk	
3/124	[Godfrey of Crowland], abbot of Peterborough	Peterborough, Saturday after Beheading of John the Baptist [31 Aug.] 1314
	F. Robert de Thorneton [Thornton], monk of abbey	
	Robert de Thorneton [Thornton], clerk	
3/125	John [of Brockhampton], abbot of Evesham	Evesham, Wednesday before feast of the Nativity of Blessed Virgin [4 Sept.] 1314
	F. William de Chirynton [Chiriton]*, monk and cellarer of Evesham	
	D. Thomas de Evesham*, clerk	
3/127	Thomas [Wouldham], bishop of Rochester [LP]	Trottesclive [Trottiscliffe], 31 Aug. 1314
	D. Henry de Plukkele [Pluckley], rector of Henlegh [Henley-on-Thames]	
	D. Peter de Fangfoss, rector of Ealdyngg [Yalding]	

21

3/128	Gilbert [Segrave], bishop of London	M. Stephen de Sancte Germain [St Germans], doctor of canon law	Clacton, 23 Aug. 1314
3/129	John [de Monmouth], bishop of Llandaff	M. David de Clitu / Anian [Sais]*, bishop of Bangor	Alvynton [Alvington], 31 Aug. 1314
3/130	A[nian Sais], bishop of Bangor	David de Buellt [Guellt], clerk	Bangor, 1 Sept. 1314
3/131	Simon [of Ghent], bishop of Salisbury	M. Hugh de Spineto*, canon of Salisbury / M. John de Blebury [Blewbury]*, rector of Neuwenham [Nuneham Courtenay]	Poterne [Potterne], 31 Aug. 1314
3/132	Ralph [de Borne], abbot of St Augustine's, Canterbury	F. Richard de Cant' [Canterbury], monk of abbey / Richard Dyering	Canterbury, 30 Aug. 1314

PARLIAMENT AT WESTMINSTER, 20 JANUARY 1315

3/133	Peter [of Chichester], abbot of Beaulieu	F. Henry de Grundewell, monk of abbey	Beaulieu, 8 Jan. 1315
3/134	[Robert de Clopcote], prior of Bath Cathedral *[LP]*	[F.] Thomas de Malmesbury, monk of priory / D. Philip de Depford [Deptford], clerk	Bath, 16 Jan. 1315
3/135	[Thomas of Sherborne], abbot of Winchcombe	Hugh de Brystoll [Bristol]	Ennestane [Enstone], Thursday after feast of St Hilary [16 Jan.] 1315

3/136	[Thomas of Sherborne], abbot of Winchcombe	[F] William de Gloucester, cellarer of Winchcombe [M.] William de Bosco [de Boys]*, clerk	[Undated]
3/137	John [of Sawtry], abbot of Ramsey	F. Simon de Eya [Eye]*, monk of abbey D. William de Corton, clerk	Ramsey, Thursday after feast of St Hilary [16 Jan.] 1315
3/138	Richard [Swinfield], bishop of Hereford	M. Robert de Ikelesham [Icklesham]*, canon of Hereford D. John de Gergrave [Gargrave]	Bosebur [Bosbury], 18 Jan. 1315
3/139	A[dam of Brokenborough], abbot of Cirencester	F. John, monk of abbey Adam le Mareschal, clerk Robert de Aston*, clerk	Cirencester, 17 Jan. 1315
3/140	[Godfrey of Crowland], abbot of Peterborough	M. Thomas de Langgetoft [Langtoft]* M. Stephen de [damaged]	Peterborough, Monday the feast of St Hilary [13 Jan.] 1315
3/141	Henry [de Brok], abbot of St Benet of Hulme	F. Robert de Smaleberghe [Smallburgh], monk of abbey	St Benet of Hulme, 18 Jan. 1315
3/142	John [of Gloucester], abbot of Hailes	D. Thomas de Evesham*, clerk Richard de Foxcote*	Hailes, [Damaged] St Hillary, [Jan.] 1315
3/143	William [Greenfield], archbishop of York	William de Rothewell [Rothwell]*, rector of Normanton John de Snaynton [Snainton]*, rector of Rudstan [Rudston]	Calke, 4 Jan. 1315

3/144	P[hilip of Barton], master of Sempringham	Gilbert de Thedelthorp [Theddlethorpe], member of order	Elton, 5 Jan. [no year]
3/145	Chapter of St Davids	[M.] Gilbert de Mosselwik [Musselwick]*, canon of St Davids Walter de la Hulle [Hull]*, canon of St Davids	St Davids Chapter House, feast of St Thomas [21 Dec.] 1314
3/146	Chapter of Carlisle	[D.] John de Crosseby [Crosby]* Robert de Santford [Sandford]*	Carlisle, 10 Jan. 1315
3/147	Dean [Robert Pickering] and Chapter of York [LP]	D. Adam de Osgotby [Osgodby]*, canon of York D. Robert de Bardelby*, canon of York D. John de Merkingfeld [Markenfield]*, canon of York	York, 28 Dec. 1314
3/148	[Thomas Wouldham, bishop of Rochester] [Damaged, but address survives on dorse of letter to identify sender]	D. Robert, rector of [Damaged – probably St Mary in Hoo]	[Damaged]
3/149	Clergy of Rochester diocese [LP]	Robert, rector of Blessed Mary in Hoo Peter de Fangefoss [Fangfoss], vicar of Ealding [Yalding]	Bromlegh [Bromley], 19 Jan. 1315
3/150A	John [Thoky], abbot of St Peter's, Gloucester [LP]	D. Thomas de Portington*, clerk D. John de Staunton*, clerk	Gloucester, 17 Jan. 1315
4/151	Thomas de Goldysburg [Goldesburgh], archdeacon of Durham [LP]	M. Ralph de Holbech [Holbeach]*, clerk M. William de Foderingay [Fotheringhay], clerk	Kyrketon in Holand [Kirton in Holland], Saturday after feast of the Epiphany [11 Jan.] 1315

4/152	William de Tothale, prior of St John of Jerusalem [LP]	F. Richard de Leycestra [Leicester]	Blacolneslee [Blakesley], 18 Jan. 1315
4/153	Thomas [Wouldham], bishop of Rochester [LP]	D. Robert, rector of St Mary in Hoo; Peter de Fangfos [Fangfoss], vicar of Ealding [Yalding]	Bromlegh [Bromley], 18 Jan. 1315
4/154	Richard [of Bishops Cleeve], abbot of Abingdon	[M.] John de Blebury [Blewbury]*	Abingdon, 16 Jan. 1315
4/155	[Richard of Sutton], abbot of Barlings	Robert Serll, rector of West Rasen; Elias de Wetheley	Barlings, St Hilary [13 Jan.] 1315
4/156	John [of Halton], bishop of Carlisle	D. William de Eyrminne [Airmyn]*, rector of Levington [Kirk Levington]; D. Hugh de Burgh*, rector of Burgo sub Mora [Brough under Stainmore]; M. Thomas de Caldebek [Caldbeck]*, rector of Clifton [Clifton]	Meleburne [Milburn], 15 Jan. 1315
4/157	Archdeacon [Gilbert de Halton] and clergy of Carlisle diocese [LP]	D. Hugh de Burgo [Burgh]*, rector of Burgo sub Mora [Brough under Stainmore]; Robert de Appelby [Appleby], rector of [Damaged], Carlisle diocese	Meleburne [Milburn], 15 Jan. 1315
4/158	John [Dalderby], bishop of Lincoln [LP]	D. Hugh de Normanton*; M. Elias de Muskham*, canon of Lincoln; M. Thomas de Langetoft [Langtoft]*, rector of Suthikam [South Hykeham]	Parcu Stowe [Stow Park], 28 Dec. 1314

4/159	Thomas [of Sherborne], abbot of Winchcombe	F. John de Cyrencestra [Cirencester], monk John de Bladintone [Bledington]	Enne [damaged – Enstone], Thursday after feast of St Hilary [16 Jan.] 1315
4/160	Simon [of Scarborough], abbot of Selby	F. Robert de Alkebargh [Alkborough], monk of abbey D. Thomas de Nova Haya [Newhay]*, clerk	Selby, [Damaged] 1315
4/161	Clergy of Ely diocese [LP]	William de Rothewell [Rothwell]*, rector of Normanton John de Snaynton [Snainton]*, rector of Ruddestan [Rudston]	Ely, Thursday after feast of the Epiphany [9 Jan.] 1315
4/162	Chapter of St Asaph	M. Richard de Oswaldestre [Oswestry]*, canon of St Asaph	St Asaph, 20 Dec. 1314
4/163	Simon [of Ghent], bishop of Salisbury	M. Richard de Bello [Battle]*, canon of Salisbury M. Hugh de Spineto*, canon of Salisbury	Sonnyngg [Sonning], 18 Jan. 1315
4/164	Thomas, abbot of Rievaulx	F. Thomas Kileber, monk of Wardon	Rievaulx, feast of St John, apostle and evangelist [27 Dec.] 1314
4/165	Geoffrey [de Feringges], abbot of Hyde near Winchester	F. Michael de Aulton [Alton], monk M. Hugh de Assherigge [Ashridge]	Hyde, 13 Jan. 1315
4/166	Ralph [de Borne], abbot of St Augustine's, Canterbury	F. Richard de Cantuaria [Canterbury], monk	Canterbury, [Damaged] 1315
4/167	Walter [of Huntingfield], abbot of St John's, Colchester	Matthew de Alneto	Colchester, 17 Jan. 1315

4/169	William [of Harvington], abbot of Pershore	Robert de la Felde, clerk Robert de Alveston [Alveston], clerk	Pershore, day of St Hilary, bishop [13 Jan.] 1315
4/170	William [of Badminton], abbot of Malmesbury	[D.] John de Bray*, clerk	Malmesbury, Sunday after feast of St Hilary [19 Jan.] 1315
4/171	Robert of Pickering, dean of York [LP]	D. Adam de Osgotby [Osgodby]* D. Robert de Bardilby [Bardelby]* D. John de Merkyngfeld [Markenfield]*	York, 18 Jan. 1315
4/172	John [Ketton], bishop of Ely	M. Geoffrey de Pakenham*, clerk D. Gilbert de Grettone [Gretton], clerk	Somersham, 17 Jan. 1315
4/173	R[ichard Kellaw], bishop of Durham	M. John de Snaynton [Snainton]* D. Roger de Saxton	Geddyng [Gedding] near Weston, 16 Jar. 1315
4/174	John [of Brockhampton], abbot of Evesham	F. William de Chyriton [Chiriton]*, monk and cellarer of Evesham D. Thomas de Evesham*, clerk	Evesham, 16 Jan. 1315
4/175	Alan [of Ness], abbot of St Mary's, York	M. John de Snaynton [Snainton]*, clerk D. John de Ayerminne [Airmyn], clerk	York, 5 Jan. 1315
4/176	Subprior and Chapter of Bath Cathedral [LP]	F. Thomas de Malmesbury, monk	Bath, 16 Jan. 1315
18/874	Simon [of Luffenham], abbot of Crowland	F. John de Ingoldeby [Ingoldsby], monk of abbey Richard de Canterbrigg [Cambridge] [D.] John de Crosseby [Crosby]*	Cotinham [Cottingham], 15 Dec. 1314

PARLIAMENT AT LINCOLN, 27 JANUARY 1316

4/177	Richard [Swinfield], bishop of Hereford	M. Robert de Ikelesham [Icklesham]*, canon of Hereford	Bosebur [Bosbury], 20 Jan. 1316
4/178	[Godfrey of Crowland], abbot of Peterborough	F. Robert de Thornton, monk Thomas Sorel of Colingham [Collingham], clerk	Peterborough, 21 Jan. 1316
4/179	Henry [de Brok], abbot of St Benet of Hulme	F. Reginald de Bliclingg [Blickling], monk	St Benet of Hulme, Saturday after feast of St Hilary [16 Jan.] 1316
4/180	Gilbert [of Crosby], prior of Carlisle	*No proctors named*	Carlisle, 13 Jan. 1316
4/181	Clergy of Rochester diocese *[LP]*	Peter de Fangefosse [Fangfoss], vicar of Ealding [Yalding] [D.] William de Burton*, vicar of Cobham	*[Illegible]*, 18 Jan. 1316
4/182	Gilbert [Segrave], bishop of London	M. Stephen de Segrave*, archdeacon of Essex	Wykham [Wickham Bishops], 15 Jan. 1316
4/183	Sylvester, subprior of Rochester Cathedral, and the Chapter	William de Dene*, clerk John Bernard, clerk	Rochester, 11 Jan. 1316
4/184	William [of Clopton], abbot of Thorney	F. William Harel, monk	Thorney, 21 Jan. 1316

4/185	John [of Brockhampton], abbot of Evesham	F. William de Chyrinton [Chiriton], monk and cellarer of Evesham* D. Thomas de Evesham*, clerk	Evesham, 20 Jan. 1316
4/186	Richard [of Hertford], abbot of Waltham	D. Roger de Sutton*, rector of Bulfeen [Bulphan] Walter de Sancto Albano [St Albans]	Waltham, 11 Jan. 1316
4/187	Hugh [of Eversden], abbot of St Albans [F]	F. William de Kirkby, prior of our cell of Bealver [Belvoir]* John de la Haie [Hay]*	St Albans, morrow of St Hilary [14 Jan.] 1316
4/188	J[ohn of Gloucester], abbot of Hailes	D. Thomas de Englham, rector of Ryshanger [Rishanger] F. Roger de Novo Castro [Newcastle], monk	Hailes, day of Holy Martyrs Fabian and Sebastian [20 Jan.] 1316
4/189	John [Ketton], bishop of Ely	M. Geoffrey de Pakenham* M. Thomas de Foxton*, doctor of canon and civil law D. Gilbert de Grettone [Gretton], clerk	Somersham, 15 Jan. 1316
4/190	John [Ketton], bishop of Ely [F]	No proctors named	Somersham, 16 Jan. 1316
4/191	Geoffrey [of Burdon], prior of Durham, and the Chapter [LP]	D. [sic] John de Butrewyk [Butterwick], monk of priory D. Robert de Tymparon*, clerk	Durham Chapter House, 17 Dec. 1315
4/192	Geoffrey [of Burdon], prior of Durham	John de Laton John de Butrewyk [Butterwick]	Durham, 1 Feb. 1316

4/193	Chapter of York [LP]	D. John de Hustwatt [Husthwayt]* D. Robert de Cotingham [Cottingham]* M. Nicholas de Ros [Ross]*	York, 24 Jan. 1316
4/194	Thomas, abbot of Rievaulx	F. William, monk	York, 18 Jan. 1316
4/195	Chapter of St Asaph [LP]	Richard de Oswalestre [Oswestry]*	St Asaph, 17 Jan. 1316
4/196	John [Dalderby], bishop of Lincoln	M. Henry de Benyngworth [Benniworth]*, subdean and canon of Lincoln M. Thomas de Bray*, canon of Lincoln D. Hugh de [Damaged – Norma]nton*, canon of Lincoln M. Thomas de Langetoft [Langtoft]*, canon of Lincoln	Parcu Stowe [Stow Park], 22 Jan. 1316
4/197	Hamo [Hethe], prior of Rochester Cathedral	William de Dene*, clerk John Bernard, clerk	Rochester, 11 Jan. 1316
4/198	Roger de Wesenham, archdeacon of Rochester [LP]	Peter de Fangfos [Fangfoss], vicar of Elding [Yalding]	Langefeld [Longfield], 16 Jan. 1316
4/199	Geoffrey [de Feringges], abbot of Hyde near Winchester	F. Nicholas de Taitorte, monk of abbey	[Illegible], feast of St Hilary [13 Jan.] 1316
4/200	John [de Monmouth], bishop of Llandaff	No proctors named	Llandaff, 15 Jan. [no year]

30

5/201	Walter [Maidstone], bishop of Worcester	M. William de Birston*, archdeacon of Gloucester M. Robert de Pirttone [Pirton], archdeacon of Gloucester's official	Hampton super Abonam [Hampton-in-Arden], 21 Jan. [*no year*]
5/202	Ralph [de Borne], abbot of St Augustine's, Canterbury	D. Richard de Aeyrminne [Airmyn]* [D.] Thomas de Braytone [Brayton]*	Canterbury, 29 Dec. [*no year*]
5/203	Chapter of Lincoln [*LP*]	M. Thomas de Langetoft [Langtoft]*, canon of Lincoln	Lincoln Chapter House, 24 Jan. 1316
5/204	John [of Sutton], abbot of Abingdon	M. John de Blebury [Blewbury]*	Abingdon, 10 Jan. 1316
5/205	Peter [of Chichester], abbot of Beaulieu	Henry, abbot of Revesby	Beaulieu, St Hilary [13 Jan.] 1316
5/206	Walter [of Huntingfield], abbot of St John's, Colchester	D. Roger de Ribbesthorp	Colchester, Saturday after feast of St Hilary [16 Jan.] 1316
5/207	A[lan of Ness], abbot of St Mary's, York	F. Adam de Thweng, monk M. William de Brampton, clerk	York, 23 Jan. 1316
5/208	Simon [of Scarborough], abbot of Selby	F. John de Alkebarow [Alkborough], monk [D.] Thomas de Brayton*, clerk	Selby, 24 Jan. 1316

5/209	Geoffrey [Fromond], abbot of Glastonbury	M. William de Selton*, clerk D. Richard de Birlaunde [Birland]* William de Stapeltone [Stapleton]	Glastonbury, 15 Jan. 1316
5/210	T[homas of Glanford Brigg], abbot of Thornton	F. Richard de Carleton [Carlton], monk	Thornton, Saturday after feast of St Vincent, martyr [23 Jan.] 1316
5/211	William [of Harvington], abbot of Pershore	M. Clement de Paston	Pershore, 19 Jan. 1316
5/212	John [of Sawtry], abbot of Ramsey	F. Simon de Eya [Eye]*	Ramsey, Thursday after feast of St Hilary, bishop [14 Jan.] 1316
5/213	Chapter of St Davids	M. Matthew de Shireford [Sherford], canon of Aberwellens [Abergwili]	St Davids Chapter House, 28 Dec. 1315
5/214	John [Thoky], abbot of St Peter's, Gloucester	M. Robert de Pirtton [Pirton], clerk D. Thomas de Portington*, clerk	Gloucester, 7 Jan. 1316
5/215	Adam [of Brokenborough], abbot of Cirencester	F. William called Savage, monk	Cirencester, 20 Jan. 1316
5/216	William [of Badminton], abbot of Malmesbury	[D.] John de Braye [Bray]*, 'clerk and proctor of your [the king's] chancery'	Malmesbury, SS Fabian and Sebastian [20 Jan.] 1316

32

5/217	Nicholas [of Whaplode], abbot of Reading	M. William de Oterhampton [Otterhampton]*, clerk	Reading, 19 Jan. 1316
5/218	Richard [of Draughton], abbot of Bury St Edmunds	F. William de Stowe [Stow], monk D. William de Cliff*	Culford, morrow of the Epiphany [7 Jan.] 1316
5/219	Thomas [of Sherborne], abbot of Winchcombe	F. John de Cyrencestr [Cirencester], monk D. Thomas de Eveshame [Evesham]*	Winchcombe, day of the Conversion of St Paul, apostle [25 Jan.] 1316
5/220	Richard [of Sutton], abbot of Barlings	F. John de Hornley, monk	Barlings, Conversion of St Paul, apostle [25 Jan.] 1316
5/221	John [de Monmouth], bishop of Llandaff	M. Richard de Melton, canon of Llandaff	Llandaff, 15 Jan. 1316
5/222	[Walter Langton], bishop of Coventry and Lichfield	M. Robert de Weston, clerk	London, Monday after feast of St Hilary [18 Jan.] 1316
5/223	John [de Monte Martini], prior of Lewes	John de Torringg, clerk	Lewes, morrow of St Vincent, martyr [23 Jan.] 1316
5/224	Thomas [Wouldham], bishop of Rochester [LP]	D. Peter de Fangfos [Fangfoss], rector of Ealding [Yalding] D. William de Burton*, rector of Cobham	Bromlegh [Bromley], 10 Jan. 1316
5/225	Gilbert [Segrave], bishop of London	M. Stephen [de Segrave]*, archdeacon of Essex	Wykham [Wickham Bishops], 15 Jan. 1316

5/226	Thomas [Wouldham], bishop of Rochester	D. Peter de Fangfoss, vicar of Ealding [Yalding] / D. William de Burton*, vicar of Cobeham [Cobham]	Bromlegh [Bromley], 10 Jan. 1316
5/227	John [de Southber], abbot of Stanley [LP]	D. John de Bray*, clerk	Stanley, 16 Jan. 1316

PARLIAMENT AT YORK, 20 OCTOBER 1318

5/229	[Simon of Luffenham], abbot of Crowland	D. John de Crosseby [Crosby]*, clerk / D. John de Sancto Paulo [St Pol]*, clerk	Crowland, 7 Oct. 1318
5/230	[Richard of Draughton], abbot of Bury St Edmunds	F. Roger de Tostok [Tostock], monk / D. Nicholas Gode	Rungeton [Runcton Holme or South Runcton], 11 Oct. 1318
5/231	William [de Chiriton], abbot of Evesham	D. Thomas de Evesham* / M. Walter de Blythe [Blyth]*	Baddeby [Badby], 13 Oct. 1318
5/233	Ralph [de Borne], abbot of St Augustine's, Canterbury	*No proctors named*	Canterbury, 5 Oct. 1318
5/234	Ralph [de Borne], abbot of St Augustine's, Canterbury	William de Herlauytone [Harlington] / [D.] Thomas de Braytone [Brayton]*	Canterbury, 5 Oct. 1318
5/235	William [of Bromley], abbot of Burton-upon-Trent	William de Mosebert, clerk	Burton-upon-Trent, Saturday after feast of St Luke, evangelist [21 Oct.] 1318

34

5/236	William [of Badminton], abbot of Malmesbury	[D] John de Bray* M. Richard de Welington [Wellington]	Malmesbury, St Luke [18 Oct.] 1318
5/237	William [of Harvington], abbot of Pershore	Hugh de Martle [Martley] Richard de Nortone iuxta Bremesgrove [Norton near Bromsgrove], 'my clerk'	Aldremoston [Aldermaston], Sunday after feast of St Luke, evangelist [22 Oct.] 1318
5/238	John [of Sutton], abbot of Abingdon	M. John de Blebury [Blewbury]*	Abingdon, morrow of St Matthew, apostle and evangelist [22 Sept.] 1318
5/239	[Simon of Eye], abbot of Ramsey	[F.] John de Grendon John de Chetingdon	Goseberkirk [Gosberton], Sunday after feast of Simon and Jude [29 Oct.] 1318
5/240	[Godfrey of Crowland], abbot of Peterborough	F. Robert de Thornton, sacristan of Peterborough Thomas Sorel [of Collingham]	Peterborough, St Luke [18 Oct.] 1318
5/241	William [de Curtlyngton], abbot of Westminster [LP]	John de Braysen, clerk John de Ildesk, clerk	Westminster, 14 Oct. 1318
5/242	Thomas [of Glanford Brigg], abbot of Thornton	[F.] Nicholas de Lyndewod [Linwood]	Thornton, St Luke [18 Oct.] 1318
5/243	Simon [of Scarborough], abbot of Selby	F. William de Donecastr [Doncaster], monk	Acastr [Acaster Malbis], 3 Nov. 1318

5/244	[William of Brackley], abbot of Croxton [Kerrial] *[LP]*	F. William de Brunne	Croxden, day of St Luke, evangelist [18 Oct.] 1318
5/245	John [of Fressingfield], prior of Ely and Chapter of Ely *[LP]*	D. Thomas de Nova Haya [Newhay]* M. Ralph Olyver [Oliver]*, rector of Malketon [Malketon] [M.] Henry de Thrippelawe [Thriplow]*, clerk	Ely, Wednesday after feast of St Matthew, apostle and evangelist [27 Sept.], 1318
5/246	*[Damaged]* of Durham	*[Damaged]* [F.] Emericus de Lumley	Durham, 21 Oct. 1318
5/247	Clergy of Surrey archdeaconry *[LP]*	D. John de Malmesburi [Malmesbury]	Clendon Regis [Clandon Regis], 2 Oct. 1318
5/248	Clergy of Winchester archdeaconry *[LP]*	[D.] John of Mucheldevere [Micheldever], rector of Chiltecommbe [Chilcombe]	Winchester, 25 Sept. 1318
5/249	John [Dalderby], bishop of Lincoln *[LP]*	M. Thomas de Langtoft*, canon of Lincoln	Lydington [Lyddington], 4 Oct. 1318
5/250	A[nian Sais], bishop of Bangor	M. Howel [Hywel] ap Ithel, canon of St Asaph M. Richard de Melton, canon of Bangor	Bangor, 11 Oct. 1318
6/251	Philip de Barton, archdeacon of Surrey *[LP]*	D. John de Malmesbury, clerk D. John de Micheldevre [Micheldever], clerk	Clendon Reg [Clandon Regis], 2 Oct. 1318
6/252	Dean and Chapter of Bangor	M. Howel [Hywel] ap Ithel, canon of St Asaph Richard de Melton, canon of Bangor	Bangor, 11 Oct. 1318

36

6/253	Richard [of Enford], prior of Winchester Cathedral [LP]	[D.] John de Malmesbury, clerk	Winchester, 12 Oct. 1318
6/254	Gilbert [of Crosby], prior of Carlisle	F. Alan de Frisington [Frizington], monk	Carlisle, 21 Oct. 1318
6/255	Clergy of York diocese [LP]	M. John de Skyrne*, rector of Marton in Craven / M. John de Lutton, rector of half of Rillington	York, 27 Oct. 1318
6/256	Chapter of Winchester Cathedral [LP]	[D.] John de Malmesbury, clerk	Winchester Chapter House, 12 Oct. 1318
6/256A	Clergy of Durham archdeaconry [LP]	Elias de Colsull [Coleshill], rector of Seaham	Durham, 17 Oct. 1318
6/256B	[John Thoky], abbot of St Peter's, Gloucester	D. Thomas de Evesham* / D. Thomas de Portynton [Portington]*	Gloucester, 27 Sept. 1318
6/257	Clergy of Ely diocese [LP]	M. Ralph Oliver*, rector of Malketon, Ely diocese / M. Henry Trippelawe [Thriplow]*, clerk	Bernewell [Barnwell], 30 Sept. 1318
6/258	Chapter of Durham	[F.] Emericus de Lumley, monk	Durham Chapter House, 22 Oct. 1318
6/259	Henry [de Brok], abbot of St Benet of Hulme	[D.] John de Norton*, clerk / John le Claver*, clerk	St Benet of Hulme, Sunday before feast of St Luke, evangelist [15 Oct.] 1318

37

6/260	Adam [Orleton], bishop of Hereford [LP]	M. Richard de Burton*, clerk	London, 20 Oct. 1318
6/261	William [of Odiham], abbot of Hyde near Winchester	William Fynamour, 'my clerk'	Hyde, 17 Oct. 1318
6/262	John [of Cockerham], abbot of Furness	Thomas de Horneby Roger le Messager	Furness, 17 Oct. 1318
6/262A	William, abbot of Rievaulx	D.John de Marton* D. William de Bardelby*	York, St Michael [29 Sept.] 1318

PARLIAMENT AT YORK, 6 MAY 1319

2/76	William [of Badminton], abbot of Malmesbury	[D.]John de Braye [Bray]* Hugh de Faryndone [Farringdon]	Malmesbury, Monday after feast of St Mark, evangelist [30 April] 1319
5/232	Richard [of Enford], prior of Winchester Cathedral [LP]	D. Geoffrey de Wileford [Wilford], clerk John Dynom	Winchester, 24 April [no year]
6/263	Clergy of Gloucester archdeaconry [LP]	John de [Illegible]cothern	[Illegible]
6/264	Clergy of Carlisle diocese [LP]	M. Robert de Southayk [Southwick], clerk M. Henry de Rillington, clerk	Carlisle, 5 May 1319

6/265	Clergy of St Davids diocese	M. Philip [de Caunton], archdeacon of St Davids, doctor of canon law William de la Roche	St Davids, 11 April 1319
6/266	Richard [of Idbury], abbot of Winchcombe	D. Thomas de Evesham* D.John de Evesham D.John Paynel*	Leicester; day of the Invention of the Holy Cross [3 May] 1319
6/267	John [of Gloucester], abbot of Hailes	Richard de Norton	Hailes, 21 April 1319
6/268	Richard [of Sutton], abbot of Barlings	D. William de Houdene [Howden], 'our dear clerk'	Barlings, 5 May 1319
6/269	Richard [of Draughton],abbot of Bury St Edmunds	F. Thomas de Wilborgham, monk D. Nicholas le Gode	Herlawe [Harlow], feast of Apostles Philip and James [1 May] 1319
6/270	Adam [of Brokenborough], abbot of Cirencester	D. Thomas de Evesham* [D.] John de Evesham	Cirencester, 6 April 1319
6/271	W[illiam of Bromley], abbot of Burton-upon-Trent	D. William de Herlaston [Harlaston]*, clerk William de Musleberd, clerk	Burton, feast of the Invention of the Holy Cross [3 May] 1319
6/272	John [Thoky], abbot of St Peter's, Gloucester	D. Adam de Eglisfeld [Eglesfeld]*, clerk D. Thomas de Portynton [Portington]*, clerk	Gloucester, 25 April 1319

6/273	William, abbot of Rievaulx	[D.] John de Marton*	York, 14 May [*no year*]
6/274	[Godfrey of Crowland], abbot of Peterborough	Thomas Sorel of Colingham [Collingham]	Peterborough, Thursday, feast of the Invention of the Holy Cross [3 May] 1319
6/275	Ralph [de Borne], abbot of St Augustine's, Canterbury	F. Richard de Cantuar [Canterbury], monk / William de Cotes*	Canterbury, 29 April 1319
6/276	Clergy of York diocese *[LP]*	M. Thomas de Cave*, clerk / William de Twyforde [Twyford], clerk	York, Sunday before feast of Apostles Philip and James [29 April] 1319
6/277	William [de Curtlyngton], abbot of Westminster	D. John de Braye [Bray]* / Henry de Seleby [Selby]	Westminster, 30 April 1319
6/278	Roger [Martival], bishop of Salisbury	[M.] Robert de Ayleston [Aylestone]*, rector of Boclonde [Buckland]	London, 27 April 1319
6/279	John [Droxford], bishop of Bath and Wells *[LP]*	D. William de Whetelay, 'our clerk'	Wynelescumb [Wivelis-combe], 29 April 1319
6/280	[Wulstan of Bransford], prior of Worcester Cathedral	F. John de Sancto Briavello [St Briavels], monk / D. Thomas de Evesham*, clerk	Worcester, 28 April 1319

6/281	Geoffrey [of Burdon], prior of Durham	M. Richard de Eryum [Airmyn]*, doctor of both laws D. [sic] Emericus de Lummeley [Lumley], monk [D.] Robert de Tymparoun [Tymparon]*, clerk	Durham, 5 April 1319
6/282	Walter [Reynolds], archbishop of Canterbury	John [Hotham], bishop of Ely, 'your chancellor' John [Sandale], bishop of Winchester	Lambeth, 1 May 1319
6/283	D[avid Martin], bishop of St Davids	Philip [de Caunton], archdeacon of St Davids, doctor of canon law	Treuedyn [Trefin], 13 April 1319
6/284	Thomas [of Glanford Brigg], abbot of Thornton	F. Nicholas de Lindewodd [Linwood], monk	Thornton, day of Invention of the Holy Cross [3 May] 1319
6/285	Walter [Coxwold], abbot of Fountains	F. John de Howyngham [Howingham], monk	Fountains, 6 May 1319
6/286	David [Dafydd ap Bleddyn], bishop of St Asaph	Hugh ap Ioh [Hywel ap Ithel], canon of St Asaph	St Asaph, 2 May 1319
6/287	John [de Monmouth], bishop of Llandaff	*No proctors named*	London, 28 April 1319
6/288	William [of Harvington], abbot of Pershore	John le Botyler of Lutletone [Littleton] John le Bruny [Brune] of Bellebroctone [Belbroughton]	Pershore, 1 May 1319
6/289	Clergy of Durham diocese *[LP]*	Elias de Colsull [Coleshill], clerk, rector of Seaham Richard de Meburn, clerk	Durham, 26 April 1319

6/290	Chapter of Worcester Cathedral	F. John de Sancto Briavello [St Briavels], monk D. Thomas de Evesham*, clerk	Worcester Chapter House, 28 April 1319
6/291	William [of Odiham], abbot of Hyde near Winchester	M. Henry de Clif [Cliffe]*, clerk	Hyde, 29 April 1319
6/292	Henry [de Brok], abbot of St Benet of Hulme	[D.] John de Norton*, clerk William de Bestone [Beeston]	St Benet of Hulme, 28 April 1319
6/293	Chapter of York [LP]	John de Brotherton, 'our chamberlain'	York, 6 May 1319
6/294	Walter [of Huntingfield], abbot of St John's, Colchester	D. Elias de Whateleye [Whateley], clerk D. Robert de Ryliston [Rylstone], clerk	Colchester, Monday [sic] the feast of the Apostles Philip and James [1 May] 1319
6/295	L[ouis de Beaumont], bishop of Durham	M. Michael de Harterla [Harclay]*, clerk M. Philip de Nassington, clerk	Grenforth [Greenford], 1 May 1319
6/296	Chapter of St Davids	Philip [de Caunton], archdeacon of St Davids, doctor of canon law	St Davids Chapter House, 12 April 1319
6/297	John [Dalderby], bishop of Lincoln [LP]	M. John Stratford*, 'our official' Sir Simon le Chaumberleyn [Chamberlain]*, knight M. Thomas de Langetoft [Langtoft]*, canon of Lincoln	Bukden [Buckden], 28 April 1319

42

6/298	Geoffrey [Fromond], abbot of Glastonbury	M. John de Bray*, clerk M. John de Kyngesbur [Kingsbury], clerk [M.] William de Seltone [Selton]*, clerk	Glastonbury, 4 April 1319
6/298A	Hugh de Statherne, archdeacon of Gloucester [LP]	John de Statherne [Stathern], clerk	Oxford, 2 May 1319
6/299	Chapter of Durham [LP]	M. Richard de Eryum, doctor of both laws [F] Emericus de Lummely [Lumley], monk [D.] Robert de Tymparoun [Tymparon]*, clerk	Durham Chapter House, 5 May 1319
6/300	Thomas [Cobham], bishop of Worcester [LP]	D. Thomas de Evesham*, rector of Baddeby M.John de Stretford [Stratford]*	Hartlebury, [Damaged] 1319
7/301	Thomas [Cobham], bishop of Worcester	*No proctors named*	Hertlebury [Hartlebury], 20 April 1319

PARLIAMENT AT YORK, 20 JANUARY 1320

7/302	A[nian Sais], bishop of Bangor	M. Howel de Hengylffylde [Hywel de Englefield], canon of St Asaph	Gogerth [Gogarth], Saturday after Epiphany [12 Jan.] 1320
7/302A	John [of Halton], bishop of Carlisle	D. Hugh [de Burgh]* de Burgo sub Mora [Brough under Stainmore], rector of the same D. Robert de Tympauroun [Tymparon]*, rector of Levington [Kirklinton]	Melburn [Melbourne], 10 Jan. 1320

7/302B	Richard [of Draughton], abbot of Bury St Edmunds	D. Nicholas le [Damaged – Gode]	Culford, 10 Jan. 1320
7/303	Adam [of Brokenborough], abbot of Cirencester	F. Philip de Weston, monk of abbey Robert de Aston*	Cirencester, 12 Jan. 1320
7/304	Hugh [of Eversden], abbot of St Albans	F. Richard de Ewyng, prior of St Albans D. William de Leycestre [Leicester]* D. John de Sancto Albano [St Albans]	St Albans, feast of St Hilary [13 Jan.] 1320

PARLIAMENT AT WESTMINSTER, 15 JULY 1321

7/305	S[imon of Eye], abbot of Ramsey	F. John de Grendon, monk of abbey D. William de Corton John de Chetingdon	Ramsey, Sunday after feast of the Translation of St Thomas, martyr [12 July] 1321
7/306	[Godfrey of Crowland], abbot of Peterborough	William de Ayschby [Ashby] William de Catteworth [Catworth]	Peterborough, 22 June 1321
7/307	John [of Cockerham], abbot of Furness	William Bartel [Damaged - Roger] le Messager	Furness, 21 June 1321
7/308	Chapter of St Asaph [LP]	Hugh ap Ithel [Hywel ap Ithel]	St Asaph, octave of the Apostles Peter and Paul [6 July] 1321

7/309	William [de Chiriton], abbot of Evesham	D. Thomas de Evesham*, clerk M. William de Bosco [Boys]*, clerk	Evesham, 10 July 1321
7/310	Ralph [de Borne], abbot of St Augustine's, Canterbury	F. Richard de Cantuar [Canterbury], monk of abbey William de Cotes*	Canterbury, 13 July 1321
7/311	Richard [of Idbury], abbot of Winchcombe	M. John de Renham, clerk M. John de Bradewas [Broadwas], clerk M. William de Bosco [Boys]*, clerk	Ennestane [Enstone], Monday after feast of the Translation of the Blessed Thomas, martyr [13 July] 1321
7/312	Philip [of Barton], master of the order of St Gilbert of Sempringham	Gilbert de Thetelthorp [Theddlethorpe], monk of order	'Our House of St Catherine outside Lincoln', 26 June [no year]
7/313	A[nian Sais], bishop of Bangor	M. Richard de Oswaldestr [Oswestry]*, clerk M. David de Buellt [Guellt], clerk	Bangor, Monday after the Apostles Peter and Paul [6 July] 1321
7/314	[Simon of Luffenham], abbot of Crowland	D. John de Crosseby [Crosby]*, clerk Nicholas de Spaldyng [Spalding]	Crowland, Tuesday after feast of [the Translation of] St Thomas, martyr [14 July] 1321
7/315	Richard [of Draughton], abbot of Bury St Edmunds	F. William de Gemingham [Gimingham], monk of abbey D. Nicholas le Gode, 'our clerk'	Culford, 13 July 1321

Ref		Persons	Place, date
7/316	Walter [Fifehead], abbot of Hyde near Winchester	Richard Benet, clerk	Hyde, 12 July 1321
7/317	[Wulstan of Bransford], prior of Worcester Cathedral	D. Thomas de Evesham*, clerk M. John Geraud*, clerk	Worcester, 4 July 1321
7/318	Chapter of Worcester Cathedral	[Damaged]	Worcester Chapter House, 4 July 1321
7/319	Robert de Thorveston, prior of St Frideswide's, Oxford [LP]	F. Hugh de Compton, canon of the monastery of Osney	Oxford Chapter House, 13 July 1321
7/320	Richard [of Charlton], abbot of Cirencester	F. Philip de Westone [Weston], monk of abbey D. Thomas de Evesham*, clerk	Cirencester, 8 July 1321
7/321	Alan [of Ness], abbot of St Mary's, York	M. William de Brampton, clerk D. Richard de Pikering [Pickering], clerk	York, 26 June 1321
7/322	John [de Crauden], prior of Ely [LP]	F. John de Conigtone [Conington], monk of priory M. Henry de Thrippelowe [Thriplow]*, clerk	Ely, 6 July 1321
7/323	Richard [of Sutton], abbot of Barlings	D. Thomas de Tynton* John de Enderby*	Barlings, 1 July 1321
7/324	John [of Halton], bishop of Carlisle	Hugh [de Burgh]*, rector of Burgo sub Mora [Burgh under Stainmore] Robert de Sandforth [Sandford]*	Carlisle, 18 June 1321

7/325	John [de Crauden], prior of Ely and the Chapter [LP]	F. John de Conigton [Conington], monk of priory; M. Henry de Thrippelowe [Thriplow]*, clerk	Ely Chapter House, 6 July 1321
7/326	Robert [de Clopcote], prior of Bath [LP]	M. John de Schoredich [Shoreditch]*, doctor of civil law	Bath, 29 June 1321
7/327	William [de Chiriton], abbot of Evesham	F. John de Stowa [Stow], monk of abbey	Evesham, 10 July 1321
7/328	Simon [of Scarborough], abbot of Selby	[D.] Thomas de Brayton*, clerk	Selby, 2 July 1321
7/329	John [Thoky], abbot of St Peter's, Gloucester	[Damaged] Thomas de Bradewelle [Bradwell], 'your clerk'; [D.] Thomas de Escrik [Escrick]*	Gloucester, [Damaged] St Benedict, Abbot [July] 1321
7/330	Geoffrey [Fromond], abbot of Glastonbury	M. William de Selton*, clerk	Glastonbury, 8 July 1321
7/331	Henry [de Brok], abbot of St Benet of Hulme	F. Thomas de Tudenham [Tuddenham], monk of abbey; [M.] Adam de Fincham*, clerk	St Benet of Hulme, 10 July 1321
7/332	[John of Gloucester], abbot of Hailes	D. Thomas de Evesham*, clerk	Hailes, 1 July 1321
7/333	William [of Bromley], abbot of Burton-on-Trent	D. William de Herlaston [Harlaston]*; D. John de Herlaston [Harlaston]	Burton[-on-Trent], 1 July 1321

47

7/334	Thomas [of Glanford Brigg], abbot of Thornton	D. Peter de Ludyngton [Luddington]* D. William de Brocklousby [Brocklesby]*	Thornton, day of the Translation of St Benedict [11 July] 1321
7/335	Subprior and Chapter of Bath Cathedral [LP]	M. John de Schoredich [Shoreditch]*, doctor of civil law	Bath Chapter House, 29 June 1321
7/336	Clergy of York diocese [LP]	M. John de Nassington*, rector of Kirkton, York diocese D. William de Wyntringham [Wintringham], rector of St George's [Fishergate], York diocese	York, Saturday before feast of the Nativity of St John the Baptist [20 June] 1321

PARLIAMENT AT YORK, 2 MAY 1322

7/337	Richard [of Draughton], abbot of Bury St Edmunds	M. Stephen de Holecote [Holcote], clerk	Rungeton [Runcton Holme or South Runcton], 24 April 1322
7/338	J[ohn of Gloucester], abbot of Hailes	Peter de Eggeswurth [Edgeworth]	Hailes, Sunday in the octave of Easter [18 April] 1322
7/339	William [of Harvington], abbot of Pershore	D. Clement de Hamptone [Hampton], rector of Enckepenum [Inkpen] Hugh de la Hulle [Hull]*	Pershore, 26 April 1322
7/340	William [of Badminton], abbot of Malmesbury	[D.] John de Bray*, clerk William, called le Messager	Malmesbury, 25 April 1322

7/341	Chapter of Winchester Cathedral [LP]	D. Geoffrey de Wyleford [Wilford] John de Dynom	Winchester Chapter House, 24 April 1322
7/342	[Adam of Boothby], abbot of Peterborough	F. Gilbert de Aslokby [Aslackby], monk of abbey William de Aysheby [Ashby]	Peterborough, Friday after feast of St Mark, evangelist [30 April] 1322
7/343	Richard [of Idbury], abbot of Winchcombe	F. William de Albenhale William de Bradewelle [Bradwell]* [MP – Worcestershire]	Winchcombe, St Mark, evangelist [25 April] 1322
7/344	Robert de Scardeburgh [Scarborough], prior of Bridlington	F. Geoffrey de Boulton, monk and cellarer of Bridlington	Bridlington, 1 May 1322
7/345	William [of Driffield], abbot of [Damaged - Kirkstall]	F. Simon de Fymmer, monk of abbey	Kirkstall, 30 April 1322
7/346	William [de Chiriton], abbot of Evesham	F. John de Stowa [Stow], monk of abbey D. Thomas de Evesham*, clerk	Evesham, 22 April 1322
7/347	[Simon de Eye], abbot of Ramsey	F. John de Grendon, monk of abbey F. Robert de Nassington*, monk of abbey D. William de Leycestr [Leicester]* John de Chetingdon	Aylington [Elton], 28 April 1322
7/348	[William of Clopton], abbot of Thorney	F. William H[damaged]l, monk of abbey and prior of Depyng [Deeping] John de Luffewyk [Lowick]*	[Damaged] 1322

7/349	Clergy of York diocese [LP]	M. John de Skyrio [Skyrne]*, rector of Marton in Craven M. Simon de Stanek*, rector of Hoconbuscell [Hutton Buscel]	York, 10 May 1322
7/350	[Richard of Charlton], abbot of Cirencester	F. Philip de Westone [Weston], monk of abbey D. Richard de Ayrminne [Airmyn]*, clerk	Cirencester, 20 April 1322
8/351	Thomas [of Dunstone], abbot of Buckland	Richard de Chissebech [Chisbridge]* [MP – Devon] John de Wetherhulle	Buckland, Sunday in the octave of Easter [18 April] 1322
8/352	Thomas [of Edenham], abbot of Barlings	D. Thomas de Tynton*, clerk D. Richard de Enderby*, clerk	Barlings, day of St Vitalis, martyr [28 April] 1322
8/353	[Nicholas of Whaplode], abbot of Reading	Adam de Gateshened [Gateshead] William de Coleshulle [Coleshill]*	Reading, 20 April 1322
8/354	Simon [of Luffenham], abbot of Crowland	F. John de Conyngton [Conington], monk of abbey D. John de Crosseby [Crosby]* Robert de Grancester [Grantchester], 'our steward'	Crowland Chapter House, 27 April 1322
8/355	Simon [of Luffenham], abbot of Crowland	F. John de Conyngton [Conington], monk of abbey D. John Crosseby [Crosby]* Robert de Grancester [Granchester], 'our steward'	Crowland, 27 April 1322
8/356	Thomas [of Glanford Brigg], abbot of Thornton	D. Peter de Ludington [Luddington]* D. William de Broclousby [Brocklesby]*	Thornton, feast of the Apostles Philip and James [1 May] 1322

8/357	Clergy of Carlisle diocese [LP]	M. Robert de Suthayk [Southwick]*, clerk M. Adam de Appelby [Appleby]*, clerk	Morland, 28 April 1322
8/358	Chapter of St Davids (to Walter, archbishop of Canterbury)	David Fraunceys*, rector of Villa Johannis in Ros [Johnston in Roose]	St Davids Chapter House, 15 April 1322
8/359	[John de Crauden], prior of Ely	F. John de Conigton [Conington], monk of abbey M. John de Spaneby [Spanby], clerk	Ely, Monday the morrow of St Mark, evangelist [26 April] 1322
8/360	[William of Brackley], abbot of Croxton	F. William de Luttheburgh [Loughborough]	Croxden, day of St George [23 April] 1322
8/361	Subprior and Chapter of Bath Cathedral [LP]	D. Philip de Bath	Bath Chapter House, 24 April 1322
8/362	William, abbot of Stanley	[D.] John de Bray*, clerk	Stanley, Sunday of St Mark, evangelist [25 April] 1322
8/363	[William of Abbotsley], abbot of Bourne [LP]	F. John de Wyneton [Winton], monk of abbey M. John de Spauneby [Spanby], rector of Southicham [South Hykeham]	Bourne, 21 April 1322
8/364	Robert [de Clopcote], prior of Bath Cathedral [LP]	M. John de Schordych [Shoreditch], doctor of civil law D. John de Bath	Bath, 24 April 1322

8/365	Abbot of Welbeck	D. Henry de Edenstowe [Edwinstowe]*, clerk	Welbeck, Thursday after St Mark, evangelist [29 April] 1322
8/366	[William of Cowton], prior of Durham	D. [sic] John de Butrewyk [Butterwick], monk of priory John de Aldsheby	Durham, 26 April 1322
8/367	Clergy of St Davids diocese (to Walter, archbishop of Canterbury)	M. David Fraunceys*, rector of Villa Johannis in Ros [Johnston in Roose] D. Philip de Lawhadeyn [Llawhaden], rector of Penbeheyr [Penboyr]	Lantefey [Lamphey], 18 April 1322
8/368	[Richard of Hertford], abbot of Waltham	F. Richard de Hertfordinggeburi [Hertfordingbury], monk of abbey [D.] Edmund de Grymmesbi [Grimsby]*, clerk	Brikendone in the county of Hertford [Brickendon], 27 April 1322
8/369	Roger [Northburgh], bishop-elect of Coventry and Lichfield [LP]	M. Robert de Baldock, archdeacon of Middlesex* William de Ayremyn [Airmyn]*, canon of Lichfield	Rochewell, 26 April 1322
8/370	John [of Speldhurst], prior of Rochester Cathedral	William de Dene*, clerk	Rochester, 20 April 1322
8/371	Chapter of Worcester Cathedral	Richard de Hauekeslowe [Hawkeslowe]* [MP – Worcestershire] D. Henry de Ouleye, clerk	Worcester Chapter House, 25 April 1322
8/372	Abbot of St James's [damaged, possibly Northampton]	Henry de Blithesworth [Blisworth]	In the monastery, 25 [damaged] 1322

8/373	Walter Wynter [Winter], archdeacon of Carmarthen (to Walter, archbishop of Canterbury)	David Fraunceys*, rector of Villa Johannis in Ros [Johnston in Roose]	St Davids, 15 April 1322
8/374	John [de Monmouth], bishop of Llandaff	No proctors named	Worleton, 24 April 1322
8/375	[Robert of Ramsbury], abbot of Sherborne	D. Thomas de Staunton*	Sherborne, 22 April 1322
8/376	Philip le Lung, archdeacon of St Davids (to Walter, archbishop of Canterbury)	M. David Fraunceys*, rector of Villa Johannis in Ros [Johnston in Roose]	Lantefey [Lamphey], 18 April 1322
8/377	David [Martin], bishop of St Davids	M. David Fraunceys*, rector of Villa Johannis in Ros [Johnston in Roose], clerk	Lantefey [Lamphey], 17 April 1322
8/378	Henry [de Brok], abbot of St Benet of Hulme	F. John de Erpingham, monk of abbey William de Tutincton [Tuttington],clerk	St Benet of Hulme, 25 April 1322
8/379	Ralph [de Borne], abbot of St Augustine's, Canterbury	F. Solomon de Rypple [Ripple], monk of abbey William de Cotes*	Canterbury, 19 April 1322
8/380	Subprior and Chapter of Rochester Cathedral	M. Thomas de Hethe, clerk F. John de Faversham, monk of abbey	Rochester Chapter House, 20 April 1322
8/381	Chapter of York [LP]	John de Tinwell, vicar choral of York	York, 1 May 1322

53

8/382	Thomas de Goldesburg [Goldesburgh], archdeacon of Durham [LP]	M. Robert de Kyele, doctor of sacred theology D. John de Polhowe [Pollow], dean of the collegiate church of Chester [-le-Street] and Langcestrie [Lanchester]	Durham, 3 May 1322
8/383	Gilbert [sic], prior of Bourne, Lincoln diocese [LP]	F. John de Wyneton [Winton], monk of abbey M. John de Spauneby [Sapnby], rector of Southicham [South Hykeham]	Bourne, 21 April 1322
8/384	Chapter of Salisbury [LP]	M. John de Everdone [Everdon]*, canon of Salisbury M. Robert de Worthe [Worth]*, canon of Salisbury M. William de Salton [Selton]*	Salisbury Chapter House, 10 April 1322
8/385	John [de Canyng], abbot of Abingdon	M. Robert de Ayleston [Aylestone]*, canon of Salisbury	[Gap has been left for place and date but not filled in] 1322
8/386	Geoffrey [Fromond], abbot of Glastonbury	D. Richard de Rodeneye [Rodney]	Glastonbury, 16 April 1322
8/387	Philip ap Howel, archdeacon of Brecon (to Walter, archbishop of Canterbury)	M. David Fraunceys*, rector of Villa Johannis in Ros [Johnston in Roose]	Brecon, 22 April 1322
8/388	Chapter of Durham [LP]	D. [sic] John de Butrewyk [Butterwick], monk of priory John de A[illegible]	Durham Chapter House, 26 April 1322

54

8/389	Roger [Marival], bishop of Salisbury	M. Robert de Ayleston [Aylestone]*, canon of Salisbury [M.] John de Blebury [Blewbury]*, clerk	Wymondeswold [Wymeswold], 28 April 1322
8/390	[Wulstan of Bransford], prior of Worcester Cathedral	D. Thomas de Evesham*, clerk [D.] John de Evesham, clerk	Worcester, 13 April 1322
8/391	Walter [Fifehead], abbot of Hyde near Winchester	M. Richard de Bartone [Barton], clerk	Hyde, Wednesday after feast of St Alphege, bishop [14 April] 1322
8/392	John [de Crauden], prior of Ely	F. John de Conigtone [Conington], monk of priory M. Nicholas de Stokton [Stockton]*	Ely, Monday the morrow of St Mark, evangelist [25 April] 1322
8/393	John [Orfreiser], abbot of Faversham [LP]	D. William de Bordenne [Borden]*, rector of Stokeberi [Stockbury]	Faversham, 24 April 1322
8/394	Edmund [of Knulle], abbot of St Augustine's, Bristol	[D.] John de Bray*, clerk	Bristol, [Illegible] April 1322
8/395	Henry [de Garland], dean of Chichester Cathedal [LP]	Ralph Pany, clerk	Chichester, 21 April 1322
8/396	[Roger of Dartford], abbot of Lessness	M. Thomas de Hethe, clerk William de Dene*, clerk	Lessness Chapter House, 20 April 1322
8/397	Philip de Vachan, archdeacon of Cardigan (to Walter, archbishop of Canterbury)	M. David Fraunceys*, rector of Villa Johannis in Ros [Johnston in Roose]	St Davids, 15 April 1322

8/398	[Roger of Dartford], abbot of Lessness	M. Thomas de Hethe, clerk William de Dene*, clerk	Lessness Chapter House, 20 April 1322
8/399	William, abbot of Stanley	D. Thomas de Stauneton [Staunton]*	Stanley, Sunday of St Mark, evangelist [25 April] 1322

PARLIAMENT AT YORK, 14 NOVEMBER 1322

8/400	Richard [of Charlton], abbot of Cirencester	D. William de Airmyn* D. Thomas de Evesham* D. Walter de Cirencester*	Cirencester, 9 Nov. 1322
9/401	John [de Canyng], abbot of Abingdon	M. Robert de Ailleston [Aylestone]* M. John de Blebury [Blewbury]*	Abingdon, 7 Nov. [no year]
9/402	Simon [of Luffenham], abbot of Crowland	M. Hugh de Walmisford [Walmesford]*, clerk D. John de Crosseby [Crosby]* Geoffrey Pampilon	Crowland, 12 Nov. 1322
9/403	[Simon of Eye], abbot of Ramsey	F. Robert de Nassington*, monk of abbey D. William de Leycester [Leicester]* Roger Hillare [Hillary]*	Ramsey, 10 Nov. 1322

9/404	Roger [Marival], bishop of Salisbury	M. Robert de Ayleston [Aylestone]*, canon of Salisbury, clerk M. John de Blebury [Blewbury]*, clerk	Poterne [Potterne], 9 Nov. 1322
9/405	David [Dafydd ap Bleddyn], bishop of St Asaph	M. Robert Vaghan, canon of St Asaph Howel [Hywel] ap Houa	St Asaph, Monday before feast of St Martin [8 Nov.] 1322
9/406	Walter [Fifehead], abbot of Hyde near Winchester	Robert Tonyld	Hyde, 7 Nov. 1322
9/407	William [de Chiriton], abbot of Evesham	F. Ralph de Wylecote [Wilcote], monk of abbey D. Thomas de Evesham*, clerk	Evesham, 7 Nov. 1322
9/408	John [de Monmouth], bishop of Llandaff	No proctors named	Lank, 7 Nov. 1322
9/409	Ralph [de Borne], abbot of St Augustine's, Canterbury	Thomas de Faversham* William de Reycolure [Reculver]*	Canterbury, 6 Nov. 1322
9/410	William [of Clopton], abbot of Thorney	D. John de Stanford*, clerk John de Luffewyk [Lowick]*	Thorney, Saturday of St Michael in Monte Tumba [16 Oct.] 1322
9/411	Thomas [Cobham], bishop of Worcester [F]	No proctors named	Hembury, 10 Oct. [no year]

9/412	Hugh [of Eversden], abbot of St Albans	D. William de Leycestre [Leicester]*, clerk D. Ralph de Dalton*, clerk	St Albans, feast of All Saints [1 Nov.] 1322
9/413	[Nicholas of Whaplode], abbot of Reading	Adam de Gateshened [Gateshead]	Reading, 2 Nov. 1322
9/414	Walter [of Huntingfield], abbot of St John's, Colchester	[D.] John de Crosseby [Crosby]*, clerk	Colchester, morrow of All Saints [2 Nov.] 1322
9/415	John [of Halton], bishop of Carlisle	M. Michael de Harcla [Harclay]*, clerk D. Hugh de Burgo [Burgh]*, clerk D. William de Kyrkeby [Kirkby]*, clerk	Hornec [Horncastle], morrow of All Souls [3 Nov.] 1322
9/416	William [de Curtlyngton], abbot of Westminster	F. Robert de Beby, monk of abbey	Westminster, Nov. 1322
9/417	Geoffrey [Fromond], abbot of Glastonbury	M. William de Selton*, clerk William de Seles*	Glastonbury, 4 Nov. 1322
9/418	[Adam of Boothby], abbot of Peterborough	F. Gilbert de Aslokby [Aslackby], monk of abbey M. Stephen de Aylington [Elton], clerk	Peterborough, Thursday of St Martin [11 Nov.] 1322
9/419	Henry [de Brok], abbot of St Benet of Hulme	[M.] Adam de Fincham*, clerk William de Tutincton [Tuttington], clerk	St Benet of Hulme, 8 Nov. 1322

9/420	Louis [de Beaumont], bishop of Durham	M. Richard de Ermyn [Airmyn]*, canon of York, clerk M. Michael de Harcla [Harclay]*, clerk	[Dating clause not filled in]
9/421	Richard [of Draughton], abbot of Bury St Edmunds	Robert de Foxton* D. John de Hunteston [Hunstanton]	Cheryngton [Chevington], 5 Nov. 1322

PARLIAMENT AT WESTMINSTER, 23 FEBRUARY 1324

9/422	William [of Cowton], prior of Durham	Thomas de Hepscot [Hepscott] John de Halnatheby*	Durham, 6 Feb. 1324
9/423	Chapter of Durham [LP]	Thomas de Hepscot [Hepscott] John de Halnatheby*	Durham Chapter House, 6 Feb. 1324
9/424	Walter [of Huntingfield], abbot of St John's, Colchester	M. John de Sculthorp [Sculthorpe], clerk	Colchester, 21 Feb. 1324
9/425	[Reginald of Waternewton], abbot of Thorney	M. Walter de Wermington [Warmington]*, clerk D. Thomas [de Sancti Petri (St Peters)], rector of St Gildlaci de Estdeping [St Guthlac of East Deeping], clerk John de Islep [Islip]	Thorney, 24 Feb. 1324

9/426	Simon [of Luffenham], abbot of Crowland	F. Robert de Burgo Sancti Petri [Peterborough], monk of abbey Robert de Grancestr [Grantchester], 'our steward'	Crowland, 16 Feb. 1324
9/427	[Adam of Boothby], abbot of Peterborough	M. Stephen de [damaged - Ayling]ton [Elton], clerk	Stanewigg [Stanwick], 20 Feb. 1324
9/428	Walter [Fifehead], abbot of Hyde near Winchester	Richard Benet, clerk	Hyde, Tuesday before feast of St Peter in cathedra [20 Feb.] 1324
9/429	William [of Badminton], abbot of Malmesbury	[D.] Philip de Bath Henry de Lamelegh [Lambley]	Malmesbury, Tuesday before feast of St Peter in cathedra [20 Feb.] 1324
9/430	Adam [of Sodbury], abbot of Glastonbury	M. William de Selton*, clerk	Glastonbury, 4 Feb. 1324
9/431	John [of Wistow II], abbot of Selby	F. Richard de Athelingflet [Adlingfleet], monk of abbey D. Peter de Ludington [Luddington]*, clerk	Selby, 19 Feb. 1324
9/432	Chapter of Norwich Cathedral (to Walter, archbishop of Canterbury)	F. John de Clipesby [Clippesby], monk of priory F. John de Berton, monk of priory M. Adam de Fincham*, clerk	Norwich Chapter House, 20 Feb. 1324
9/433	S[imon of Haltwhistle], prior of Carlisle	Robert de Sandford* [MP, Westmorland]	Carlisle, 1 Feb. 1324

	Recipient	Proctors/Names	Place and date
9/434	[Wulstan of Bransford], prior of Worcester Cathedral	M. Robert de Hemeltone, doctor of civil law D. Simon de Evesham*, clerk	Worcester, 29 Jan. 1324
9/435	Chapter of Carlisle [LP]	John de Capella [Chapel]* of Carlisle	Carlisle, 31 Jan. 1324
9/436	Richard [of Charlton], abbot of Cirencester	F. William Hereward*, monk of abbey D. Adam de Ayrmynne [Airmyn]*, clerk	Cirencester, 20 Feb. 1324
9/437	Robert [Pickering], dean, and Chapter of York [LP]	M. Henry de Cliff [Cliffe]*, canon of York M. Gilbert de Bruerio [Brewer], canon of York	York, 9 Feb. 1324
9/438	John [of Halton], bishop of Carlisle	M. William de Kendale [Kendal]*, rector of Salkeld [Great Salkeld], clerk D. Robert de Tymparon*, rector of Levington [Kirklinton], clerk	Horncaster, 17 Feb. 1324
9/439	Chapter of St Asaph [LP]	Richard [damaged] M. [damaged]vychan	St Asaph, feast of the Purification of Mary [2 Feb.] 1324
9/440	Thomas [of Edenham], abbot of Barlings	D. Thomas de Tynton* Richard de Bolyngbrok [Bolingbroke]*	Barlings, 6 Feb. 1324
9/441	A[nian Sais], bishop of Bangor	M. Stephen de Kettlebury [Kettleburgh]* [M.] David de Guellt, canon of Bangor	Gogerth prope Conewey [Gogarth near Conwy], 14 Feb. 1324
9/442	Henry [de Brok], abbot of St Benet of Hulme	F. Reginald de Bliclingg [Blickling], monk of abbey Robert de Spaunton	St Benet of Hulme, Sunday after feast of St Valentine [18 Feb.] 1324

9/443	Dean and Chapter of Bangor	M. Madoc de Engelfeld [Matthew de Englefield]* [M.] David de Buellt [Guellt]	Bangor, 14 Feb. 1324
9/444	[Dafydd ap Bleddyn], bishop of St Asaph	M. Henry de Clif [Cliffe]* M. Richard de Oswaldestr [Oswestry]*	Shrewsbury, 17 Feb. 1324
9/445	John [Thoky], abbot of St Peter's, Gloucester	F. Hugh de Harsfeld [Haresfield], monk of abbey	Gloucester, 19 Feb. 1324
9/446	Ralph [de Borne], abbot of St Augustine's, Canterbury	William de Tilmanestone [Tilmanstone], monk of abbey William de Cotes*	Canterbury, 19 Feb. 1324
9/447	Chapter of Worcester	F. Robert de Cliftone [Clifton], monk of abbey	Worcester Chapter House, 29 Jan. 1324
9/448	William [of Grasby], abbot of Thornton	D. William de Broclousby [Brocklesby]* [D.] Edmund de Grymesby [Grimsby]*	Thornton, 19 Feb. 1324
9/449	Alan [of Ness], abbot of St Mary's, York	D. Hugh de Burgo [Burgh]*, clerk D. Richard de Pykeryng [Pickering], clerk	York, 10 Feb. 1324
9/450	Clergy of Carlisle diocese *[LP]*	M. W[illiam] de Kendale [Kendal]*, rector of Salkeld [Great Salkeld] D. John de Meteborn [Metburn], rector of Merten [Long Marton]	Carlisle, 11 Feb. 1324
10/451	Henry [of Leicester], prior of Coventry *[LP]*	D. Richard de Kyngton [Kington], clerk Roger Hillary*, clerk	Coventry, 19 Feb. 1324

10/452	Ralph [de Borne], abbot of St Augustine's, Canterbury	F. Robert de Fekenham [Feckenham], monk of abbey William de Cotes*	Canterbury, 15 Oct. 1324
10/453	[Adam of Boothby], abbot of Peterborough	M. Stephen de Aylington [Elton], clerk	Peterborough, Wednesday after feast of St Luke, evangelist [24 Oct.] 1324

PARLIAMENT AT WESTMINSTER, 25 JUNE 1325

10/454	Henry [of Leicester], prior of Coventry	D. Richard Hillary, clerk F. Roger, monk of priory	Coventry [damaged] June 1325
10/455	Adam [of Sodbury], abbot of Glastonbury	M. William de Seltone [Selton]* [D.] John de Briggewater [Bridgwater]*	Glastonbury, [Undated]
10/456	[Simon of Eye], abbot of Ramsey	F. John de Burgo [Burgh], monk of abbey D. William de Corton, clerk D. William de Leycester [Leicester]*, clerk D. John de Clayton, clerk	Barton, 23 June [no year]
10/457	Richard [of Charlton], abbot of Cirencester	F. Ralph de Escote [Eastcote]*, monk of abbey Robert [Illegible]	Cirencester, 22 June 1325
10/458	A[nian Sais], bishop of Bangor	Matthew de Engylfeld [Englefield]*, canon of Bangor [M.] David de Buellt [Guellt], canon of Bangor	Lamas, 13 June 1325

10/459	Henry [of Casewick], abbot of Crowland	D. John de Crosseby [Crosby]* Hasculf de Wytewell [Whitewell]*	Crowland, 15 June 1325
10/460	Adam [of Boothby], abbot of Peterborough	D. Thomas de Sybthorp [Sibthorp]*, clerk M. Stephen de Aylington [Elton]	Peterborough, Wednesday after feast of St Botolph [19 June] 1325
10/461	Walter [of Huntingfield], abbot of St John's, Colchester	John *called* Parles* of Colchester	Mondon, 20 June 1325
10/462	William [de Chiriton], abbot of Evesham	F. Peter de Wyk [Wick], monk and cellarer of Evesham D. Thomas de Evesham*, clerk	Evesham, 20 June 1325
10/463	Richard [of Draughton], abbot of Bury St Edmunds	D. John de Cavenham, clerk	Rongeton [Runcton Holme *or* South Runcton], 20 June 1325
10/464	Walter [Fifehead], abbot of Hyde near Winchester	Richard Benet, clerk	Hyde, 20 June 1325
10/465	W[illiam of Grasby], abbot of Thornton	Peter de Ludyngton [Luddington]* [D.] Edmund de Grymesby [Grimsby]*	Thornton, 20 June 1325
10/466	Ralph [de Borne], abbot of St Augustine's, Canterbury	F. Robert de Fekenham [Feckenham], monk of abbey William de Cotes*	Canterbury, Saturday before feast of John the Baptist [22 June] 1325
10/467	John [Thoky], abbot of St Peter's, Gloucester	F. Hugh de Harsfeld [Haresfield], monk of abbey	Gloucester, ii Non. April [*sic* in MS – 4 April] 1325

64

10/468	[Reginald of Waternewton], abbot of Thorney	D. Thomas, rector of Estdepping [East Deeping] John de Islep [Islip]* John de Luffewyk [Lowick]*	Thorney, 1 June 1325
10/469	Alan [of Ness], abbot of St Mary's, York [LP]	D. Richard de Pykering [Pickering], clerk Adam de Bonay, clerk	York, 3 June 1325
10/470	John [of Wistow II], abbot of Selby	D. Thomas de Brayton*, clerk James de Billingburgh [Billingborough]	Selby, 11 June 1325
10/471	[Dafydd ap Bleddyn], bishop of St Asaph	M. Matthew de Englefield*, clerk John de Horneby, clerk	Ruthelan [Rhuddlan], 13 June 1325
10/472	John [of Wistow II], abbot of Selby	D. Richard de Ayremynne [Airmyn]*, clerk	Acaster [Acaster Malbis], 12 June 1325

PARLIAMENT AT WESTMINSTER, 18 NOVEMBER 1325

10/473	Ralph [de Borne], abbot of St Augustine's, Canterbury	F. Robert de Fekenham [Feckenham], monk of abbey William de Cotes* William de Raculvre [Reculver]*	Canterbury, 15 Nov. 1325
10/474	Richard [of Charlton], abbot of Cirencester	F. Ralph de Estcote [Eastcote]*, monk of abbey M. John Swayn, clerk	Cirencester, 13 Nov. 1325

10/475	John [de Crauden], prior of Ely	F. Nicholas de Copmanford [Coppingford] / M. William de Burton*, rector of Neuton [Newton], Ely diocese	Ely, Monday of St Martin [11 Nov.] 1325
10/476	Chapter of Durham *[LP]*	[D.] Thomas Surtays [Surtees]* / John de Halnatheby*	Durham, 10 Nov. 1325
10/477	Chapter of St Davids	M. Stephen Nest, canon of Aberwell [Abergwili]	Landogy [Llandygwydd], 2 Nov. 1325
10/478	Dean and Chapter of Bangor	[M.] David de Buellt [Guellt], canon of Bangor	Bangor, 10 Nov. 1325
10/479	Llywelyn [ap Hwfa], archdeacon of St Asaph *[LP]*	M. Matthew de Englyfeld [Englefield]*	St Asaph, 11 Nov. 1325
10/480	Reginald [of Waternewton], abbot of Thorney	D. Reginald de Leyton / John de Luffewyk [Lowick]*	Thorney, morrow of St Martin [12 Nov.] 1325
10/481	Walter [of Huntingfield], abbot of St John's, Colchester	John *called* Parles*	Mondon, 16 Nov. 1325
10/482	Adam [de la Hok], abbot of Malmesbury	F. John de Tynterna [Tintern]*, monk of abbey / Hugh de Lameleghe [Lambley], clerk	Malmesbury, 15 Nov. 1325
10/483	John [Thoky], abbot of St Peter's, Gloucester	F. Hugh de Harsfeld [Haresfield], monk of abbey	Gloucester, 31 Oct. 1325
10/484	Roger [Marival], bishop of Salisbury	M. William de Lubbenham [Lubenham]	Potne [Potterne], 15 Nov. 1325

10/485	Henry [of Casewick], abbot of Crowland	D. John de Crosseby [Crosby]* Hasculf de Whitewell* [MP – Rutland]	Crowland, 10 Nov. 1325
10/486	[William de Dene], archdeacon of Rochester [LP]	D. John [Tilton], perpetual vicar of Horton [Horton Kirby], Rochester diocese	Oxford, 13 Nov. 1325
10/487	Richard, subprior of Winchester [LP]	F. Nicholas de Eneford [Enford], monk of priory	Winchester Chapter House, 19 Nov. 1325
10/488	Chapter of York [LP]	M. Richard de Er[myn] [Airmyn]*, canon of York M. Richard de Baldock*, canon of York	York, 10 Nov. 1325
10/489	Madoc ap Nova, dean of St Asaph [LP]	M. Matthew de Englyfeld [Englefield]*, canon of Bangor	St Asaph, 11 Nov. 1325
10/490	A[nian Sais], bishop of Bangor	M. Madoc de Engglyffeld [Matthew de Englefield]*, canon of Bangor M. David de Buelli [Guellt], canon of Bangor	Bangor, 10 Nov. 1325
10/491	Chapter of St Asaph [LP]	M. Matthew de Englefeld [Englefield]*	St Asaph, 11 Nov. 1325
10/492	William [de Chiriton], abbot of Evesham	F. Peter de Wyk [Wick], monk of abbey D. Thomas de Evesham*, clerk	Evesham, 14 Nov. 1325
10/493	[Wulstan de Bransford], prior of Worcester	D. Reginald de Evesham	Worcester, 14 Nov. 1325
10/494	Henry [de Brok], abbot of St Benet of Hulme	F. Thomas de Tudenham [Tuddenham], monk of abbey William de Tutington [Tuttington], clerk	St Benet of Hulme, 12 Nov. 1325

67

10/495	David [Dafydd ap Bleddyn], bishop of St Asaph	M. Matthew de Englefeld [Englefield]* John de Horneby	Lanteglaa [Llandegla], 9 Nov. 1325
10/496	Richard [of Draughton], abbot of Bury St Edmunds	Robert de Foxton* [D.] John de Cavenham	Herlawe [Harlow], 17 Nov. 1325
10/497	Walter [Fifehead], abbot of Hyde near Winchester	Richard Benet, clerk	Hyde, Sunday after All Saints [3 Nov.] 1325
10/498	Louis [de Beaumont], bishop of Durham	D. Roger de Waltham*, canon of St Paul's, London Mausus Marmyon, rector of Stanhop [Stanhope]	Stokton [Stockton-on-Tees], 10 Nov. 1325
10/499	Alan [of Ness], abbot of St Mary's, York [LP]	F. John de Thornton [D.] Richard de Pikeryng [Pickering]	Popelton [Poppleton], 10 Nov. 1325
10/500	John [de Crauden], prior of Ely	F. Nicholas de Copmanford [Coppingford] M. William de Burton*, rector of Neuton [Newton], Ely diocese	Ely, Monday of St Martin [11 Nov.] 1325
11/501	William [of Cowton], prior of Durham	[D.] Thomas Surtays [Surtees] John de Halnatheby*	Durham, 10 Nov. 1325
11/502	David [Martyn], bishop of St Davids	M. Stephen Nest, canon of Aberwellen [Abergwili] collegiate church	Landogy [Llangadog], 2 Nov. 1325
11/503	John [of Wistow II], abbot of Selby	D. Thomas de Brayton* D. Hugh de Bardelby* James de Bilingburgh [Billingborough]	Selby, 10 Nov. 1325

11/504	Adam [of Boothby], abbot of Peterborough	D. Thomas de Sibthorp*, clerk M. Stephen de Aylington [Elton]	Peterborough, Thursday after St Bricius [14 Nov.] 1325
11/505	Robert [de Clopcote], prior of Bath Cathedral [LP]	John de Sevenhampton*	Bath, 12 Nov. 1325
11/506	Subprior and Chapter of Bath Cathedral [LP]	John de Sevenhampton*	Bath Chapter House, 12 Nov. 1325
11/507	Adam [of Sodbury], abbot of Glastonbury	M. William de Selton*, clerk [D.] John de Bruggewater [Bridgwater]*, clerk	Glastonbury, 12 Nov. 1325
11/508	Clergy of London archdeaconry [LP]	M. Hugh de Mortone [Morton]*, rector of Garsington and official of the archdeacon of London M. Andrew de Offord*, clerk, commissary general of the official of the archdeacon of London	London, 14 Nov. 1325
11/509	Clergy of Rochester diocese [LP]	D. John Tilbon, vicar of Horton [Horton Kirby], Rochester diocese John de Brampton, vicar of Estgrenewych [East Greenwich], Rochester diocese	Derteford [Dartford], 9 Nov. 1325
11/510	Chapter of Worcester Cathedral	D. Thomas de Evesham*, clerk	Worcester Chapter House, 14 Nov. 1325

11/511	Clergy of Durham diocese [LP]	D. Thomas de Bamburgh*, rector of Ovyngeham [Ovingham] John de Pollowe [Pollow], dean of prebendal church of Langcestre [Lanchester]	Stocketon [Stockton-on-Tees], Sunday before feast of St Martin [10 Nov.] 1325
11/512	Adam [de la Hok], abbot of Malmesbury (to Hugh Despenser) [F]	No proctors named	[Undated]

PARLIAMENTS OF EDWARD III

PARLIAMENT AT LINCOLN, 15 SEPTEMBER 1327

11/515	Walter [Fifehead], abbot of Hyde near Winchester [LP]	Richard Benyt [Benet]	Hyde, 9 Sept. 1327
11/516	Prior of Carlisle	M. Richard Averioun (?), clerk	Carlisle, 6 Sept. 1327
11/517	John, prior of [damaged] [LP]	[Damaged]	[Illegible] Id. Sept. 132[illegible]
11/518	Chapter of Durham [LP]	D. [sic] John de Butrewyk [Butterwick], monk of priory	Durham Chapter House, 4 Sept. 1327
11/519	Hamo [Hethe], bishop of Rochester	No proctors named	Hallyng [Halling], 10 Sept. 1327

11/520	Alan [of Ness], abbot of St Mary's, York [LP]	F. Thomas de Dalton, monk of abbey D. Richard de Pykeryng [Pickering], clerk	York, 10 Sept. 1327
11/521	Chapter of Lincoln Cathedral [LP]	M. Thomas de Luda [Louth], treasurer of Lincoln	Lincoln Chapter House, 13 Sept. 1327
11/522	Hugh, subprior of Coventry Cathedral, and the Chapter [LP]	[M.] John de Thoresby*, clerk D. Richard de Kyngton [Kington], clerk	Coventry Chapter House, 3 Sept. 1327
11/523	Chapter of Carlisle [LP]	Richard Pyioun	Chapter House, 6 Sept. 1327
11/524	Ralph [de Borne], abbot of St Augustine's, Canterbury	M. Walter de Stourene [Stauren] William de Cotes*	Canterbury, 7 Sept. [no year]
11/525	Adam [of Sodbury], abbot of Glastonbury	M. Henry de Clyf [Cliffe]*, clerk [D.] John de Briggewater [Bridgwater]*, clerk	Glastonbury, 10 Sept. 1327
11/526	[Roger Martival], bishop of Salisbury	M. William de Lubbenham [Lubenham], 'our clerk'	Potne [Potterne], 1 Sept. 132 [damaged]
11/527	Hamo [Hethe], bishop of Rochester	D. Thomas de Alkham, rector of Suthflet [Southfleet], Rochester diocese, 'our clerk' Thomas de Hethe, 'our clerk'	Hallyng [Halling], 10 Sept. 1327
11/528	John [of Wistow II], abbot of Selby	F. Richard de Athelingflet [Adlingfleet], monk of abbey D. Hugh de Bardelby*, clerk	Selby, 30 Sept. 1327

71

11/529	John [Droxford], bishop of Bath and Wells *[LP]*	M. Walter de Hull*, 'our clerk'	Wyvelescomb [Wivelis-combe], 4 Sept. 1327
11/530	A[nian Sais], bishop of Bangor	M. Matthew [Madoc Hedwich], archdeacon of Anglesey	Bangor, feast of the Nativ-ity of the Blessed Virgin Mary [8 Sept.] 1327
11/532	Alan [de Retlyng], abbot of Battle	F. John de Bello [Battle], monk of abbey F. Thomas Aubrei [Aubrey], monk of abbey	Battle, 5 Sept. 1327
11/533	William [of Cowton], prior of Dur-ham *[LP]*	D. [*sic*] John de Butrewyk [Butterwick], monk of priory	Durham, 4 Sept. 1327
11/534	[Edmund London], archdeacon of Bedford	D. John de Martone [Marton]*, rector of Westillburi [West Tilbury] M. John de [*illegible*]	[*Illegible*]
11/535	Stephen [Gravesend], bishop of London	M. Richard de Brencheslee [Brenchley]*, canon of London	Claketon [Clacton], 9 Sept. 1327
11/536	Henry [of Leicester], prior of Cov-entry Cathedral	M. John de Thoresby*, clerk D. Richard de Kyngton [Kington], clerk	Coventry, 3 Sept. 1327

72

PARLIAMENT AT YORK, 7 FEBRUARY 1328

11/513	Dean and Chapter of Bangor	Madoc [Hedwich], archdeacon of Anglesey Madoc de Egylfylde [Matthew de Englefield]*	Bangor, Sunday before feast of the Purification of the Blessed Virgin Mary [30 Jan.] 1328
11/514	Walter [Fifehead], abbot of Hyde near Winchester [LP]	Richard Benet	Hyde, 14 Jan. 1328
11/537	Adam [of Sodbury], abbot of Glastonbury	M. Henry de Clif [Cliffe]*, clerk [D.] John de Bruggewauter [Bridgwater]*, clerk	Glastonbury, 2 Jan. 1328
11/538	Edmund [of Knulle], abbot of St Augustine's, Bristol [LP]	Hugh called le Hunt, clerk Thomas de Gloucester, clerk	Bristol Chapter House, 19 Feb. 1328
11/539	Chapter of Durham [LP]	D. [sic] John de Butrewyk [Butterwick], monk of priory John de Halnatheby*	Durham Chapter House, 3 Feb. 1328
11/540	Richard [of Draughton], abbot of Bury St Edmunds	M. Richard de Herlingge [Harling]*	Bury St Edmunds, 2 Feb. 1328
11/541	[Richard of Charlton], abbot of Cirencester	[Illegible]	[Damaged and illegible]
11/542	Roger [Martival], bishop of Salisbury	M. William de Lubbenham [Lubenham], 'our clerk'	Remmesbury [Ramsbury], 18 Dec. 1327

11/543	David [Martyn], bishop of St Davids	D. Thomas de Cotingham [Cottingham]*, rector of Angulo, St Davids diocese D. John de Wittenhulle [Wettenhall], rector of Merthirkelir, St Davids diocese	Gloucester, Monday the feast of St Thomas, apostle [21 Dec.] 1327

PARLIAMENT AT NORTHAMPTON, 24 APRIL 1328

11/544	Dean and Chapter of York *[LP]*	M. Henry de Clyff [Cliffe]*, canon of York D. John Gyffard [Giffard]*, canon of York D. Nicholas de Hugate [Hungate]*, canon of York	York, 19 April 1328
11/545	Louis [de Beaumont], bishop of Durham	M. Richard de Wyteworth [Whitworth], doctor of civil law, rector of Braunaspath [Brancepeth], Durham diocese William de Quiny	*[No place]*, 15 April 1328
12/600A	Subprior and Chapter of Rochester Cathedral *[LP]*	M. William de Middeltone [Middleton], vicar of Haddenham	Rochester, 15 April 1328

PARLIAMENT AT YORK, 31 JULY 1328

11/546	[Richard of Draughton], abbot of Bury St Edmunds	M. Richard de Herlinge [Harling]* *[Damaged]*	Meleford [Long Melford], 25 July 1328

11/547	Richard [of Charlton], abbot of Cirencester	D. Thomas de Evesham*, clerk Walter de Anneford, clerk	Cirencester, feast of St James, apostle [25 July] 1328
11/548	W., abbot of [damaged]	[Damaged] [Damaged]ham, clerk	[Damaged] St Mary Magdalene [July] 1323
11/549	Thomas [de Goldesburgh], archdeacon of Durham	William de Hunmanby, clerk Richard de Hyde	Esington [Easington], Durham diocese, 27 July 1328
11/550	[Simon of Eye], abbot of Ramsey	D. Thomas de E[illegible], 'our clerk' D. John de Feribi [Ferriby], 'our clerk' Nicholas de Styuecle* [MP – Huntingdonshire]	26 July [no year]
12/551	Stephen [Gravesend], bishop of London	D. William de Munden	Claketon [Clacton], 22 July 1328
12/552	David [Dafydd ap Bleddyn], bishop of St Asaph	M. Henry de Clyf [Cliffe]* [D.] Anias de Leyc [Leicester]	[Damaged], 28 July 1328
12/553	Roger [Martival], bishop of Salisbury	[M.] William de Lubbe [damaged – Lubenham]	Bodeford, 21 July 1328
12/554	William [de Curtlyngton], abbot of Westminster	D. William de Harlaston*, clerk [Damaged]	Piriford [Pyrford], 21 July 1328

12/555	Henry [Gower], bishop of St Davids	D. William de Harleston [Harlaston]*, clerk	Warblynton [Warblington], Monday the feast of St James, apostle [25 July] 1328
12/556	Richard [of Wallingford], abbot of St Albans	F. Richard de Hedesete [Hethersett], monk of abbey D. Ralph de Dalton*, clerk	St Albans, 23 July – *damaged* 1328
12/557	Chapter of York *[LP]*	M. Richard de Cestr [Chester]*, canon of York M. Richard de Crume[well], canon of York D. John Giffard*, canon of York	York, 24 July 1328
12/558	John de Craudene [Crauden], prior of Ely and the Chapter *[LP]*	M. William de Ayrton [Airton] M. Richard de Barton	Ely, Friday after feast of the Translation of St Thomas, martyr [8 July] 1328
12/559	John de Crauden, prior of Ely *[LP]*	M. William de Ayrton [Airton] M. Richard de Barton	Ely, Friday after feast of the Translation of St Thomas, martyr [8 July] 1328
12/560	Adam [of Boothby], abbot of Peterborough	D. Henry de Edenestowe [Edwinstowe]*, clerk Robert de Lufwyk [Lowick]* John de Munkel[*damaged*]	Peterborough, feast of St Mary Magdalene [22 July] 1328

PARLIAMENT AT SALISBURY, 16 OCTOBER 1328

12/561	Richard [of Draughton], abbot of Bury St Edmunds	[Damaged]	Cheuington [Chevington], [Damaged]
12/562	J[ohn of Wigmore], abbot of St Peter's, Gloucester	D. Thomas de Evesham*, clerk	Gloucester, Friday after feast of the Translation of St Edward, king [14 Oct.] 1328
12/563	Simon [of Eye], abbot of Ramsey	D. William de Leycestre [Leicester]* D. Thomas de Escrik [Escrick]* Nicholas de Styuecle*	Ramsey, [damaged] 1328
12/564	Richard [of Charlton], abbot of Cirencester	D. Thomas de Evesham*, clerk Walter de Anneford, clerk	Cirencester, 14 Oct. 1328
12/565	William [de Curdlyngton], abbot of Westminster	[F.] John de Tothale	Westminster, 5 Oct., [damaged]
12/566	William [de Chiriton], abbot of Evesham	F. Peter de Wyke [Wick], monk of abbey D. Thomas de Evesham*, clerk	Evesham, 9 Oct. 1328
12/567	John [Langton], bishop of Chichester [LP]	M. John de Mitford*, clerk [Damaged] de Burgh, clerk	Aldyngbourne, 13 Oct. [damaged]
12/568	[Ralph de Borne], abbot of St Augustine's, Canterbury	M. Walter de Stourene [Stauren] [Damaged]	Canterbury, [damaged] 1328

12/569	Richard [of Wallingford], abbot of St Albans	F. Richard de Hedersete [Hethersett], monk of abbey D. Simon [*damaged*]wode	St Albans, 11 Oct. 1328
12/570	Adam [de la Hok], abbot of Malmesbury	F. John de Tynterna [Tintern]*, monk of abbey Nicholas Pruet, clerk	Malmesbury, 14 Oct. 1328
12/571	Hamo [Hethe], bishop of Rochester [*LP*]	M. John de Secheford [Sedgeford], rector of Faukeham [Fawkham], Rochester diocese	Hallyng [Halling], 12 Oct. 1328
12/572	Clergy of Worcester archdeaconry [*LP*]	D. Thomas de Evesham*, clerk	Worcester, 12 Oct. 1328
12/573	Walter [Fifehead], abbot of Hyde near Winchester [*LP*]	Richard de la More, rector of Kyngeston Sayntmour [Kingston Seymour], Bath and Wells diocese	Hyde, Friday after feast of St Dionysius [14 Oct.] 1328
12/574	William [Melton], archbishop of York [*LP*]	D. Richard de Ayrmynne [Airmyn]*, canon of Lincoln, rector of Elveley D. Henry de Edenestowe [Edwinstowe]*, canon of Suwell [Southwell] D. Michael de Wath*, rector of Wath, York diocese	Thorp by York [Bishopthorpe], [*damaged*]
12/575	Adam [of Boothby], abbot of Peterborough	D. Henry de Edenestowe [Edwinstowe]*, clerk D. William de Lund, clerk	Peterborough, Tuesday after feast of St Michael [4 Oct.] 1328
12/576	M[atthew de Englefield], bishop of Bangor	[D.] Thomas de Capynhurst [Capenhurst]*, clerk	Troflogan, Thursday the feast of St Michael [29 Sept.] 1328

12/577	Chapter of St Asaph [LP]	M. Richard de Oswaldestre [Oswestry]*, canon of St Asaph	St Asaph, 29 Sept. 1328
12/579	Louis [de Beaumont], bishop of Durham	M. Richard de Eryom [Airmyn]*, doctor of both laws	Aukeland [Bishop Auckland], 3 Oct. 1328
12/580	Adam de Ayremynne [Airmyn], archdeacon of Norfolk [LP]	D. Thomas de Evesham*, rector of Badby, Lincoln diocese D. William de Emeldon*, rector of Bothal [Northumberland], Durham diocese	Cambridge, 8 Oct. 1328
12/581	David [Dafydd ap Bleddyn], bishop of St Asaph	M. Henry de Clyf [Cliffe]*, clerk M. Richard de Oswaldester [Oswestry]*, clerk	St Asaph, 27 Sept. 1328
12/582	John [de Crauden], prior of Ely [LP]	M. Nicholas de Stocton [Stockton]*, clerk M. Richard de Barton, clerk	Ely, Friday after feast of St Matthew, apostle [23 Sept.] 1328
12/583	Dean and Chapter of Bangor	Gervase, clerk, rector of Llangian	Bangor, Thursday the feast of Fides, virgin [6 Oct.] 1328
12/584	John [de Crauden], prior of Ely and the Chapter [LP]	M. [Damaged]	Ely, Friday after feast of St Matthew, apostle [23 Sept.] 1328
12/585	Adam de Sandwyco [of Sandwich], archdeacon of Worcester	D. Thomas de Evesham*, clerk	Worcester, 12 Oct. 1328

12/586	Chapter of Norwich [LP]	M. Roger de Breus [Bruce], clerk William de Ayreminne [Airmyn]*, clerk	Chapter House, 13 Oct. 1328
12/587	Alan [of Ness], abbot of St Mary's, York [LP]	F. John de Thornton, monk of abbey	Overton, 8 Oct. 1328
12/588	John [Grandisson], bishop of Exeter	M. John Gloyou, 'our official' M. William de Seton, canon of Lincoln M. William de Nassington*, canon of collegiate church of Osmunderlee [Osmotherley], York diocese	Lawhitton in Cornwall, 10 Oct, 1328
12/589	John [de Eclescliff], bishop of Llandaff	D. William de Herlaston [Harlaston]*, canon of Llandaff	Lank', 14 Oct. 1328
12/590	Dean and Chapter of York [LP]	M. Richard de Hardyngg [Harding], canon of York M. Richard de Eryum [Airmyn]*, canon of York D. John Giffard*, canon of York	York, 9 Oct. 1328
12/591	[Wulstan of Bransford], prior of Worcester Cathedral	D. John de Stok [Stoke]*, rector of Seggesberwe [Sedgeberrow]	Worcester, 12 Oct. 1328
12/592	Robert de Wodhous [Wodehouse], archdeacon of Richmond [LP]	D. William de Harlaston*, canon of Llandaff D. Henry de Edenestowe [Edwinstowe]*, canon of Suthwell [Southwell]	Metheleye [Methley], 23 Sept. 1328
12/593	John [of Aylsham], abbot of St Benet of Hulme	D. Thomas de Egefeld [Edgefield], clerk John Claver*	St Benet [damaged], 2 Oct. 1328

12/594	William [of Caxton], prior of Norwich Cathedral [LP]	M. Roger de Breus [Bruce], clerk William de Ayreminne [Airmyn]*, clerk	Norwich, 13 Oct. 1328
12/595	John [of Wistow II], abbot of Selby	F. Geoffrey de Gadesby [Gaddesby]*, monk of abbey D. Thomas de Brayton*, clerk	Selby, 7 Oct. 1328

PARLIAMENT AT WESTMINSTER, 9 FEBRUARY 1329 (SECOND SESSION OF OCTOBER 1328 PARLIAMENT)

12/578	J[ohn of Appleford], abbot of Reading	Adam de Gateshened [Gateshead]	Reading, 8 Feb. 1329
12/596	Thomas La[damaged], prior of St John of Jerusalem in England [LP]	Thomas de Colt	[Illegible], 3 Feb. 1329
12/597	Louis [de Beaumont], bishop of Durham	M. Richard de Erium [Airmyn]*, canon of York, [not stated] of both laws M. Richard de Bynteworth [Bintworth]*, canon of prebendal church of Aukeland [Bishop Auckland]	Durham, 28 Jan. 1329
12/598	Henry [Gower], bishop of St Davids [LP]	M. Griffin de Cawntiton [Gruffudd Caunton]*, clerk D. William de Holynes, clerk	Great Malvern, 8 Feb. 1329
12/599	Chapter of St Asaph [LP]	D. Anias Leyc [Leicester]	St Martin's, 3 Feb. 1329
12/600	Dean and Chapter of York [LP]	M. Henry de Clif [Cliffe]*, canon of York D. John Gyffard [Giffard]*, canon of York	York, 1 Feb. 1329

| 13/602 | David [Dafydd ap Bleddyn], bishop of St Asaph | D. Anias Leycester [Leicester], clerk
D. Thomas de Kapinhurst [Capenhurst]*, clerk | [St] Martin's, 3 Feb. 1329 |
| 13/610 | Richard [of Draughton], abbot of Bury St Edmunds | M. Richard de Herlingg [Harling]*, clerk | Bury St Edmunds, 17 Jan., 3 Edward III [1330, *recte* 1329] |

GREAT COUNCIL AT WINDSOR, 23 JULY 1329

| 13/604 | [Richard of Wallingford], abbot of St Albans | F. Richard de Hedersete [Hethersett], monk of abbey | St Albans, the vigil of St James, apostle [24 July] 1329 |

PARLIAMENT AT WINCHESTER, 11 MARCH 1330

13/603	Louis [de Beaumont], bishop of Durham	D. Thomas Surtesye [Surtees], knight M. Richard de Bynteworth [Bintworth]*, clerk, doctor of civil law	Middleham Manor, 1 April 1329
13/605	[Simon of Eye], abbot of Ramsey	F. John de Gretford [Greatford], monk of abbey John de Chetingdon	Broughton, 8 March 1330
13/606	William [de Curtlyngton], abbot of Westminster	F. John de Tothale, monk D. John de Muchedevre [Micheldever], clerk	Westminster, 8 March 1330

13/607	William [of Grasby], abbot of Thornton	D. Edmund de Grymesby [Grimsby]* Thomas de Ulseby [Ulceby]	Thornton, [*illegible*] March 1330
13/608	Chapter of Worcester Cathedral	D. Thomas de Evesham*, clerk	Worcester Chapter House, 8 March 1330
13/609	Adam [de la Hok], abbot of Malmesbury	F. John de Tynterna [Tintern]*, monk of abbey D. Thomas de Evesham*, clerk	Malmesbury, 9 March 1330
13/611	Alan [of Ness], abbot of St Mary's, York [*LP*]	F. Roger de Aselakby [Aslackby], monk of abbey D. Hugh de Burgh*, clerk	Popelton [Poppleton], 1 March 1330
13/612	Adam [of Sodbury], abbot of Glastonbury	M. Henry de Clyf [Cliffe]*, clerk [D.] John de Briggewater [Bridgwater]*, clerk	Glastonbury, 20 Feb. 1330
13/613	Richard [of Charlton], abbot of Cirencester	D. Thomas de Evesham*, clerk Richard Benet	Cirencester, 9 March 1330
13/614	William [Melton], archbishop of York	M. John de Thoresby*, canon of Wells M. John de Aton [Acton]*, canon of Lincoln M. Ralph de Yarwell, rector of Cotum [Cottam], York diocese	Thorp by York [Bishopthorpe], 2 March 1330
13/615	Richard [of Wallingford], abbot of St Albans	F. Adam de Newerk [Newark], monk of abbey [D.] Thomas de Escrik [Escrick]*, clerk	St Albans, 10 March 1330
13/616	Archdeacon of Brecon, St Davids diocese	[M.] Giffard de Kamiteton [Gruffudd Caunton], canon of St Davids	Brecon, 9 March 1330

13/617	Ralph [de Borne], abbot of St Augustine's, Canterbury	Henry de Edenestowe [Edwinstowe]*, clerk	Canterbury, 6 March 1330
13/618	Adam [of Boothby], abbot of Peterborough	D. Henry de Edenestowe [Edwinstowe]*, clerk M. John Trivet, clerk	Northampton, 5 March 1330
13/619	Hamo [Hethe], bishop of Rochester [LP]	M. John de Secheford [Sedgeford], rector of Faukeham, Rochester diocese	Hallyng [Halling], 7 March 1330
13/620	John [of Appleford], abbot of Reading	Adam de Gateshened [Gateshead]	Reading, 9 March 1330
13/621	John [of Wigmore], abbot of St Peter's, Gloucester	D. Thomas de Evesham*, clerk	Gloucester, 5 March 1330
13/622	Alan [de Retlyng], abbot of Battle	D. Elias de Grymmesby [Grimsby]*, clerk	Battle, 7 March [no year]
13/623	John [of Wistow II], abbot of Selby	D. Thomas de Brayton*, clerk D. Hugh de Bardelby*, clerk	Selby, 3 March 1330
13/624	Thomas [Charlton], bishop of Hereford [LP]	M. John de Lancestone [Launceston], clerk M. John de Bartone [Barton], clerk	Ros [Ross-on-Wye], 7 March 1330
13/625	John [Langton], bishop of Chichester [LP]	M. John de [le] Brabazon*, canon of Chichester	Bysshopestone [Bishop-stone], 4 March 1330
13/626	Robert [of Garford], abbot of Abingdon	F. Richard de Hildesleye [Hildesley], monk of abbey	Abingdon, 5 March [no year]

84

13/627	Roger [Martival], bishop of Salisbury	M. William de Lubbenham [Lubenham], 'our clerk'	Potnere, 9 March 1330
13/628	Dean and Chapter of Bangor	D. William de Werdale [Weardale], rector of Aberfraw [Aberffraw], Bangor diocese D. Robert de Biwell [Bywell], rector of Aber, Bangor diocese	Bangor, Sunday after feast of St Cedd, bishop [4 March] 1330
13/629	Matthew [de Englefield], bishop of Bangor	[D.] Thomas de Capnest [Capenhurst]*, clerk Griffin ap Tudur [Tudor], clerk	Esseby Folvill [Ashby Folvill], Thursday before feast of St Gregory, pope [8 March] 1330
13/630	Dean [Robert Pickering] and Chapter of York [LP]	M. Henry de Clyff [Cliffe]*, canon of York M. Gilbert de la Bruere [Brewer], canon of York M. Nicholas de Ludlowe [Ludlow], canon of York	York, 1 March 1330
13/631	[Wulstan of Bransford], prior of Worcester Cathedral	D. Walter de Bradeweye [Broadway], chaplain Adam de Braunfeld [Brayfield], clerk	Worcester, 8 March 1330
13/632	Thomas Larchier, prior of the Hospital of St John of Jerusalem in England [LP]	F. John de Bymbrok [Binbrok], monk of order Thomas de Collum, clerk	Hetheryngton [Hetherington], 1 March 1330
13/633	Chapter of St Davids	[M.] Gruffinus Cautyton [Gruffudd Caunton]*, canon of St Davids	St Davids Chapter House, 28 Feb. 1330

85

13/634	[Dafydd ap Bleddyn], bishop of St Asaph [LP]	D. Kenrick Loyt, rector of Lanveyr [Llanvair]	St Asaph, 1 March 1330
13/635	Richard [of Draughton], abbot of [damaged – Bury St Edmunds]	F. Walter de Pincebek [Pinchbeck], monk of abbey	Culeford [Culford], 6 March 1330
13/636	John [of Aylsham], abbot of St Benet of Hulme	Either D. John de Norton*, rector of Bradele Magna [Great Bradley] or Roger de Merkeshale [Markshall]	St Benet of Hulme, 4 March 1330
13/637	Philip, archdeacon of Cardigan	M. Griffin de Caunton [Gruffudd Caunton]*, canon of St Davids	Kinerdyn, Saturday after feast of Blessed David, confessor [3 March] 1330
13/638	John [Ross], bishop of Carlisle	D. Adam de Stayngreve [Stonegrave]* of Wyggeton [Wigton]; M. Thomas de Goldyngton [Goldington], rector of Musgrave; M. John de Estsex [Essex] of Sancto Albano [St Albans]; M. William Lengleys [English], armiger [gentleman]*	Rosa [Rose], 3 March 1330
13/639	David [Dafydd ap Bleddyn], bishop of St Asaph	[D.] Thomas de Capynhurst [Capenhurst]*, 'our clerk'; Kenrick Loyt, 'our clerk'	Eyton, 3 March 1330
13/640	Simon [Meopham], archbishop of Canterbury	M. John de Radeswell [Ridgewell], clerk; M. Laurence Fastolf*, clerk	Mortelak [Mortlake], 8 March 1330

PARLIAMENT AT NOTTINGHAM, 15 OCTOBER 1330

13/641	Adam [of Boothby], abbot of Peterborough	D. Henry de Edenestowe [Edwinstowe]* Peter [illegible] Robert de Lufwyk [Lowick]*	Peterborough, [damaged] before feast of St Michael, archangel, 133c [Sept. 1330]
13/642	Ralph [de Borne], abbot of St Augustine's, Canterbury	M. Walter de Stourenne [Stauren], archdeacon of Stow D. Henry de [damaged]	Canterbury, 9 Oct. 1 [damaged]
13/643	[Ralph of Shrewsbury], bishop of Bath and Wells	[Damaged – Henry] de Clyf [Cliffe]*, clerk D. Thomas de Evesham*, clerk	[Damaged] 1330
13/644	John [of Aylsham], abbot of St Benet of Hulme	Roger de Merkyshal [Markshall]	St Benet of Hulme, 8 Oct. 1330
13/645	Adam [of Sodbury], abbot of Glastonbury	M. Henry de Clif [Cliffe]* [D.] John de Bruggewauter [Bridgwater]*	Glastonbury, 1 Oct. 1330
13/646	Walter [Fifehead], abbot of Hyde near Winchester	Robert de Bukyngeham [Buckingham]	Hyde, 3 Oct. 1330
13/647	Louis [de Beaumont], bishop of Durham	M. Richard de Bynteworth [Bintworth]*, doctor of civil law	Welburn, 10 Oct., 1330
13/648	Richard [of Wallingford], abbot of St Albans	F. Robert [illegible], monk of abbey D. Thomas de Escrik [Escrick]*, clerk	St Albans, 12 Oct. 1330

13/649	Simon [Meopham], archbishop of Canterbury [LP]	M. Laurence Fastolf*, 'our clerk'	Mortelak [Mortlake], 7 Oct. 1330
13/650	Robert [of Garford], abbot of Abingdon	D. Thomas de Evesham*, clerk Benedict de Normanton, clerk	Abingdon, [illegible] Oct. [no year]
14/651	John [of Wigmore], abbot of St Peter's, Gloucester	D. Thomas de Evesham*, clerk	Gloucester, 8 Oct. 1330
14/652	Adam [de la Hok], abbot of Malmesbury	D. Thomas de Evesham*, clerk	Malmesbury, 30 Sept. 1330
14/653	[Alan of Ness], abbot of St Mary's, York	F. Roger de Thorp, monk of abbey Roger Sturdy	Popilton [Poppleton], 9 Oct. 1330
14/654	Matthew [of Englefield], bishop of Bangor	[D.] Thomas de Capenhust*, clerk Griffin ap Tudor, clerk	Gogerth [Gogarth], Wednesday after St Diony- sius, martyr [10 Oct.] 1330
14/655	William [de Curdyngton], abbot of Westminster	D. Henry de Edenestowe [Edwinstowe]*, clerk M. William de Bampton, clerk	Westminster, 9 Oct., 4 Edward III [1330]
14/656	[Simon of Eye], abbot of Ramsey	[F.] John de Gretford [Greatford], monk of abbey D. Thomas de Escrik [Escrick]*	Ramsey, 12 Oct. [no year]
14/657	William [de Chiriton], abbot of Evesham	F. Peter de Wyke [Wick], monk D. Thomas de Evesham*, clerk	Evesham, feast of St Michael [29 Sept.] 1330

14/658	Richard [of Charlton], abbot of Cirencester	D. Thomas de Evesham*, clerk Richard de Tetlebury	Cirencester, 8 Oct. 1330
14/659	Richard [of Draughton], abbot of Bury St Edmunds	F. Walter de Pinchebek [Pinchbeck]	Elmeswell [Elmswell], 10 Oct. 1330
14/660	[Adam of Boothby], abbot of Peterborough	D. Richard de Whytewell [Whitwell], clerk D. John Coleman, clerk M. John Tryvet [Trivet], clerk	Peterborough, Friday after St Dionysius [12 Oct.] 1330
14/661	J[ohn of Appleford], abbot of Reading	Adam Gatteshened [Gateshead]	Reading, 5 Oct. 1330
14/662	John [of Wistow II], abbot of Selby	F. Geoffrey de Gaddesby*, monk of abbey D. Thomas de Brayton*, clerk	Selby, 12 Oct. [no year]
26/1288	Louis [de Beaumont], bishop of Durham [F]	No proctors named	[Undated]

PARLIAMENT AT WESTMINSTER, 26 NOVEMBER 1330

14/663	Walter [Fifehead], abbot of Hyde near Winchester [LP]	[Damaged] le Botiler, monk of abbey	Hyde, Thursday after feast of St Katherine, virgin [29 Nov.] 1330

14/664	John [Ross], bishop of Carlisle	M. John Bigge, rector of [St Nicholas] Feltewell [Felt-well], Norwich diocese, clerk of the bishop's household D. Richard de Enderby*, rector of Riseangle [Rish-angles], Norwich diocese D. Thomas de Eynton, rector of 'Midekyngton', Lincoln diocese	Horncaster [Horncastle], 14 Nov. 1330
14/665	[Alan of Ness],abbot of St Mary's, York	F. Roger de Thorp, monk of abbey D. Richard de Pickering, clerk	Popilton [Poppleton], 17 Nov. 1330
14/666	[William of Cowton], prior, and Chapter of Durham	M. John de Hirlaw, clerk M. John de Bekyngham [Beckingham], clerk	Durham, 12 Nov. 1330
14/667	Dean and Chapter of Bangor	M. David de Guellt, canon of Bangor	Bangor, Monday on the morrow of St Martin, bishop, [12 Nov.] 1330
14/668	Henry [of Leicester], prior of Coventry [LP]	D. John de Leycestr [Leicester], canon of Lichfield F. John called de Sutham [Southam], monk of priory	Coventry, 23 Nov. 1330
14/669	Adam [of Boothby], abbot of Peterborough	D. Henry de Edenestowe [Edwinstowe]* [CoP] M. Philip de Kilkenni [Kilkenny]* Robert de Lufwyk [Lowick]*	Peterborough, Friday the feast of St Clement [23 Nov.] 1330
14/670	John [de Eclescliff], bishop of Llandaff	M. Thomas Sampson', canon of Llandaff D. Henry de Edenestowe [Edwinstowe]*, canon of Llandaff [CoP]	Lank', 21 Nov. 1330

14/671	Joceus [de Kinebauton], archdeacon of Gloucester [LP]	D. Adam de Aylinton [Ellington] / M. Thomas de Bradewelle [Bradwell]	Sobur' [Sodbury], 22 Nov. 1330
14/673	William [of Grasby], abbot of Thornton	[F.] Alan de Clee, monk of abbey	Thornton, xvii Kal. Dec. [15 Nov.] 1330
14/674	Chapter of St Asaph [LP]	M. Richard de Oswaldestr' [Oswestry]*, canon of St Asaph	St Asaph, [illegible] 1330
14/675	John [of Aylsham], abbot of St Benet of Hulme	[D.] John de Norton*, clerk / John Claver*	St Benet of Hulme, 20 Nov. 1330
14/676	[Richard of Idbury], abbot of Winchcombe	F. Robert de Ippewelle [Ipwell]*, prior of Winchcombe	Winchcombe, Friday the feast of St Clement [23 Nov.] 1330
14/677	John [of Wistow II], abbot of Selby	F. Geoffrey de Gaddesby*, monk of abbey / [D.] Thomas de Brayton*, clerk	Selby, 18 Nov. 1330
14/678	[Robert of Garford], abbot of Abingdon	D. Thomas de Evesham* / [F.] Richard de Hildesley, monk of abbey	Abingdon, 20 Nov. [no year]
14/679	[Simon of Eye], abbot of Ramsey	[F.] John de Gretford [Greatford], monk of abbey / John de Chetingdon / D. Thomas de Escrik [Escrick]* / [D.] Simon de Glynton [Glinton]*	Broughton, 21 Nov. [no year]
14/680	Adam [de la Hok], abbot of Malmesbury	F. John de Tintern*, monk of abbey / D. Thomas de Evesham*, clerk	Malmesbury, [illegible] Nov. 1330

14/681	William [of Cowton], prior of Durham	M John de Hirlaw, clerk M. John de Bekyngham [Beckingham], clerk	Durham, 12 Nov. 1330
14/682	John [of Appleford], abbot of Reading	Adam Gateshened [Gateshead]	Reading, 21 Nov. 1330
14/683	John [Langton], bishop of Chichester [LP]	M. John [le] Brabazon*, canon of Chichester John de [illegible]ford [Mitford]*, canon of Chichester	Aldyngbourne [Aldingbourne], 23 Nov. 1330
14/684	Richard [of Draughton], abbot of Bury St Edmunds	F. Walter de Pincebeck [Pinchbeck]	Culeford [Culford], 23 Dec. 1330
14/685	Richard [of Wallingford], abbot of St Albans	F. Richard Broun, monk of abbey F. Richard de Hederset [Hethersett], monk of abbey [D.] Thomas de Escrik [Escrick]*, clerk	St Albans, 24 Nov. [no year]
14/686	[Wulstan of Bransford], prior of Worcester	F. Robert de [Damaged]tone, monk and sacristan of Worcester	Worcester, 18 Nov. 1330
14/688	Clergy of Worcester archdeaconry [LP]	M. John de Lude*	Worcester, 17 Nov. 1330
14/689	Reginald [of Waternewton], abbot of Thorney	M. John [de Stanford]*, rector of Giddingg [Little Gidding] John de Luffewyk [Lowick]* Richard de Islep [Islip]	Thorney, Monday after St Edmund, king and martyr [26 Nov.] 1330

14/690	Louis [de Beaumont], bishop of Durham	D. Thomas Surteyse [Surtees], knight M. Richard de Bynteworth [Bintworth]*, doctor of civil law	Alington, 24 Nov. 1330
14/691	Richard [of Charlton], abbot of Cirencester	D. Thomas de Evesham*, clerk	Cirencester, 22 Nov. 1330
14/692	John [of Wigmore], abbot of St Peter's, Gloucester	D. Thomas de Evesham*, clerk	Hardepure [Hartpury], 9 Nov.1330
14/693	Chapter of Worcester	D. Reginald de Evesham, rector of Kyselingbury [Kislingbury], Lincoln diocese D. John de Stoke*, rector of Seggeberrow [Sedgeberrow], Worcester diocese	Worcester Chapter House, 18 Nov. 1330
14/694	Clergy of Durham archdeaconry [LP]	M. John de Bekyngham [Beckingham], clerk	Durham, 14 Nov. 1330
14/695	Subprior and Chapter of Coventry [LP]	M. John de Thoresby*, clerk F. John called de Sutham [Southam], monk of priory Henry de Shulton*, clerk	Coventry Chapter House, 22 Nov. 1330
14/696	Clergy of Northumberland archdeaconry [LP]	M. John de Hyrlawe [Hirlaw], clerk	Durham, 14 Nov. 1330
14/697	Ralph [de Borne], abbot of St Augustine's, Canterbury	Thomas de Lincolna [Lincoln]* [F.] Solomon de Ripple, monk of abbey [F.] Thomas de Natingdone [Nackington], monk of abbey	Canterbury, 21 Nov. 1330

93

PARLIAMENT AT WESTMINSTER, 30 SEPTEMBER 1331

14/698	Walter [of Halton], prior of Spalding	M. John de Hawe	Spalding, Sunday after St Matthew, apostle [22 Sept.] 1331
14/699	Walter [Fifehead], abbot of Hyde near Winchester [LP]		Hyde, 26 Sept. 1331
14/700	Ralph [de Borne], abbot of St Augustine's, Canterbury	M. Henry de Clyf [Cliffe]*, canon of Salisbury Richard Beneyt [Benet]	Canterbury, v Kal. [damaged] 1331
15/701	Clergy of Carlisle diocese [LP]	M. Robert de Wigornia [Worcester]*, doctor of civil law Thomas de Lincolna [Lincoln]*	Carlisle, feast of the Exaltation of the Holy Cross [14 Sept.] 1331
15/702	Wulstan [of Bransford], prior of Worcester Cathedral	M. Adam de Appelby [Appleby]*, rector of Caldbeck Robert de Tympauron, rector of Kirkyngton [Kirklinton], Carlisle diocese	Worcester, 26 Sept. 1331
15/703	Matthew [of Englefield], bishop of Bangor	F. John de Westbury, monk of priory	Bangor, the morrow of St Matthew, apostle [22 Sept.] 1331
15/704	Richard [of Wallingford], abbot of St Albans	M. Matthew [Madoc Hedwich], archdeacon of Anglesey, clerk [M.] David de Guellt, canon of Bangor, clerk	St Albans, Saturday after St Matthew, apostle [28 Sept.] 1331
15/705	Chapter of Worcester Cathedral	F. Richard de Hedersete [Hethersett], monk of abbey D. Thomas de Escrik [Escrick]*, clerk	Worcester Chapter House, 25 Sept. 1331
		D. Reginald de Evesham, rector of Kyselingbury [Kislingbury]	

94

15/706	John [of Aylsham], abbot of St Benet of Hulme	D. Michael de Wath*, clerk Robert de Spaunton	St Benet of Hulme, 25 Sept. 1331
15/707	Richard [of Draughton], abbot of Bury St Edmunds	D. John de Cavenham	Culeford [Culford], 24 Sept. 1331
15/708	[Adam of Sodbury], abbot of Glastonbury	M. Henry de Clyf [Cliffe]*, clerk D. John de Briggewater [Bridgwater]*, clerk	Glastonbury, 14 Sept., 1331
15/709	Ralph [of Shrewsbury], bishop of Bath and Wells	M. Henry de Clyf [Cliffe]* Simon de Bristol [Bristol]*	Dogmersfield [Dogmersfield], Sunday the feast of St Michael [29 Sept.] 1331
15/710	Louis [de Beaumont], bishop of Durham	M. Richard de Bynteworth [Bintworth]*, prebend and canon of the prebendal church of Aukland [Bishop Auckland], Durham diocese, and doctor of civil law	Aukland [Bishop Auckland], 18 Sept. 1331
15/711	John [of Wistow II], abbot of Selby	F. Geoffrey de Gaddesby*, monk of abbey D. Thomas de Brayton*, clerk	Selby, 18 Sept. 1331
15/712	Robert [of Garford], abbot of Abingdon	M. Robert Dayleston [de Aylestone]*, clerk D. Thomas de Evesham*, clerk	Abingdon, Sunday before St Matthew, apostle [15 Sept.] 1331
15/713	Adam [de la Hok], abbot of Malmesbury	F. John de Tynterna [Tintern]*, monk of abbey D. Thomas de Evesham*, clerk	Malmesbury, 24 Sept. 1331
15/714	John [of Wigmore], abbot of St Peter's, Gloucester	D. Thomas de Evesham*, clerk	Gloucester, 21 Aug. 1331

15/715	John [de Eclescliff], bishop of Llandaff	D. Henry de Edenestowe [Edwinstowe]*, canon of Llandaff [CoP] M. John de Carleton [Carlton]*, clerk	Lank', 21 Sept. 1331
15/716	Richard [of Charlton], abbot of Cirencester	D. Thomas de Evesham*, clerk Richard de la Hale*	Cirencester, 25 Sept. 1331
15/717	David [Dafydd ap Bleddyn], bishop of St Asaph	Louis [Llywelyn ap Madoc ab Ellis]*, archdeacon of St Asaph	Alltmelydyn [Meliden], 23 Sept. 1331
15/718	[Thomas of Moulton], abbot of St Mary's, York [LP]	F. Roger de Aselakby [Aslackby], monk of abbey [D.] Richard de Pykering [Pickering]	Meton, 21 Sept. 1331
15/719	William [Melton], archbishop of York	M. Richard de Havering*, canon of York M. John de Thoresby*, canon of Suwell [Southwell] M. John de Barneby [Barnby], canon of Suwell [Southwell]	Suwell [Southwell], 24 Sept. 1331, 14th year of archbishop's pontificate
15/720	Dean and Chapter of Bangor	M. David de Guellt, canon de Bangor	Bangor, Saturday the vigil of St Matthew, apostle [21 Sept.] 1331
15/721	Chapter of St Asaph [LP]	Louis [Llywelyn ap Madoc ab Ellis]*, archdeacon and canon of St Asaph	St Asaph, 23 Sept. 1331

PARLIAMENT AT WESTMINSTER, 20 JANUARY 1332

15/726	William [de Chiriton], abbot of Evesham	F. Peter de Wyke [Wick], monk of abbey D. Thomas de Evesham*, clerk	Evesham, feast of St Hilary [13 Jan.] 1332
15/727	Ralph [de Borne], abbot of St Augustine's, Canterbury	Thomas de Lyncolna [Lincoln] F. Thomas de Natyndone [Nackington], monk of abbey	Canterbury, 17 Jan. 1332
15/728	Thomas [of Moulton], abbot of St Mary's, York [LP]	D. Richard de Pykering [Pickering], clerk John de Pykering [Pickering], clerk	York, 12 Jan. 1332
15/729	Robert [of Garford], abbot of Abingdon	M. Robert Dayleston [de Aylestone]* D. Thomas de Evesham*	Abingdon, 13 Jan. 1332
15/730	John [of Wigmore], abbot of St Peter's, Gloucester	D. Thomas de Evesham*, clerk	Gloucester, 3 Jan. 1332
15/732	Richard [of Draughton], abbot of Bury St Edmunds	D. John de Cavenham	Herlawe [Harlow], 18 Jan. 1332
15/733	Adam [de la Hok], abbot of Malmesbury	D. Thomas de Evesham*, clerk M. John de Badmyntone [Badminton]*, clerk	Malmesbury, 15 Dec. 1331
15/734	Leonard de Tibert, prior of the hospital of St John of Jerusalem in England [LP]	D. Henry de Edenestowe [Edwinstowe]*, clerk F. Simon Faucon, monk of order	York, 12 Jan. 1332

15/735	Richard [of Wallingford], abbot of St Albans	F. Richard de Hederset [Hethersett], monk of abbey D. Thomas de Escrik [Escrick]*, clerk	St Albans, 19 Jan. 1332
15/736	Adam [of Boothby], abbot of Peterborough	D. Henry de Edenestowe [Edwinstowe]*, clerk Peter fil' Warin [Fitzwarren], clerk Robert de Lufwyk [Lowick]*, clerk	Peterborough, Friday the feast of St Anthony [17 Jan.] 1332
15/737	Matthew [of Englefield], bishop of Bangor	M. David de Guellt, canon of Bangor [D.] Thomas de Capenhurst*, clerk	Norton, 10 Jan. 1332
15/738	David [Dafydd ap Bleddyn], bishop of St Asaph	M. Llywelyn Ardan Matthew de Trefrawr [Trefor]*, canon of St Asaph	Oswestry, morrow of St Thomas, apostle [22 Dec.] 1331
15/739	William [of Grasby], abbot of Thornton	D. William de Broclousby [Brocklesby]*, clerk D. Edmund de Grymesby [Grimsby]*, clerk D. John de Rasen, clerk	Thornton, 11 Jan. 1332
15/740	John [de Eclescliff], bishop of Llandaff	D. Henry de Edenestowe [Edwinstowe]*, canon of Llandaff M. John de Carleton [Carlton]*, 'our clerk'	Lank', 17 Jan. 1332

98

15/742	John [de Crauden], prior of Ely, and the Chapter [LP]	F. Richard de Copmanford [Coppingford], monk of priory M. Nicholas de Stocton [Stockton]*, clerk	Ely, Friday the morrow of St Gregory, pope [13 March] 1332
15/743	John [de Crauden], prior of Ely	F. Richard de Copmanford [Coppingford], monk of priory M. Nicholas de Stocton [Stockton]*, clerk	Ely, Thursday the feast of St Gregory, pope [12 March] 1332
15/744	[Robert of Langdon], abbot of Burton-upon-Trent	D. Michael de Wath*, clerk	[Damaged] March, 1332
15/746	Philip [of Barton], master of Sempringham	Peter de Sempringham, doctor of sacred theology F. William de Nesse, monk of order	Our house of Ellerton near York, 4 March [no year]
15/747	Alan [de Retlyng], abbot of Battle	F. John de Bello [Battle], monk of abbey D. Elias de Grymesby [Grimsby]*, clerk	Battle, 13 March 1332
15/748	Edmund [of Knulle], abbot of St Augustine's, Bristol [LP]	M. John de Cleoburi [Cleobury], canon of Llandaff F. John de Schaston [Shaftesbury], monk of abbey	Bristol, 10 March 1332
15/749	Adam [Knoll], prior of St Stephen's, Launceston	John de Altestowe*	Launceston, 10 March 1332
15/750	Richard, prior of St German's, Cornwall	John Bylloun [Billoun]*	St German's, 23 Feb. 1332

99

16/751	John [de Thorpe], prior of Coxford	Simon de Reynham [Raynham]	Coxford, 8 March 1332
16/752	John [of Gloucester], abbot of Hailes	D. Reginald de Evesham, rector of Kiselingbury [Kislingbury] Laurence Bruton* of Chepingnorton [Chipping Norton]	Hailes, Thursday the feast of St Gregory, pope [12 March] 1332
16/753	John [de Cotes], abbot of Tewkesbury	D. John le Smale M. William de Keneneriton	Tewkesbury, 7 March 1332
16/754	Chapter of St Asaph	M. Matthew de Trefvaur [Trefor]*, canon of cathedral	St Asaph, 3 March 1332
16/755	Ralph [de Borne], abbot of St Augustine's, Canterbury	Thomas de Lincolnia [Lincoln]* Stephen de Hakyntone [Hackington], monk of abbey [F.] Thomas de Natyndone [Nackington], monk of abbey	Canterbury, 9 March 1332
16/756	William [de Banville], prior of Wilmington [LP]	Adam de [Damaged]	Wilmington, Thursday the feast of St Gregory, pope [12 March] 1332
16/757	John [of Wigmore], abbot of St Peter's, Gloucester	D. Thomas de Evesham*, clerk	Gloucester, 4 March 1332
16/758	John [of Aylsham], abbot of St Benet of Hulme	[D.] Michael de Wath*, clerk John Claver*	St Benet of Hulme, 8 March 1332
16/759	Thomas [of Witherley], abbot of Bordesley	F. William de Wenden, monk of abbey	Bordesley, Monday before feast of St Gregory, pope [9 March] 1332

16/760	Richard [of Wallingford], abbot of St Albans	F. Richard de Hedersete [Hethersett], monk of abbey D. Thomas de Escrik [Escrick]*, clerk	St Albans, day of St Gregory, pope [12 March] 1332
16/761	Richard [of Charlton], abbot of Cirencester	M. Richard de Chaddesle [Chaddesley]*, clerk D. Thomas de Evesham*, clerk	Cirencester, 9 March 1332
16/762	Adam [of Skerne], abbot of Meaux	D. Michael de Wath*, clerk Robert de Cayton	Melsa [Meaux], 8 March 1332
16/763	Ralph [Courait], prior of Lancaster [LP]	Henry de Haydock* John de Muncketon [Monkton]	Lancaster, 6 March 1332
16/764	John [of Kilkhampton], prior of Bodmin in Cornwall	John Byllon [Billoun]*	Bodmin, Monday before feast of St Gregory, pope [9 March] 1332
16/765	Thomas [sic], prior of St Oswald's, Nostell	[D.] Thomas Baumburge [Bamburgh]* [D.] Michael de Wath*	St Oswald's, 20 Feb. 1332
16/766	Robert [Pickering], dean of York and the Chapter [LP]	M. Henry de Clyf [Cliffe]*, canon of York D. John Gyffard [Giffard]*, canon of York D. Robert de Valoignes [Valognes]*, canon of York	York, 22 Feb. 1332
16/767	John [de Sancto Albino], prior of Tutbury	Nicholas de Acton* William Curteys [Curtis]	Tutbury, 6 March 1332
16/768	Richard [Tours], abbot of Leicester	F. William Geryn, monk of abbey F. William de Exham, monk of abbey	Our abbey of Leicester, 9 March 1332

101

16/769	[Peter de Carville], prior of St Michael's Mount	John Ceylon	St Michael's Mount, 5 March 1332
16/770	William [of Ingelby], abbot of Rievaulx	D. John de Marton* Richard de Marton*	Rievaulx, 4 March 1332
16/771	Clergy of Carlisle diocese [LP]	F. Adam de Dalton, prior of Wedrehal [Wetheral] D. Robert de Tymperon [Tymparon]*, rector of Kirkington [Kirklinton], Carlisle diocese	Merton, 26 Feb. 1332
16/772	Peter [of Chichester], abbot of Beaulieu	F. William de Lynkenholte [Linkenholt], monk of abbey	Beaulieu, feast of St Gregory, pope [12 March] 1332
16/773	Thomas [of Moulton], abbot of St Mary's, York [LP]	F. Roger de Aslakby [Aslackby], monk of abbey [D.] Richard de Pykering [Pickering], clerk	York, 4 March 1332
16/774	Gilbert [of Whaplode], prior of Westacre, Norwich diocese	Richard de Swafham [Swaffham], clerk	Westacre, 8 March 1332
16/775	Walter [Coxwold], abbot of Fountains	D. Adam de Stayngreue [Stonegrave]*, clerk D. William de Kettelby [Kettleby], clerk	Kyrkested [Kirkstead], Thursday the feast of St Gregory, pope [12 March] 1332
16/776	[Reginald of Waternewton], abbot of Thorney	D. John [Balne], rector of Stibbington D. John [de Stanford]*, rector of Parva Giddingge [Little Giding] John de Luffewyk [Lowick]*	Thorney, 10 March 1332

102

16/777	Adam [of Boothby], abbot of Peterborough	D. Henry de Edenestowe [Edwinstowe]*, clerk [CoP] Robert de Lufwyk [Lowick]*, clerk William de Stavern, clerk	Peterborough, Thursday the feast of Gregory, pope [12 March] 1332
16/778	Walter [of Halton], prior of Spalding	F. John de Hatfeld [Hatfield], monk of priory F. John de Hagh, monk of priory	Spalding, Wednesday before feast of St Gregory, pope [11 March] 1332
16/779	John [Langton], bishop of Chichester [LP]	M. John le Brabauzon [Brabazon]*, canon of Chichester, clerk [M.] John de Mitford*, clerk	Ferryngg [Ferring], 10 March 1332
16/780	[Robert of Hathern], prior of Thurgarton [LP]	F. Thomas de Barkeby [Barkby], monk of priory	Thurgarton, Thursday the feast of St Gregory, pope [12 March] 1332
16/781	[William of Muckley], abbot of Shrewsbury [LP]	F. Thomas de Acton, monk of abbey M. Roger de Aston*, clerk	Shrewsbury, Thursday the feast of St Gregory, pope [12 March] 1332
16/782	Robert [of Scarborough], prior of Bridlington	D. Michael de Wath*, clerk D. Robert de Sprottele [Sproatley], clerk	Bridlington, 27 Feb. 1332
16/783	Ralph [of Ticknall], prior of Repton	D. Thomas de Evesham*, clerk	Repton, 13 March 1332
16/784	[Thomas of Wellingore], abbot of Wellow	[Damaged]	[Damaged], 7 March 133[damaged]

16/785	John [of Wistow II], abbot of Selby	F. Geoffrey de Gaddesby*, monk of abbey D. Thomas de Brayton*, clerk	Selby, [Damaged] March 1332
16/786	William [of Grasby], abbot of Thornton	D. Edmund de Grymesby [Grimsby]*, rector of Graynesby [Grainsby] Thomas de Ulseby [Ulceby], clerk	Thornton, 10 March 1332
16/787	David [Dafydd ap Bleddyn], bishop of St Asaph	[Damaged] wicum, 'our clerk' Matthew de Trefuaur [Trefor]*	Shrewsbury, 5 March [damaged]
16/788	Chapter of Lincoln [LP]	M. Simon de Islep [Islip]*, archdeacon of Stow M. William Bacheler, canon of Lincoln D. Richard de Whitewelle [Whitewell], canon of Lincoln	Lincoln, 6 March 1332

PARLIAMENT AT WESTMINSTER, 9 SEPTEMBER 1332

2/83	Richard [of Charlton], abbot of Cirencester	M. [sic] Thomas de Evesham*, clerk Richard de la Hale*	Cirencester, 6 Sept. 1332
16/789	Matthew [of Englefield], bishop of Bangor	M. David de Guellt, canon of Bangor [D.] Thomas de Capenhurst*, clerk	Bangor, morrow of St Bartholomew, apostle [25 Aug.] 1332
16/791	Ralph [de Borne], abbot of St Augustine's, Canterbury	F. Richard de Cantuaria [Canterbury], monk of abbey Thomas de Lincoln* Stephen Donet*	Canterbury, 4 Sept. 1332

16/792	William [de Chiriton], abbot of Evesham	[F] Peter de Wyke [Wick], monk of abbey D. Thomas de Evesham*, clerk	Evesham, 2 Sept. 1332
16/793	John [of Aylsham], abbot of St Benet of Hulme	D. Michael de Wath*, clerk D. John de Norton*, clerk	St Benet of Hulme, feast of the Beheading of John the Baptist [29 Aug.] 1332
16/794	David [Dafydd ap Bleddyn], bishop of St Asaph	Llywelyn [ap Madog ab Ellis]*, archdeacon of St Asaph [D.] Thomas de Capunhurst [Capenhurst]*, canon of St Asaph	Alltmelyd [Meliden], 28 Aug. 1332
16/795	Thomas [of Moulton], abbot of St Mary's, York [LP]	F. Roger de Aselakby [Aslackby], monk of abbey	York, 27 Aug, 1332

PARLIAMENT AT YORK, 4 DECEMBER 1332

16/796	Louis [de Beaumont], bishop of Durham	M. Ralph de Holbech [Holbeach]*, canon of Lichfield D. William de Emeldon*, rector of Stamfordham	Aukeland [Bishop Auckland], 30 Nov. 1332
16/797	Adam [of Boothby], abbot of Peterborough	D. Henry de Edenestowe [Edwinstowe]*, clerk D. Robert de Rasen*, clerk	Peterborough, Sunday the vigil of St Andrew, apostle [29 Nov.] 1332
16/798	John [of Wigmore], abbot of St Peter's, Gloucester	D. Thomas de Evesham*, clerk	Gloucester, 12 Nov. 1332
16/799	David [Dafydd ap Bleddyn], bishop of St Asaph	D. Thomas de Capinhurst [Capenhurst]*, canon of St Asaph	[Damaged], Nov. 1332

105

16/800	[Richard of Gainsborough], abbot of Bardney [LP]	D. Thomas de Sibthorp* D. Thomas de Tynton* William de Morton	Bardney, 1 Dec. 1332
17/801	Richard [of Charlton], abbot of Cirencester	D. Thomas de Evesham*, clerk	Cirencester, 18 Nov. 1332
17/802	Ralph [de Borne], abbot of St Augustine's, Canterbury	D. Henry, rector of Elmston [Elmstone] William Kaythorp [Caythorpe]	Canterbury, 24 Nov. 1332
17/803	Adam [of Sodbury], abbot of Glastonbury	M. Henry de Clif [Cliffe]* D. John de Bruggewauter [Bridgwater]*	Glastonbury, Friday after feast of St Andrew [4 Dec.] 1332
17/804	[John of Appleford], abbot of Reading	Adam de Gateshened [Gateshead] Richard de Beenham	Reading, 24 Nov. 1332
17/805	William [de Curtlyngton], abbot of Westminster	D. Henry de Edenestowe [Edwinstowe]*, clerk D. William de Muskham*, clerk	Piriford, 26 Nov. 1332
17/806	Matthew [of Englefeld], bishop of Bangor	[D.] Thomas de Capenhurst*, clerk [D.] William de Werdal [Weardale], clerk	Bangor, Friday before feast of Andrew, apostle [27 Nov.] 1332
17/807	Ralph [of Shrewsbury], bishop of Bath and Wells	M. Henry de Clyf [Cliffe]* D. Thomas de Evesham*	Banewelle [Banwell], 24 Nov. 1332
17/808	Reginald [of Waternewton], abbot of Thorney	M. John de Balne, rector of Stibbington [Stibbington]	Thorney, Tuesday after feast of St Clement, [24 Nov.] 1332

106

17/809	Henry [of Casewick], abbot of Crowland	F. Alan de Sancto Botulph [St Botulph], monk of abbey [D.] Nicholas de Stamford*, clerk	Crowland, vigil of St Andrew [29 Nov.] 1332
17/810	Richard [of Wallingford], abbot of St Albans	F. Richard de Hedersete [Hethersett], monk of abbey D. Thomas de Escryk [Escrick]*, clerk	St Albans, Saturday after feast of St Katherine, Virgin [28 Nov.] 1332
17/812	John [Hotham], bishop of Ely *[LP]*	D. Robert de Tauton*, clerk D. Henry de Edenestowe [Edwinstowe]*, clerk M. William de Birton, clerk Nicholas de Cantebrigia [Cambridge]*, clerk	Dudington [Doddington], 22 Nov. 1332
17/813	John [Stratford], bishop of Winchester	M. Robert de Stratford*, canon of Lincoln M. Richard de Chaddesleye [Chaddesley]*, doctor of canon law	Farnham, 18 Nov. 1332
17/814	[Simon of Eye], abbot of Ramsey	M. Thomas de Potesbury [Potterspury]* D. Thomas de Escrik [Escrick]* Richard de Burgo [Burgh]	Broughton, 28 Nov. 1332
17/815	William [of Grasby], abbot of Thornton	F. Alan de Clee, monk of abbey	Thornton, 2 Dec. 1332
17/816	William [Cummor], abbot of Abingdon	D. Thomas de Evesham* D. William de Tewe	Abingdon, 16 Nov. 1332
17/817	William [de Chiriton], abbot of Evesham	D. Thomas de Evesham*, clerk D. John de Stoke*, clerk	Evesham, feast of St Katherine, virgin, [25 Nov.] 1332

17/818	Richard [of Draughton], abbot of Bury St Edmunds	D. John de Cavenham	Herlawe [Harlow], 19 Nov. 1332
17/819	John [of Aylsham], abbot of St Benet of Hulme	D. Michael de Wath*, clerk Robert de Spaunton	St Benet of Hulme, Friday the feast of St Edmund, king and martyr [20 Nov.] 1332
17/820	Walter [of Halton], prior of Spalding	F. John de Hattefeld [Hatfield], monk of priory John de Trehampton*, prior's steward	Spalding, feast of St Katherine, virgin [25 Nov.] 1332
17/821	Adam [de la Hok], abbot of Malmesbury	F. John de Tynterna [Tintern]*, monk of abbey D. Thomas de Evesham*, clerk	Malmesbury, 16 Nov. 1332
32/1558	Walter [Fifehead], abbot of Hyde near Winchester	Richard Beneyt [Benet]	Hyde, feast of St Katherine, virgin [25 Nov.] 1332

PARLIAMENT AT YORK, 20 JANUARY 1333 (PROROGATION OF DECEMBER 1332 SESSION)

15/722	Stephen [Gravesend], bishop of London	D. Walter de London, canon of London Adam atte Water, 'our clerk'	Pelham, 13 Jan. 1333
15/723	John [Grandisson], bishop of Exeter	M. Robert de Nassington*, doctor of civil law D. Thomas de Evesham*, canon of prebendal church of Crediton [RoP] [M.] Philip de Nassington, rector de Asshcombe [Ashcombe], Exeter diocese	Chuddelegh [Chudleigh] Manor, 10 Jan. 1333

15/724	Richard [Tours], abbot of Leicester	M. Richard de Chaddesl' [Chaddesley]* / Thomas de Morton	Leicester, 16 Jan. 1333
15/731	John [Langton], bishop of Chichester [LP]	M. John de Mitford*, canon of Chichester	Aumble, 5 Jan. 1333
15/741	Richard [of Wallingford], abbot of St Albans	F. Nicholas de Flamsted [Flamstead], monk and prior of abbey / F. Richard de Hedersete [Hethersett], monk of abbey / D. Thomas de Escryk [Escrick], Clerk* / M. John de Barnet, clerk*	St Albans, Wednesday the feast of St Hilary [13 Jan.] 1333
17/811	Ralph [de Borne], abbot of St Augustine's, Canterbury	M. John de Shordwich [Shoreditch]*, 'our clerk' / D. Henry, rector of Elmerstone [Elmstone], Canterbury diocese / William Caythorp [Caythorpe]	Canterbury, 29 Dec. 1332
17/822	William [de Chiriton], abbot of Evesham	F. Ralph de Wilcote, monk of abbey / D. Thomas de Evesham*, clerk [RoP]	Evesham, feast of the Epiphany [6 Jan.] 1333
17/823	Henry [Gower], bishop of St Davids	D. Thomas de Cotingham [Cottingham]*	Lantefey [Lamphey], 12 Jan. 1333
17/824	[Adam of Boothby], abbot of Peterborough	D. Henry de Edenestowe [Edwinstowe]*, clerk [CoP] [RoP] / D. Robert de Rasen*, clerk	Peterborough, Monday before feast of St Hilary [11 Jan.] 1333
17/825	Matthew [of Englefield], bishop of Bangor	M. David de Guellt, archdeacon of Bangor / [D.] Thomas de Capenhuste [Capenhurst]*, clerk	Bangor, morrow of St Hilary [14 Jan.] 1333

17/826	Louis [de Beaumont], bishop of Durham	[M.] Ralph de Holbech [Holbeach]*, canon of Lichfield [M.] John de Bekyngham [Beckingham], rector of Blyburgh [Blyborough], Lincoln diocese	Aukland [Bishop Auckland], 15 Jan. 1333
17/827	David [Dafydd ap Bleddyn], bishop of St Asaph	M. Loddaicus [Llywelyn ap Madoc ab Ellis]*, archdeacon and canon of St Asaph D. Thomas de Capinhurst [Capenhurst]*, canon of St Asaph	Alltmelyd [Meliden], 5 Jan. 1333
17/828	[Reginald of Waternewton], abbot of Thorney	D. John de Staunford [Stanford]*, rector of Parva Gidding [Little Gidding], clerk Thomas de Clyf [Cliff]*, clerk	Thorney, Thursday the morrow of St Hilary [14 Jan.] 1333
17/829	William [de Curtlyngton], abbot of Westminster	M. John de Schordich [Shoreditch]*, clerk D. Henry de Edenestowe [Edwinstowe]*, clerk [CoP] [RoP]	Westminster, 2 Jan. 1333
17/830	Simon [Meopham], archbishop of Canterbury	D. Stephen [Gravesend], bishop of London John [Hotham], bishop of Ely Henry [Burghersh], bishop of Lincoln Thomas [Charlton], bishop of Hereford	Maghefeld [Mayfield], 1 Jan. 1333
17/831	Henry [Gower], bishop of St Davids	M. Henry de Edenestowe [Edwinstowe]* [CoP] [RoP]	Lantefey [Lamphey], 12 Jan. 1333
17/832	Richard [of Draughton], abbot of Bury St Edmunds	D. John de Cavenham	Herlawe [Harlow], morrow of St Hilary [14 Jan.] 1333

17/833	Walter [Fifehead], abbot of Hyde near Winchester [LP]	M. Henry de Clif [Cliffe]*, clerk; Richard Beneyt [Benet]	Hyde, 10 Jan. 1333
17/834	[John of Appleford], abbot of Reading	Adam de Gateshened [Gateshead]; Richard de Beenham	Reading, 12 Jan. 1333
17/835	John [of Wymondham], abbot of St John's, Colchester	D. John de Marton*, clerk; D. John de Norton*, clerk	Colchester, 4 Jan. 1333
17/836	John [of Wigmore], abbot of St Peter's, Gloucester	D. Thomas de Evesham*, clerk [RoP]	Hynehame [Highnam], 23 Dec. 1332
17/837	Hamo [Hethe], bishop of Rochester	D. Thomas de Stowe, clerk; D. Thomas de Whattone [Whatton]*, clerk	Trottestlyve [Trottiscliffe], 3 Jan. 1333
17/839	John [of Aylsham], abbot of St Benet of Hulme	D. Michael de Wath*; Robert de Spaunton	St Benet of Hulme, Wednesday the feast of St Hilary [13 Jan.] 1333

PARLIAMENT AT YORK, 21 FEBRUARY 1334

17/838	Richard [of Charlton], abbot of Cirencester	M. Richard de Cheddesleye [Chaddesley]*, clerk; D. Thomas de Evesham*, clerk	Cirencester, 2 Jan. 1334
17/840	John [Langton], bishop of Chichester [LP]	M. John de Hyldeslegh [Hildesley]*, canon of Chichester, clerk; D. William de Langeton [Langton], clerk	Aumble [Ambley], 10 Feb. 1334

111

17/841	[John of Appleford], abbot of Reading	William de Wyttenham [Wittenham]* Martin Chaunceus	Reading, Monday the feast of St Valentine, martyr [1 Feb.] 1334
17/842	H[amo Hethe], bishop of Rochester	D. John de Langetone [Langton] D. William de Boyleston [Boylestone] D. Thomas de Hethe, rector of Nettlested [Nettlestead], Bromlegh [Bromley] and Snodelond [Snodland], Rochester diocese	Trotestlie [Trottiscliffe], 9 Feb. 1334
17/843	Adam [of Boothby], abbot of Peterborough	D. Henry de Edenestowe [Edwinstowe]*, clerk M. John Trivet, clerk	Peterborough, Wednesday after feast of St Valentine [16 Feb.] 1334
17/844	Adam [de la Hok], abbot of Malmesbury	D. Thomas de Evesham*, clerk Gilbert de Tinedene [Tyndene]*	Malmesbury, 12 Feb. 1334
17/845	[Wulstan of Bransford], prior of Worcester	D.John de Stoke*, rector de Seggesberewe [Sedgeberrow]	Worcester, 2 Feb. 1334
17/846	John [de Sheppey], prior of Rochester	Thomas le Hoy [F.] John de Faveresham [Faversham]	Rochester, 13 Feb. 1334
17/847	John [of Aylsham], abbot of St Benet of Hulme	D. Ralph de Wolvyngham [Wellingham], clerk Robert de Spainton [Spaunton]	St Benet of Hulme, 14 Feb. 1334
17/848	David [Dafydd ap Bleddyn], bishop of St Asaph	D. Thomas de Capenhurst*, canon of St Asaph M. Lodewycus [Llywelyn] de Bromfield, canon of St Asaph	Asfomelydyn, 15 Feb. 1334

17/849	Dean and Chapter of Bangor	M. David [de Guellt], archdeacon of Bangor [D.] Thomas de Capenhurst*, clerk	Bangor, 14 Feb. 1334
17/849A	Clergy of York diocese [LP]	Richard de Snoweshull [Snowshill], rector of Huntyngton [Huntington] William de Neusom [Newsham], advocate of the court of York	York, 14 Feb. 1334
17/849B	Richard [of Gainsborough], abbot of Bardney [LP]	D. Thomas de Sibthorp* F. William de Barton, monk of abbey William de Morton, clerk	Bardney, 15 Feb. 1334
17/850	Reginald [of Waternewton], abbot of Thorney [LP]	Richard de Islep [Islip], clerk Thomas de Clif [Cliff]*, clerk William de Luffewyk [Lowick], clerk	Thorney, Mon. day after feast of St Agatha, virgin [7 Feb.] 1334
18/851	Ralph [of Shrewsbury], bishop of Bath and Wells	D. Henry de Carleton [Carlton]* [D.] John de Westmannecote [Westmancote]* M. Robert de Chigewell [Chigwell]*, clerk	Banewell [Banwell], 12 Feb. 1334
18/852	Henry [Gower], bishop of St Davids	D. Henry de Edenestowe [Edwinstowe]*, canon of St Asaph	Lantefey [Lamphey], 14 Feb. 1334
18/853	William [Cumnor], abbot of Abingdon	D. Thomas de Evesham* [D.] William de Tewe	Abingdon, 19 Dec. [no year]
18/854	Chapter of Worcester	D. Thomas de Evesham* Peter de Grete* [MP – Worcestershire]	Worcester Chapter House, 14 Feb. 1334

113

18/855	Henry [of Leicester], prior of Coventry [LP]	Henry de Shulton*, clerk Simon de Shulton, his brother, clerk	Coventry, 7 Feb. 1334
18/856	Chapter of Carlisle [LP]	F. John de Byghton [Bighton], canon [monk] of Carlisle	Carlisle, Tuesday after feast of St Valentine, martyr [15 Feb.] 1334
18/857	Water [Fifehead], abbot of Hyde near Winchester [LP]	Peter de Ho, rector of Lassham [Lasham], Winchester diocese William de Cristchurche [Christchurch]	Hyde, 4 Feb. 1334
18/858	Clergy of Northumberland archdeaconry, Durham diocese [LP]	M. Ralph de Blaykeston [Blakeston], clerk	Durham, 12 Feb. 1334
18/859	Hugh, subprior of Coventry and the Chapter [LP]	Henry de Shulton*, clerk William de Cestria [Chester], clerk	Coventry Chapter House, 7 Feb. 1334
18/860	Stephen [Gravesend], bishop of London	D. Walter de London, canon of London [D.] Thomas de Stowe, 'our clerk'	Crindon [Crondon], 12 Feb. 1334
18/861	John [Hotham], bishop of Ely	M. Alan de Hotham [Hotham]* D. Thomas de Stowe D. John de Ellerker*	Glemesford [Glemsford], 13 Feb. 1334
18/862	Clergy of Carlisle diocese [LP]	D. Robert Coyville, rector of Thoresby [Thursby] M. John de Hakthorp [Hackthorpe]*, clerk	Louther [Lowther], 10 Feb. 1334

18/863	Leonard de Tibert, prior of St John of Jerusalem in England [LP]	F. Simon le Fauconer, monk of order D. Henry de Edenestowe [Edwinstowe]*, clerk D. William de Langeford [Langford], clerk	London, 14 Feb. 1334
18/864	Chapter of St Asaph [LP]	M. Louis [Llywelyn] de Bromfeld [Bromfield], canon of St Asaph	Alltmelyd [Meliden], 18 Jan. 1334
18/865	Matthew [of Englefield], bishop of Bangor	M. David [de Guellt], archdeacon of Bangor, clerk [D.] Thomas de Capenhurst*, clerk	Bangor, 14 Feb. 1334
18/866	Thomas [Charlton], bishop of Hereford [LP]	M. John de Hyldeslee [Hildesley]*, canon of Chichester, clerk M. John de Barton, archdeacon of Hereford, clerk D. Robert de Hemyngburg [Hemmingburgh]*, clerk	Whytebourn [Whitbourne], 31 Jan. 1334
18/867	Chapter of Rochester	Thomas le Hoy [F.] John de Faveresham [Faversham]	Rochester, 13 Feb. 1334
18/868	Richard [of Draughton], abbot of Bury St Edmunds	D. John de Cavenham	Bury St Edmunds, 10 Feb. [no year]
18/869	John [of Wigmore], abbot of St Peter's, Gloucester	D. Thomas de Evesham*, clerk	Gloucester, 4 Feb. 1334
18/870	Clergy of Durham archdeaconry [LP]	M. William de Vallibus, clerk	Durham, 12 Feb. 1334
18/871	Richard [of Wallingford], abbot of St Albans	F. Richard de Hedersete [Hethersett], monk of abbey D. Thomas de Escryk [Escrick]*, clerk	St Albans, Tuesday after St Valentine [15 Feb.] 1334

18/872	[Simon of Eye], abbot of Ramsey	[F.] John de Gretford [Greatford] Robert de Sadyngton [Sadington]* D. Thomas Descrik [de Escrik]*	Ramsey, 16 Feb. 1334
18/873	John [de Crauden], prior of Ely	D. Henry de Edenestouwe [Edwinstowe]*, rector of Orford D. Henry de Teford, rector of 'Troye'	Ely, 11 Feb. 1334
18/874A	Adam [of Sodbury], abbot of Glastonbury	D. John de Sancto Paulo [St Pol]*, clerk D. John de Bruggewater [Bridgwater]*, clerk	Glastonbury, 8 Feb. 1335 [sic, recte 1334]

PARLIAMENT AT WESTMINSTER, 19 SEPTEMBER 1334

The twenty-six surviving proxy letters for this parliament have been misfiled in TNA C 219 (parliamentary election returns). Each letter has a number pencilled onto the back, but the documents are bound into the file in the order below rather than in numerical order.

C 219/5/17/23	William [Cumnor], abbot of Abingdon	F. William de Salesburys [Salisbury], monk of abbey M. John de Colleshull [Coleshill]*	Abingdon, Friday after feast of the Exultation of the Holy Cross [16 Sept.] 1334
C 219/5/17/4	David [ap Bleddyn], bishop of St Asaph	M. Thomas de Capenhurst*, canon of St Asaph	St Asaph, 6 Sept. 1334
C 219/5/17/3	Dean and Chapter of Bangor	[M.] David [de Guellt], archdeacon of Bangor Griffin ap Tudur [Tudor], canon of Bangor	Bangor, Thursday the feast of the Nativity of the Blessed Virgin Mary [8 Sept.] 1334

C 219/5/17/9	John [Langton], bishop of Chichester [LP]	M. John de Mitford*, canon of Chichester	Aldyngbourn [Aldingbourne], 17 Sept. 1334
C 219/5/17/22	Richard [of Charlton], abbot of Cirencester	F. Ralph de Estcote [Eastcote]*, monk of abbey D. Thomas de Evesham*, clerk	Cirencester, 11 Sept. 1334
C 219/5/17/10	Thomas [of Moulton], abbot of St Mary's, York	F. John de Tyverington [Terrington], monk of abbey Thomas de Kendale, clerk	Airmynne [Airmyn], 11 Sept.1334
C 219/5/17/11	Clergy of York diocese [LP]	M. John de Thoresby*, canon of collegiate church of Suwell [Southwell], York diocese John de Barneby [Barnby], rector of Barneby [Barnby Dun], York diocese	York, 3 Sept. 1334
C 219/5/17/19	William [de Chiriton], abbot of Evesham	D. Thomas de Evesham*, clerk D. John de Stoke*, clerk	Evesham, Tuesday after feast of the Nativity of the Blessed Mary [13 Sept.] 1334
C 219/5/17/20	John [of Wigmore], abbot of St Peter's, Gloucester	D. Thomas de Evesham*, clerk	Gloucester, 9 Sept. 1334
C 219/5/17/26	John [of Aylsham], abbot of St Benet of Hulme	D. Ralph de Wolyngham [Wellingham], clerk Robert de Spaunton, attorney	St Benet of Hulme, 15 Sept. 1334
C 219/5/17/27	[Damaged – Walter Fifehead], abbot of Hyde near Winchester [LP]	D. Nicholas de Yystele [alias Churchill], rector of Lyngefeld [Lingfield], Winchester diocese Richard Beneyt [Benet]	Hyde, 10 Sept. 1334

C	Person/Office	Witnesses	Place and date
C 219/5/17/17	Geoffrey, prior of Carlisle, and the Chapter [LP]	D. David de Wolhore [Wollore]*, rector of Cnaresdal [Knarsdale]	Carlisle Chapter House, 8 Sept. 1334
C 219/5/17/21	Richard [Tours], abbot of Leicester	D. John de Stoke*, clerk [D.] William de Newenham*, clerk F. William de Hexham, monk of abbey F. [Illegible]	Leicester, 13 Sept. 1334
C 219/5/17/18	[Adam de la Hok], abbot of Malmesbury	D. Thomas de Evesham*, clerk F. John de Tynterna [Tintern]*, monk of abbey	Malmesbury, feast of the Exaltation of the Holy Cross [14 Sept.] 1334
C 219/5/17/5	Clergy of Northumberland archdeaconry [LP]	D. William de Emyldon [Emeldon]*, clerk D. John Wawaym*, clerk	Durham, 3 Sept. 1334
C 219/5/17/8	Adam [of Boothby], abbot of Peterborough	D. Henry de Edenestowe [Edwinstowe]*, clerk M. [Damaged – Philip de] Kilkenny*, clerk	Peterborough, 14 Sept. 1334
C 219/5/17/7	[John of Appleford], abbot of Reading	Martin de Chaunceaux [Chaunceus] William de Wittenham*	Reading, 15 Sept. 1334
C 219/5/17/15	John [of Wistow II], abbot of Selby	D. Thomas de Brayton*, clerk	Selby, 7 Sept. 1334
C 219/5/17/16	Richard [of Wallingford], abbot of St Albans	F. Richard de Hedersete [Hethersett], monk of abbey D. Thomas de Escryk [Escrick]*, clerk	St Albans, morrow of the Exaltation of the Holy Cross [15 Sept.] 1334

C 219/5/17/24	Richard [of Draughton], abbot of Bury St Edmunds	D. John de Cavenham	Chevyngton [Chevington], 16 Sept. 1334
C 219/5/17/13	[Reginald of Waternewton], abbot of Thorney	Thomas de Clyf [Cliff]*, clerk; John de Luffewyk [Lowick]*; Richard de Islep [Islip]	Thorney, Tuesday before feast of the Exaltation of the Holy Cross [13 Sept.] 1334
C 219/5/17/1	[William of Grasby], abbot of Thornton	F: [Damaged – Alan] de Clee	Thornton, on the Exaltation of the Holy Cross [14 Sept.] 1334
C 219/5/17/2	Simon [Montacute], bishop of Worcester	M. John de Hildesle [Hildesley]*, canon of Chichester	Hamsted Marschal [Hamstead Marshall], 15 Sept. 1334
C 219/5/17/25	[Wulstan of Bransford], prior of Worcester	D. Henry Geraud, clerk	Worcester, 8 Sept. 1334
C 219/5/17/6	Chapter of Worcester	D. Thomas de Evesham*, clerk	Worcester Chapter House, 7 Sept. 1334
C 219/5/17/12	Clergy of Worcester diocese [LP]	M. William de Adel[damaged], clerk; D. Thomas de Donynton [Donington], vicar of Grafton	Worcester, 10 Sept. 1334

PARLIAMENT AT YORK, 26 MAY 1335

18/900	Adam [de la Hok], abbot of Malmesbury	D. Thomas de Evesham*, clerk Gilbert de Tyndene*	Malmesbury, 22 May 1335
19/901	Clergy of Carlisle diocese [LP]	[M.] Thomas de Halghton, rector of Kyrkeland [Kirkland] Richard de Craystok [Greystoke], vicar of Crossethwayt [Crosthwaite]	Carlisle, 11 May 1335
19/902	[Document gives nothing to identify sender]	D. Walter Power*	Kempele [Kempley], 11 May 1335
19/903	Chapter of St Asaph [LP]	D. Thomas de Capenhurst*, canon of St Asaph	St Asaph, 27 April 1335
19/904	John [de Breynton], abbot of Glastonbury	D. John de Sancto Paulo [St Pol]*, clerk D.John de Bruggewater [Bridgwater]*, clerk	Glastonbury, 18 May 1335
19/905	Robert [Wyvil], bishop of Salisbury	M. Thomas de Asteley [Astley]*, canon of Salisbury M. Robert de Worth*, canon of Salisbury D. Thomas de Evesham*	Sonnyn [Sonning] Manor, 18 May 1335
19/906	Dean and Chapter of Bangor	M. David [de Guellt], archdeacon of Bangor D. Thomas de Cappenhurst [Capenhurst]*, clerk	Bangor, Saturday the morrow of St Dunstan, bishop and confessor [20 May] 1335

19/907	Matthew [of Englefield], bishop of Bangor	M. David [de Guellt], archdeacon of Bangor D. Thomas de Cappenhurst [Capenhurst]*, clerk	Bangor, Saturday the morrow of St Dunstan, bishop and confessor [20 May] 1335
19/908	Hamo [Hethe], bishop of Rochester [LP]	D. Nicholas North, rector of Catmere [Catmore], Salisbury diocese Robert de Langetone [Langton], rector of Nettlested [Nettlestead], Rochester diocese	Trotteslline [Trottiscliffe], 27 April 1335
19/909	Richard [Tours], abbot of Leicester	M. Ralph de Thurvill F. William de Hexham, monk of abbey M. [sic – recte F.] Ralph de Thurleston [Thurlaston]*, monk of abbey	Our abbey of Leicester, 22 May 1335
19/910	Chapter of Worcester	John de Dombelton [Dumbleton], rector of Sedgeberrow	Worcester Chapter House, 12 May 1335
19/911	John [de Eclescliff], bishop of Llandaff	M. Thomas Sampson*, doctor of civil law D. Henry de Edenestowe [Edwinstowe]*, canon of Llandaff	Marthue [Mathern], 17 May 1335
19/912	Ralph [of Shrewsbury], bishop of Bath and Wells [LP]	D. Michael Wath* D. Thomas de Evesham*	Pokercherche [Pucklechurch], 15 May 1335
19/913	John [Grandisson], bishop of Exeter	M. William de la Zouche*, canon of Exeter M. Thomas de Astelegh [Astley]*, canon of Exeter	Clyst [Bishop's Clyst], 15 May 1335

121

19/914	John [de Crauden], prior of Ely	F. Robert de Aylesham [Aylsham], monk of priory	Ely, 9 May 1335
19/915	[John de Crauden], prior, and Chapter of Ely [LP]	F. Robert de Aylesham [Aylsham], monk of priory D. Henry de Clyf [Cliffe]*, clerk	Ely Chapter House, 9 May 1335
19/916	[Wulstan of Bransford], prior of Worcester	D. Thomas de Evesham*, clerk	Worcester, 27 April 1335
19/917	Richard [of Charlton], abbot of Cirencester	D. Thomas de Evesham*, clerk Richard de la Hale*	Cirencester, 19 May 1335
19/918	Thomas [Poucyn], abbot of St Augustine's, Canterbury	D. John de Westmancote* William de Waure*	Stureye [Sturry], feast of St Mark, evangelist [25 April] 1335
19/919	Richard [of Wallingford], abbot of St Albans	F. Adam de Newerk [Newark], monk of abbey Richard de Kuleshulle [Kelshall]*	St Albans, Saturday after feast of Apostles Philip and James [6 May] 1335
19/920	William [de Chiriton], abbot of Evesham	D. Thomas de Evesham*, clerk D. John de Stoke*, clerk	Evesham, feast of St Dunstan [19 May] 1335
19/921	John [of Wigmore], abbot of St Peter's, Gloucester	D. Thomas de Evesham*, clerk	Gloucester, 1 May 1335
19/922	Thomas [de Henle], abbot of Westminster	D. Henry de Edenestowe [Edwinstowe]* D. [sic – recte F.] John de Tothale	Westminster, 3 May 1335
19/923	David [Dafydd ap Bleddyn], bishop of St Asaph	D. Thomas de Capenhurst*, canon of St Asaph	St Asaph, 27 April 1335

19/924	Thomas [Charlton], bishop of Hereford *[LP]*	M. John de Hyldesleye [Hildesley]*, clerk John de Wortham	Crughowel [Crickhowell], 1 May 1335
19/925	Simon [Montacute], bishop of Worcester	M. John de Hildesleye [Hildesley]*, canon of Chichester D. John le Smale, canon of Ripon	Hertlebur' [Hartlebury], 22 May 1335
19/926	John de Pollow, dean of Collegiate Church of Langcestre [Lanchester] *[LP]*	M. William de Alverton, vicar of Akley [Aycliffe], Durham diocese	Durham, 17 May 1335
19/927	Roger [of Thame], abbot of Abingdon	D. John de Sancto Paulo [St Pol]* D. Thomas de Evesham*	Abingdon, 3 May 1335
19/928	John [Langton], bishop of Chichester *[LP]*	D. Michael de Waht [Wath]*, clerk D. William de Langetone [Langton], clerk	Duryngwyk [Drungewick], 19 May 1335
19/929	Chapter of Durham *[LP]*	M. Robert de Neunham [Newenham], clerk	Durham Chapter House, 20 May 1335
19/930	Hamo Geler, dean of Collegiate Church of Auckland, Durham diocese *[LP]*	M. William de Alverton, vicar of Akley [Great Aycliffe], Durham diocese	Durham, 18 May 1335
19/931	William [of Cowton], prior of Durham	M. Robert de Neunham [Newenham], clerk	Durham, 20 May 1335
19/932	John [of Appleford], abbot of Reading	Martin Chaunson [Chaunceus]	Reading, morrow of St Dunstan, bishop [20 May] 1335

19/933	John [of Aylsham], abbot of St Benet of Hulme	D. Thomas de Cotyngham [Cottingham]*, clerk D. Ralph de Wolyngham [Wellingham], clerk	St Benet of Hulme, 14 May 1335
19/934	Clergy of York diocese [LP]	M. Richard de Wath, advocate of the Court of York M. Robert de Ruddeby [Rudby], rector de Goushill [Goxhill], York diocese	York, 23 May 1335
19/935	[Simon of Eye], abbot of Ramsey	D. Thomas de Sibthorp* Robert de Sadyngton [Sadington]* Richard de Burgo [Burgh]	Ramsey, 22 May 1335
19/936	Adam [of Boothby], abbot of Peterborough	D. Henry de Edenestowe [Edwinstowe]*, clerk Robert de Lufwyk [Lowick]*, clerk	Peterborough, 19 May 1335
19/937	[Reginald of Waternewton], abbot of Thorney	John de Luffewyk [Lowick]* [MP – Huntingdonshire] Richard de Islep [Islip]	Thorney, Thursday before feast of St Dunstan [18 May] 1335
19/938	Walter [Fifehead], abbot of Hyde near Winchester [LP]	William de Bromham, monk of abbey D. Robert de Keleseie [Kelsey]*, clerk	Hyde, 14 May 1335
19/939	William [of Grasby], abbot of Thornton	[F.] Alan de Clee, [monk of abbey]	Thornton, 24 May 1335
19/940	Chapter of York [LP]	M. Richard de Haveryng [Havering]*, canon of York D. John Gyffard [Giffard]*, canon of York D. Nicholas de Hongate [Hungate]*, canon of York	York, [Damaged] June 1335

19/941	Henry [Gower], bishop of St Davids	D. Henry de Edenestowe [Edwinstowe]*, clerk in king's court (curia) D. William de Kyldesby [Kilsby]*, clerk in your court (curia)	Aberwell, 1 May 1335
19/942	John [of Wymondham], abbot of St John's, Colchester	D.John de Marton*, clerk	Colchester, Thursday after St Mark, evangelist [27 April] 1335
19/943	John [Langton], bishop of Ely	M. Alan de Hotham*, clerk D. Henry de Hedenestowe [Edwinstowe]*, clerk	Dounham [Little Downham], 8 May [no year]
19/944	Clergy of Durham archdeaconry [LP]	William de Alverton, perpetual vicar of Acley [Great Aycliffe], Durham diocese	Durham, 17 May 1335

PARLIAMENT AT WESTMINSTER, 11 MARCH 1336

18/875	Clergy of York diocese [LP]	M. John de Burton, rector of Stokesley [Stokesley], York diocese M. John de Barneby [Barnby], rector of Barneby super Dene [Barnby Dun], York diocese	York, 1 March 1336
18/876	Dean and Chapter of York [LP]	M. John de Warenna [Warenne], canon of York D. Robert de Valoygnes [Valognes]*, canon of York M. Thomas [illegible], canon of York	York, 19 Feb. 1336

125

18/877	John [de Eclescliff], bishop of Llandaff	D. Henry de Edenestowe [Edwinstowe]*, canon of Llandaff M. John de Blebury [Blewbury]*, canon of Llandaff	Lank, 5 March 1336
18/878	Richard [Tours], abbot of Leicester	M. William de Lec' [Leicester]* D. John de Kynwell [Gynwell]*, clerk	In the abbey, [illegible] 1336
18/879	Clergy of Northumberland archdeaconry [LP]	M. Ralph de Blakiston [Blakeston], clerk	Durham, 20 March 1336
18/880	Adam [of Boothby], abbot of Peterborough	D. Henry de Edenestowe [Edwinstowe]*, clerk Peter Fitzwarin [Fitzwarren], clerk	[Damaged], Friday after feast of St Perpetua [8 March] [damaged]
18/881	Richard [of Gainsborough], abbot of Bardney [LP]	M. John de [Damaged], clerk [Damaged – William] de Saundeby [Saundby], clerk	Bardney, 10 March 1336
18/882	John [Grandisson], bishop of Exeter	D. Ralph [of Shrewsbury], bishop of Bath and Wells M. Adam Murymouth [Murimuth]*, precentor of Exeter M. Thomas de Nassington*, archdeacon of Exeter M. William de Nassington*, canon of Exeter	Chuddelegh [Chudleigh], 2 March 1336
18/883	William [Melton], archbishop of York	D. Henry de Edenestowe [Edwinstowe]*, canon of Suwell [Southwell] M. Adam de Haselbech*, archbishop's chancellor, canon of Houden [Howden] M. John de Thoresby*, canon of Suwell [Southwell] John de Barneby [Barnby], rector of Barneby [Barnby Dun], York diocese	Cawode [Cawood], 4 March 1336

18/884	John [of Wymondham], abbot of St John's, Colchester	D. John de Martone [Marton]*, clerk John Parles* of Colchester [MP – Colchester]	Colchester, 12 March 1336
18/885	William [de Chiriton], abbot of Evesham	F. Peter de Wyke [Wick], cellarer of Evesham D. Thomas de Evesham*, clerk	Evesham, 4 March 1336
18/886	Clergy of Durham archdeaconry	[Damaged - Mausus] Marmyon, rector of Houghton [Houghton-le-Spring], Durham diocese	[Damaged]
18/887	William [Hereward], abbot of Cirencester	[Damaged]	[Damaged]
18/888	[Thomas Poucyn], abbot of St Augustine's, Canterbury	[Damaged – William] de Waure*	Canterbury, 9 March 133[damaged]
18/889	Thomas [of Moulton], abbot of St Mary's, York	Henry de Edenstow [Edwinstowe]* F. John de Tyverington [Terrington], monk of abbey	York, penultimate day [damaged] 1336
18/890	John [of Heslington], abbot of Selby	F. Richard de Athelmaslet, monk of abbey F. Geoffrey de Gaddesby*, monk of abbey D. Thomas de Brayton*, clerk	Selby, 2 March [illegible]
18/891	Ralph [of Shrewsbury], bishop of Bath and Wells	D. Michael Wath* [D.] Thomas de Evesham* M. Robert de Chigewelle [Chigwell]*	Kynggesbury [Kingsbury Episcopi], 28 Feb. 1336
18/892	[Adam de la Hok], abbot of Malmesbury	F. John de Tynterna [Tintern]*, monk of abbey Gilbert de Tynedene [Tyndene]*	Malmesbury, 8 March 1336

18/893	John [Langton], bishop of Chichester	M. Peter de Scolacley [School Aycliffe], treasurer of Chichester M. John de Mitford*, canon of Chichester	Aumble [Amberley], 7 March 1336
18/894	Chapter of Worcester	F. Simon Crompe*, sacristan of Worcester	Worcester Chapter House, 5 March, 1336
18/895	[Damaged]	Richard de B[damaged]	[Damaged], 8 March [no year]
18/896	John [Hotham], bishop of Ely	M. John de Offord*, archdeacon of Ely M. Alan de Hothom [Hotham]*, canon of St Paul's, London M. Richard de Baddewe [Badew]*, bishop's official	Dodyngton [Doddington], 4 March 1336
18/897	John [of Wigmore], abbot of St Peter's, Gloucester	D. Thomas de Evesham*, clerk	Gloucester, 1 March 1336
18/898	[Wulstan of Bransford], prior of Worcester	D. Thomas de Evesham*, clerk	Worcester, 5 March 1336
18/899	Dean of St Asaph [LP]	D. Louis [Llywelyn ap Madoc ab Ellis]*, archdeacon and canon of St Asaph	St Asaph, 3 March 1336
19/945	David [Dafydd ap Bleddyn], bishop of St Asaph	D. Louis [Llywelyn ap Madoc ab Ellis]*, archdeacon and canon of St Asaph D. Thomas de Capenhurst*, canon of St Asaph	St Asaph, 2 March 1336

19/947	John [de Breynton], abbot of Glastonbury	D. John de Sancto Paulo [St Pol]*, clerk D. John de Bruggewater [Bridgwater]*, clerk	Glastonbury, 4 March 1336
19/948	[Roger of Thame], abbot of Abingdon	D. John de Sancto Paulo [St Pol]* F. William de Salisbury, monk of abbey	Abingdon, 10 March 1336
19/949	Walter [Fifehead], abbot of Hyde near Winchester [LP]	F. John de Blancchmal, monk of abbey D. Robert de Keleseye [Kelsey]*, clerk	Hyde, 5 March 1336
19/950	Chapter of St Asaph [LP]	[Damaged]	[Damaged] 1336
20/951	Henry [Gower], bishop of St Davids	D. Henry de Edenstowe [Edwinstowe]*, clerk John, clerk	Lanwadeyn [Llawhaden], [Damaged] 1336

GREAT COUNCIL AT NOTTINGHAM, 23 SEPTEMBER 1336

19/946	Robert de Wodehous [Wodehouse], archdeacon of Richmond [LP]	M. John de Thoresby* D. Henry de Edenestowe [Edwinstowe]* D. John de Hoicton*	Keten, day of St Matthew, apostle [21 Sept.] 1336
20/952	William [of Grasby], abbot of Thornton	[F.] Alan de Clee, [monk of abbey]	Thornton, Sunday after the Nativity of Blessed Virgin Mary [15 Sept.] 1336
20/953	[Richard Tours], abbot of Leicester	M. Ralph Thurvile [Thurvill] F. William de Hextildesham [Hexham], monk of abbey F. Ralph de Thurleston [Thurlaston]*, monk of abbey	Leicester, feast of St Matthew, apostle [21 Sept.] 1336

20/958	John [of Wymondham], abbot of St John's, Colchester	D. John de Martone [Marton]*, rector of Westillebery [West Tilbury]	Colchester, Tuesday after the Exaltation of the Holy Cross [17 Sept.] 1336
20/959	Thomas [Charlton], bishop of Hereford [LP]	M. Laurence Fastolf* M. Michael de Wath*	Castro Epi' [Bishops Castle] Manor, 20 Sept. 1336
20/960	[Simon of Eye], abbot of Ramsey	D. Thomas de Sibbethorp [Sibthorp]*, clerk D. Hugh de Bardelby*, clerk D. Simon de Glynton [Glinton]*, clerk	Ramsey, 21 Sept. 1336
20/961	Chapter of St Asaph [LP]	D. Thomas de Capenhurst*, canon of St Asaph	[Undated]
20/962	John [de Breynton], abbot of Glastonbury	D. John de Sancto Paulo [St Pol]*, clerk D. John de Bruggewater [Bridgwater]*, clerk	Glastonbury, [Damaged] Sept. 1336
20/963	William [de Bernham], abbot of Bury St Edmunds	D. William de Cotton*, clerk	Bury St Edmunds, 18 Sept. 1336
20/964	Roger [of Thame], abbot of Abingdon	D. Edmund de la Beche* D. John de Sancto Paulo [St Pol]*	Abingdon, 12 Sept. 1336
20/965	Robert [Wyvil], bishop of Salisbury	D. Edmund de la Beche* D. Thomas de Evesham* D. John de Sancto Paulo [St Pol]*	Clidestok, 16 Sept., 1336

130

PARLIAMENT AT WESTMINSTER, 3 MARCH 1337

20/954	Reginald [of Waternewton], abbot of Thorney	D. Reginald de Leigthone [Leyton], clerk John de Luffewyk [Lowick]* [MP – Huntingdonshire]	Thorney, 27 Feb. 1337
20/955	John [of Heslington], abbot of Selby	F. Geoffrey de Gaddesby*, monk of abbey D. Thomas de Brayton*, clerk	Selby, 17 Feb. 1337
20/956	Adam [of Boothby], abbot of Peterborough	D. Henry de Edenestowe [Edwinstowe]* M. Philip de Kilkenny* Robert de Lufwyk [Lowick]*	Peterborough, 28 Feb. 1337
20/957	Chapter of Worcester	D. Thomas de Evesham*, clerk	Worcester Chapter House, 23 Feb. 1337
20/966	Thomas [of Nassington], prior of Spalding [LP]	D. Roger de Exton, clerk	Spalding, Sunday the vigil of St Matthias [23 Feb.] 1337
20/967	John [de Eclescliff], bishop of Llandaff	D. Henry de Edenestowe [Edwinstowe]*, canon of Llandaff D. Gilbert de Wygeton [Wigton]*, canon of Llandaff M. John de Carleton [Carlton]*, canon of Wells and of Llandaff M. Richard de Haversham*, canon of Wells and of Llandaff	Lank, 24 Feb. 1337

131

20/968	John [of Aylsham], abbot of St Benet of Hulme	M. Ralph de Wolyngham [Wellingham], clerk M. Henry de Ingylby [Ingleby]*, clerk	St Benet of Hulme, 26 Feb. 1337
20/969	Clergy of Durham archdeaconry	D. John de Thoresby*, rector of Ellewyk [Elwick], Durham diocese	Durham, 17 Feb. 1337
20/970	[Richard of Idbury], abbot of Winchcombe	D. Thomas de Evesham* D. William de Pershore	[Undated]
20/971	Walter [Fifehead], abbot of Hyde near Winchester [LP]	D. Robert de Keleseye [Kelsey]*, rector of Exton, Winchester diocese F. Richard de Diketon, monk of abbey	Hyde, 26 Feb. 1337
20/972	[Wulstan of Bransford], prior of Worcester	D. Henry Geraud, rector of Overbury	Worcester, 23 Feb. 1337

GREAT COUNCIL AT WESTMINSTER, 26 SEPTEMBER 1337

20/973	[Reginald of Waternewton], abbot of Thorney	M. Ralph Turfuile [Thurvill], clerk John de Luffewyk [Lowick]* [MP – Huntingdonshire]	Thorney, Tuesday after St Matthew, apostle [23 Sept.] 1337
20/974	John [de Breynton], abbot of Glastonbury	D. John de Sancto Paulo [St Pol]*, clerk M.John de Blebury [Blewbury]*, clerk	Glastonbury, Monday the morrow of St Matthew, apostle [22 Sept.] 1337

Ref.	Abbot/Prior	Members	Place and date
20/975	John [of Aylsham], abbot of St Benet of Hulme	[D.] Ralph de Welyngham [Wellingham], clerk	St Benet of Hulme, Monday the morrow of St Matthew, apostle [22 Sept.] 1337
20/976	[William Prestwold], prior of Sempringham	F. Roger de Stanes, monk of order F. John de Lethworth [Letchworth], monk of order William de Ravendale*, clerk	Sempringham, 20 Sept. 1337
20/977	[Richard Tours], abbot of Leicester	M. Ralph Turvile [Thurvill], clerk F. William de Heytildesham [Hexham], monk of abbey F. Ralph de Thurleston [Thurlaston]*, monk of abbey	In our abbey of Leicester, feast of St Matthew, apostle and evangelist [21 Sept.] 1337
20/978	[Roger of Thame], abbot of Abingdon	D. Edmund de la Beche*, clerk D. John de Sancto Paulo [St Pol]*	Abingdon, Monday after feast of St Matthew, apostle [22 Sept.] 1337
20/979	William [de Chiriton], abbot of Evesham	D. Thomas de Evesham*, clerk F. Robert de Bray, monk of abbey	Evesham, Sunday the feast of St Matthew, apostle [21 Sept.] 1337
20/980	William [Hereward], abbot of Cirencester	D. Thomas de Evesham*, clerk	Cirencester, feast of [damaged], 11 Edward III
20/981	Adam [of Staunton], abbot of St Peter's, Gloucester	D. Thomas de Evesham*, clerk	Gloucester, Monday the morrow of St Matthew, apostle [22 Sept.] 1337

133

20/982	John [de Eclescliff], bishop of Llandaff	M. John de Blebury [Blewbury]*, clerk M. John de Carleton [Carlton]*, clerk M. Richard de Haversham*, clerk D. Geoffrey de Olneye [Olney], clerk	Lank, 18 Sept. 1337
20/983	Adam [of Staunton], abbot of St Peter's, Gloucester	William de Cheltenham*	Gloucester, Monday the morrow of St Matthew, apostle [22 Sept.] 1337
20/984	William [de Bernham], abbot of Bury St Edmunds *[LP]*	D. William de Manthorpe, rector of Cottone [Cotton], Norwich diocese	Bury St Edmunds, 24 Sept. 1337
20/985	Henry [Gower], bishop of St Davids	D. John de Sancto Paulo [St Pol]* D. Henry de Edenestowe [Edwinstowe]*	St Davids, 17 Sept. 1337
20/986	Thomas [Hemenhale], bishop of Worcester	M. Andrew de Offord*, doctor of civil law, 'our chancellor'	Kemeseye [Kempsey], 16 Sept. 1337
20/987	Ralph [of Shrewsbury], bishop of Bath and Wells	M. Richard de Benteworth [Bintworth]* M. John de Carleton [Carlton]* M. Robert de Chikewelle [Chigwell]*	Wells, 16 Sept. 1337
20/988	[Wulstan of Bransford], prior of Worcester	D. Thomas de Evesham*, clerk D. Henry Geraud, clerk	Worcester, 19 Sept. 1337
20/989	J[ohn of Appleford], abbot of Reading	William de Wyttenham [Wittenham]*	Reading, [*Undated*]

134

20/990	William [of Grasby], abbot of Thornton	D. Edmund de Grimsby*, rector of Greynesby [Grainsby]; William de Ravendale*, clerk	Thornton, feast of St Matthew, apostle [21 Sept.] 1337
20/991	Richard [of Gainsborough], abbot of Bardney	D. Thomas de Sibthorp*; M. John de Langetoft [Langtoft]*	Bardney, feast of St Matthew, apostle [21 Sept.] 1337
20/992	Adam [de la Hok], abbot of Malmesbury	D. Thomas de Evesham*, clerk; Gilbert de Tyndene*	Malmesbury, 21 Sept. 1337
20/993	John [of Heslington], abbot of Selby	F. Geoffrey de Gaddesby*, monk of abbey; D. Thomas de Brayton*, clerk	Selby, 18 Sept. 1337
20/994	Walter [Fifehead], abbot of Hyde near Winchester [LP]	D. Robert de Kellesye [Kelsey]*, clerk; Nicholas de Chynham [Chineham]	Hyde, 25 Sept. 1337
20/995	Thomas [of Moulton], abbot of St Mary's, York	D. John de Wodhous [Wodehouse]*, 'our clerk'; F. John de Tyverington [Terrington], monk of abbey	York, 22 Sept. [no year]
20/996	Thomas [Poucyn], abbot of St Augustine's, Canterbury	F. John de Ripple, monk of abbey; D. John de Westmancote*, clerk; William de Waure*	Canterbury, 23 Sept. 1337
20/997	David [Dafydd ap Bleddyn], bishop of St Asaph	D. Thomas de Capenhurst*, canon of St Asaph	Alkemelyd [Meliden], 20 Sept. 1337

20/998	[Richard of Idbury], abbot of Winchcombe	F. William de Gloucester, cellarer of Winchcombe M. William de Adelmyntone [Admington], 'our clerk'	[Undated]
20/999	Matthew [of Englefield], bishop of Bangor	D. Thomas de Cappenhurst [Capenhurst]*, canon of St Asaph	Bangor, vigil of St Matthew, apostle [20 Sept.] 1337
20/1000	Thomas [of Nassington], prior of Spalding	M. Thomas de Nassington*, archdeacon of Exeter D. Roger de Exton, 'our clerk'	Spalding, day of St Matthew, apostle [21 Sept.] 1337
21/1001	[Adam of Boothby], abbot of Peterborough	F. Henry de Morcote [Morcott]*, monk of abbey M. Philip de Kilkenny*, clerk	Peterborough, Tuesday after St Matthew, apostle [23 Sept.] 1337

PARLIAMENT AT WESTMINSTER, 3 FEBRUARY 1338

21/1002	Henry [Gower], bishop of St Davids	D. John de Sancto Paulo [St Pol]*, clerk [D.] Thomas de Bamburgh*, clerk	Lantefey [Lamphey], 17 Jan. 1338
21/1004	[William of Harvington], abbot of Pershore	[D.] Henry de Stretforda [Stratford]*, rector of Overbury	Pershore, 25 Jan. 1338
21/1005	Adam [of Boothby], abbot of Peterborough	D. Henry de Edenstowe [Edwinstowe]*, canon of Lincoln F. Henry de Morcote [Morcott]*, monk of abbey	Peterborough, Friday after feast of the Conversion of St Paul [30 Jan.] 1338

21/1006	William [Melton], archbishop of York	M. John de Aton [Acton]*, official of archbishop's court M. Thomas de Neuikk [Newick], doctor of civil law D. William de Poppleton [Poppleton], rector of Harewode [Harewood] M. John de Barneby, rector of Barneby super Dene [Barnby Dun]	Cawode [Cawood], 23 Jan. 1338
21/1007	John [of Heslington], abbot of Selby	F. Geoffrey de Gadesby [Gaddesby]*, monk of abbey D. Thomas de Brayton*, clerk	Selby, 22 Jan. 1338
21/1008	Chapter of St Asaph *[LP]*	D. Thomas de Capenhurst*, canon of St Aspah	Alkemelyd [Meliden], [*illegible*] Jan. 1338

GREAT COUNCIL AT NORTHAMPTON, 26 JULY 1338

21/1009	[Adam of Boothby], abbot of Peterborough *(to Prince Edward, duke of Cornwall, earl of Chester and custodian of the realm)*	F. Henry de Morcote [Morcott]*, monk of abbey [M.] Philip de Kilkenny* Peter Fitzwarin [Fitzwarren]	Peterborough, feast of St James, apostle [25 July] 1338
21/1010	*[Damaged]* – Henry Gower, bishop of St Davids	John de Sweynes, rector of Iltuti [Ilston], 'our diocese' *[Damaged]*	Lawadeyn [Llawhaden], 20 July 1338

GREAT COUNCIL AT WESTMINSTER, 5 NOVEMBER 1338

21/1011	Adam [of Staunton], abbot of St Peter's, Gloucester	D. Thomas de Evesham*, clerk M. Thomas de Ewyas, clerk	Gloucester, 1 Nov. 1338
21/1012	William [de Bernham], abbot of Bury St Edmunds (to king and Prince Edward)	D. William [de Manthorpe], rector of Cotton and 'our clerk'	Culford, 3 Nov. 1338
21/1013	Anthony [Bek], bishop of Norwich (to Prince Edward, duke of Cornwall and custodian of the realm)	M. John de Brynchull [Brinkhill], doctor of civil law D. Michael de Haynton, rector of Matlok [Matlock], Lichfield diocese	Blofeld [Blofield], 31 Oct. 1338
21/1014	Adam [of Boothby], abbot of Peterborough (to Prince Edward, duke of Cornwall and custodian of the realm)	D. Gervase de W[damaged]d [Wilford] D. W[damaged – William] de Lound [London]*	Peterborough, 2 Nov. 1338
21/1015	Thomas [Hemenhale], bishop of Worcester	Stephen de Ketelbury [Kettleburgh]*, doctor of civil law, bishop's official	Hertlebury [Hartlebury], 3 Nov. 1338
21/1016	Robert [Stratford], bishop of Chichester [LP]	M. Richard de Chaddesley*, doctor of civil law M. Henry de Iddesworth [Idsworth], canon of St Paul's, London	Aldyngbury [Aldingbourne], 2 Nov. 1338
21/1017	Robert [Stratford], bishop of Chichester [LP]	M. Richard de Chaddesle [Chaddesley]*, doctor of canon law M. Henry Geraud de Stretford, canon of St Davids	Aldyngbury [Aldingbourne], 2 Nov. 1338

21/1018	[Simon of Eye], abbot of Ramsey	[F.] John de Gretford [Greatford] D. Simon de Glynton [Glinton]*, clerk	Ramsey, 1 Nov. 1338
21/1019	William [de Chiriton], abbot of Evesham *(to the king or the one holding his place in England)*	D. Thomas de Evesham*, clerk D. John de Stoke*, clerk	Evesham, Tuesday after feast of All Saints [3 Nov.] 1338
21/1020	John [de Breynton], abbot of Glastonbury *(to Prince Edward, duke of Cornwall and custodian of the realm)*	D. John de Sancto Paulo [St Pol]*, clerk D. William de Tilney, clerk	Glastonbury, 1 Nov. 1338
21/1021	Walter [Fifehead], abbot of Hyde near Winchester *[LP]*	John de Aultone [Alton]* Nicholas de Chynham [Chineham]	Hyde, 30 Oct. 1338
21/1022	[Roger of Thame], abbot of Abingdon	D. John de Sancto Paulo [St Pol]*, clerk James de Wodestok [Woodstock]*	Abingdon, Sunday the feast of All Saints [1 Nov.] 1338
21/1023	Michael [of Mentmore], abbot of St Albans *(to Prince Edward, duke of Cornwall, earl of Chester and keeper of the realm)*	F. Adam de Wyttenham [Wittenham], monk of abbey D. John de Langeton [Langton], clerk	St Albans, Tuesday after feast of All Saints [3 Nov.] 1338
21/1024	William [Melton], archbishop of York	*No proctors named*	Cawode [Cawood], 4 Nov. 1338

21/1026	Matthew [of Englefield], bishop of Bangor *(to king or Edward, duke of Cornwall and custodian of the realm)*	Stephen de Ketelburgh [Kettleburgh]*, preacher in the church of Castri Kybii [Caergybi, Holyhead] D. Thomas de Cappenhurst [Capenhurst]*, canon of St Asaph	Gogerth [Gogarth], morrow of the Conversion of St Paul, apostle [26 Jan.] 1339
21/1027	[Roger of Thame], abbot of Abingdon	D. Edmund de la Bech [Beche]*, clerk D. John de Sancto Paulo [St Pol]*, clerk	Abingdon, Tuesday after feast of the Conversion of St Paul [26 Jan.] 1339
21/1028	Henry [Gower], bishop of St Davids	D. John Goch [Gogh]*, clerk M. Thomas de Mar, clerk	St Clarus [St Clares], 21 Jan., 1339
21/1029	John [of Wymondham], abbot of St John's, Colchester	M. Gilbert de Meleford [Melford], clerk Adam de Ayrdale [Airedale]	Colchester, Tuesday the feast of the Purification of Blessed Virgin Mary [2 Feb.] 1339
21/1030	Walter [Fifehead], abbot of Hyde near Winchester [LP]	Robert de Kelesey [Kelsey]*, rector of Exton, Winchester diocese [M.] John de Langetoft [Langtoft]*, rector of Lyngefeld [Lingfield], Winchester diocese	Hyde, 25 Jan. [no year]
21/1031	John [of Aylsham], abbot of St Benet of Hulme	D. Thomas de Cotyngham [Cottingham]*, clerk D. Ralph de Wolyngham [Wellingham], clerk	St Benet of Hulme, 30 Jan. 1339
21/1032	Chapter of York [LP]	M. Thomas Sampson*, canon of York D. John de Sancto Paulo [St Pol]*, canon of York	York, 1 Feb. 1339

21/1033	Robert de Wodehous [Wodehouse], archdeacon of Richmond [LP]	[D.] John de Thorp, rector of Buay, York diocese and Flamstede [Flamstead], Lincoln diocese	[Damaged], 27 Jan. 1339
21/1034	William [de Bernham], abbot of Bury St Edmunds (to Prince Edward, duke of Cornwall, earl of Chester and custodian of the realm)	D. William [de Manthorpe], rector of Cotton	Bury St Edmunds, 28 Jan. 1339
22/1072	Thomas [de Henle], abbot of Westminster	D. John de Shordich [Shoreditch], knight F. Richard de Winton [Winchester], monk of abbey	Piriford [Pyrford], 13 Feb. 1339

PARLIAMENT AT WESTMINSTER, 13 OCTOBER 1339

21/1037	John [de Eclescliff], bishop of Llandaff	M. John de Carleton [Carlton]*, canon of Wells and Llandaff M. Richard de Haversham*, canon of Wells and Llandaff	Lank, 4 Oct. 1339
21/1038	William [de Bernham], abbot of Bury St Edmunds	D. William [de Manthorpe], rector of Cotton, clerk	In the monastery, 8 Oct. 1339
21/1039	John [de Breynton], abbot of Glastonbury	D. John de Sancto Paulo [St Pol]*, clerk D. John de Bruggewater [Bridgwater]*, clerk	Glastonbury, 8 Oct. 1339
21/1040	Chapter of York [LP]	D. John Gyffard [Giffard]*, canon of York D. John de Sancto Paulo [St Pol]*, canon of York D. John de Wodehous [Wodehouse]*, canon of York	York, 28 Sept. 1339

21/1041	Henry [of Casewick], abbot of Crowland	D. Adam de Steyngrave [Stonegrave], clerk F. Roger de Freston, monk of abbey	Crowland, 9 Oct. 1339
21/1042	Thomas [of Moulton], abbot of St Mary's, York (to Prince Edward, duke of Cornwall, earl of Chester and custo-dian of the realm)	D. Thomas de Bamburgh*, clerk F. John de Maungby [Maunby], monk of abbey	In the monastery, 6 Oct. 1339
21/1043	John [of Wymondham], abbot of St John's, Colchester (to king or custodian of the realm)	D. John de Mertone [Merton]* M. Gilbert de Meleforde [Melford]	Colchester, Tuesday after feast of St Dionysius [12 Oct.] 1339
21/1044	William [Melton], archbishop of York	D. Thomas de Malghum [Malham], rector of Thornton in Lonesdale [Thornton in Lonsdale], York diocese D. William de Wirkesworth [Wirksworth], rector of Slay-tebury [Slaidburn], York diocese	Cawode [Cawood], 4 Oct. 1339
21/1045	Robert de Wodehous [Wodeshouse], archdeacon of Richmond [LP]	D. Philip de Houton D. Thomas de Mallom [Malham] D. Philip de Chesterfeld [Chesterfield]	Nortwell [Norwell], 28 Sept. 1339
21/1046	William [Hereward], abbot of Cirencester	D. Thomas de Evesham*, clerk William Bromwich	Cirencester, feast of mar-tyrs Cosmas and Damian [27 Sept.] 1339
21/1047	[Roger of Thame], abbot of Abingdon	D. John de Sancto Paulo [St Pol]*, clerk D. Thomas de Evesham*, clerk	Abingdon, Sunday after feast of St Dionysius [10 Oct.] 1339

21/1048	John [of Heslington], abbot of Selby	F. Geoffrey de Gaddesby*, monk of abbey D. Thomas de Brayton*, clerk	Selby, 2 Oct. 1339
21/1049	Richard [of Gainsborough], abbot of Bardney [LP]	D. William de Broklesby [Brocklesby]* M. John de Langetoft [Langtoft]* D. Thomas de Sybthorp [Sibthorp]*	Bardney, 2 Oct. 1339
21/1050	Anthony [Bek], bishop of Norwich (to king or Prince Edward)	M. John de Fenton*, archdeacon of Suffolk, clerk [M.] Gilbert de Welton*, clerk	Hoxne, 6 Oct. 1339
22/1051	[Richard of Idbury], abbot of Winchcombe	M. William de Bosco [Boys]*, clerk John de Sponleye [Spoonley]	[Undated]
22/1052	[Simon of Eye], abbot of Ramsey	D. John de Sancto Paulo [St Pol]* F. John de Gretford [Greatford], monk D. Thomas de Sibthorp*	Ramsey, 10 Oct. 1339
22/1053	William [de Chiriton], abbot of Evesham	F. Robert de Bray, monk of abbey D. Thomas de Evesham*, clerk	Evesham, Sunday after feast of St Fides, Virgin [10 Oct.] 1339
22/1054	Walter [Fifehead], abbot of Hyde near Winchester [LP]	D. Robert de Kelleseye [Kelsey]* William de Cristchurche [Christchurch]	Hyde, 5 Oct. 1339
22/1055	John [of Aylsham], abbot of St Benet of Hulme	D. Thomas de Cotingham [Cottingham]*, clerk D. Ralph de Welyngham [Wellingham], clerk	St Benet of Hulme, 10 Oct. 1339

143

22/1057	Simon [le Botiller], prior of Worcester	D. Thomas de Evesham*, clerk	Worcester, 8 Oct. 1339
22/1058	Adam [of Staunton], abbot of St Peter's, Gloucester	D. Thomas de Evesham*, clerk William de Cheltenham*	Gloucester, 26 Sept. 1339
22/1059	Michael [of Mentmore], abbot of St Albans	F. Robert de Schyrbourne [Sherbourne], monk of abbey D. John de Langetone [Langton], clerk	St Albans, Monday after feast of St Dionysius, bishop and martyr [11 Oct.] 1339
22/1060	Thomas [Poucyn], abbot of St Augustine's, Canterbury	F.John Grete, monk of abbey	Menstre [Minster Abbey] Manor on the Isle of Thanet, 5 Oct. 1339
22/1061	Richard [Tours], abbot of Leicester	M. Ralph Turvile [Thurvill] [F] Ralph de Thurleston [Thurlaston]*	Leicester, 28 Sept. 1339
22/1062	Henry [of Morcott], abbot of Peterborough	D. Gervase de Wylford [Wilford], clerk F. Gilbert de Aslokby [Aslackby], monk of abbey Richard de Islep [Islip]	Stiucek [Stukeley] near Huntington, 11 Oct., 1339
22/1063	Chapter of Worcester	F. Simon Crumpe [Crompe]*, monk and sacristan of cathedral	Worcester Chapter House, 8 Oct. 1339
22/1064	Clergy of York diocese	M. Thomas de Harpham*, advocate of the court of York M. Robert de Newenham, proctor of the court of York	York, 30 Sept. 1339

144

PARLIAMENT AT WESTMINSTER, 20 JANUARY 1340

21/1025	Clergy of York diocese	M. William de Kendale [Kendal]*, clerk M. Robert de Neuwenham [Newenham], clerk	York, 10 Jan. 1340
22/1065	Wulstan [of Bransford], bishop of Worcester	M. Robert de Chigewell [Chigwell]*, canon of London	Hertlbury [Hartlebury], 9 Jan. 1340
22/1066	Reginald [of Waternewton], abbot of Thorney	M. Ralph Turvill [Thurvill] John de Luffewyk [Lowick]*	Thorney, Monday after feast of St Hilary, bishop [16 Jan.] 1340
22/1067	Richard [of Gainsborough], abbot of Bardney [LP]	F. William de Barton, monk of abbey [D.] Thomas de Sibbethorp [Sibthorp]* M. John de Langetoft [Langtoft]*, clerk William de Saundeby [Saundby], clerk	Bardney, Sunday after feast of St Hilary [15 Jan.] 1340
22/1068	Richard [Tours], abbot of Leicester	M. Ralph Turvile [Thurvill] F. Ralph de Thurleston [Thurlaston]*, monk [canon] of abbey Adam de [Damaged - ?Cradley]	In the monastery, [Damaged] Feb. 1340
22/1069	Anthony [Bek], bishop of Norwich (to king or Prince Edward as keeper of the realm)	M. John de Brynkhull [Brinkhill], clerk M. Gilbert de Welton*, clerk	Hoxne, 14 Jan., 1340
22/1070	Henry [of Morcott], abbot of Peterborough	D. Gervase de Willeforde [Wilford] F. John de [Damaged] Richard de Islep [Islip]	Peterborough, [Damaged] Jan. 1340

145

22/1071	Henry [Gower], bishop of St Davids	[D.] Henry de Strateford [Stratford]*, canon of St Davids [D.]John Goch [Gogh]*, clerk	Lawadyn [Llawhaden], 10 Jan. 1340
22/1073	[Roger of Thame], abbot of Abingdon	M. John de Hildeslegh [Hildesley]*, clerk D. John de Sancto Paulo [St Pol]*, clerk James de Woodstok [Woodstock]*	Abingdon, Wednesday after feast of the Epiphany [11 Jan.] 1340
22/1074	John [Grandisson], bishop of Exeter	D. John de Sancto Paulo [St Pol]*, canon of Exeter Benedict de Paston, canon of collegiate church of St Probus	Chuddelegh [Chudleigh], 15 Jan. 1340
22/1075	David [Dafydd ap Bleddyn], bishop of St Asaph	D. Thomas de Capenhurst*, canon of St Asaph M. Stephen de Ketylbri [Kettleburgh]*, doctor of laws	Alkton, 11 Jan. 1340
22/1076	Matthew [of Englefield], bishop of Bangor	M. Stephen de Kettelbery [Kettleburgh]*, provost of the church of Castri Kybii [Caergybi, Holyhead] D. Thomas de Cappenhurst [Capenhurst]*, canon of St Asaph	Gogerth [Gogarth], morrow of the Epiphany [7 Jan.] 1340
22/1077	Thomas [of Moulton], abbot of St Mary's, York (to Prince Edward)	D. Thomas de Bamburgh*, clerk Robert de Brounby	In the monastery, 5 Jan. 1340
22/1078	John [de Breynton], abbot of Glastonbury	D. John de Sancto Paulo [St Pol]*, clerk D. John de Bruggewater [Bridgwater]*, clerk	Glastonbury, 15 Jan. 1340

22/1079	Michael [of Mentmore], abbot of St Albans (to *Prince Edward as keeper of the realm*)	F. Adam de Wyttenham [Wittenham], monk of abbey D. John de Langeton [Langton], clerk	St Albans, Wednesday after feast of St Hilary [18 Jan.] 1340
22/1080	[Simon Crompe], prior of Worcester	D. Thomas de Evesham*, clerk D. Henry Geraud, clerk	Worcester; 8 Jan. 1340
22/1081	Dean and Chapter of Bangor	Henry de E[*damaged*], rector of Caernarfon Kyffnorth de Grion, clerk	Bangor; Monday after the Epiphany [9 Jan.] 1340
22/1082	[Simon of Eye], abbot of Ramsey	D. John de Sancto Paulo [St Pol]* F. John de Gretford [Greatford], monk of abbey D. Thomas de Sibthorp*	Ramsey; 17 Jan., 13 Edward III [1340]
22/1083	John [of Aylsham], abbot of St Benet of Hulme	D. Thomas de Cotyngham [Cottingham]*, clerk [D.] R[alph] Wolyngham [Wellingham], clerk	St Benet of Hulme, [*Damaged*] Jan. 1340

PARLIAMENT AT WESTMINSTER, 29 MARCH 1340

| 21/1035 | David [Dafydd ap Bleddyn], bishop of St Asaph | M. Richard de Oswaldestr [Oswestry]*, canon of St Asaph | Alkton, 20 March 1340 |
| 21/1036 | Chapter of St Asaph [*LP*] | M. Richard de Oswaldestr [Oswestry]*, canon of St Asaph M. Thomas de Capenhurst*, canon de St Asaph | Alkton, 20 March 1340 |

22/1084	Walter [Fifehead], abbot of Hyde near Winchester [LP]	F. John Blancchmal, monk of abbey M. John de Langetoft [Langtoft]* [RoP]	Hyde, Monday after feast of the Annunciation [27 March] 1340
22/1085	Wulstan [of Bransford], bishop of Worcester	M. Robert de Chikwell [Chigwell]*, canon of London	Hertlebury [Hartlebury], 22 March 1340
22/1086	Chapter of York [LP]	D. John Gyffard [Giffard]*, canon of York M. Thomas Sampson*, canon of York M. John de Sancto Paulo [St Pol]*, canon of York M. John de Wodhous [Wodehouse]*, canon of York	York, 21 March 1340
22/1087	John [de Breynton], abbot of Glastonbury	D. John de Sancto Paulo [St Pol]*, clerk F. John de Cant' [Canterbury], monk of abbey	Glastonbury, Sunday in the middle of Lent [26 March] 1340
22/1088	[Roger of Thame], abbot of Abingdon	D. John de Sancto Paulo [St Pol]*, clerk D. Edmund de la Beche*, clerk	Abingdon, 25 March 1340
22/1089	John [of Aylsham], abbot of St Benet of Hulme	D. Thomas de Cotyngham [Cottingham]*, clerk D. Ralph de Welyngham [Wellingham], clerk	St Benet of Hulme, 26 March 1340
22/1090	Chapter of Worcester	D. Thomas de Evesham*, clerk [RoP] D. Henry Geraud, clerk	Worcester Chapter House, 23 March 1340
22/1091	Adam [of Staunton], abbot of St Peter's, Gloucester	D. Thomas de Evesham*, clerk [RoP] William de Cheltenham*	Gloucester, 11 March 1340

22/1092	William [de Bernham], abbot of Bury St Edmunds	D. William [de Manthorpe], rector of Cotton	Bury St Edmunds, 26 March 1340
22/1093	Henry [Gower], bishop of St Davids	D. John de Sancto Paulo [St Pol]*, clerk D. Henry de Stratford*, clerk [RoP]	Lawadeyn [Llawhaden], 16 March 1340
22/1094	John [of Wymondham], abbot of St John's, Colchester	D. John de Marton*, rector of [Damaged – West Tilbury], clerk M. Gilbert de Melford, clerk	Colchester, Tuesday after the middle Sunday of Lent [28 March] 1340
22/1095	John [of Appleford], abbot of Reading	John de Freolond [Freeland]* John de Cophath*	[No place], 27 March 1340
22/1096	[Simon of Eye], abbot of Ramsey	D. John de Sancto Paulo [St Pol]* D. Thomas de Sibthorp* F. John de Gretford [Greatford], monk of abbey John de Stiuecle [Stukeley]	Ramsey, 26 March 1340
22/1097	Reginald [of Waternewton], abbot of Thorney	M. Ralph Turvill [Thurvill], clerk F. Ralph de Brampton, monk of abbey John de Luffewyk [Lowick]*	Thorney, morrow of the Annunciation [26 March] 1340
22/1098	Clergy of York diocese	M. Robert de Neuwenham [Newenham], clerk M. John de Aslakby [Aslackby], clerk	York, 18 March 1340
22/1099	Robert de Wodehous [Wodehouse], archdeacon of Richmond [LP]	D. John de Houton*, clerk D. John de Thorp, clerk D. John de Chesterfeld [Chesterfield]*, clerk	Methleye [Me:hley], 15 March 1340

149

22/1100	Thomas [of Moulton], abbot of St Mary's, York	D. Thomas de Bamburgh*, clerk [RoP] F. John de Eyveryngton [Everington], monk of abbey	In the monastery, 23 March 1340
23/1101	[Simon Crompe], prior of Worcester	M. John Geraud*, clerk F. Robert de Weston, monk and cellarer of Worcester	Worcester, 23 March 1340
23/1102	Ralph [of Shrewsbury], bishop of Bath and Wells	D. Thomas de Evesham* [RoP] M. John de Carleton [Carlton]*	Kyngesbury [Kingsbury Episcopi], 21 March 1340
23/1103	John [de Eclescliff], bishop of Llandaff	M. John de Carleton [Carlton]*, canon of Wells and Llandaff M. Richard de Haversham*, canon of Wells and Llandaff	Lank, 23 March 1340
23/1104	Thomas [of Nassington], prior of Spalding	D. John de Cotyngton [Cottington], rector of Geytburton [Gate Burton] John de Hautebarge [Alkborough], clerk	Spalding, 26 March 1340
23/1105	William [of Grasby], abbot of Thornton	[F] Alan de Clee, monk of abbey John de Grimesby [Grimsby], clerk	Thornton, feast of St Benedict, abbot [21 March] 1340
23/1106	Henry [of Morcott], abbot of Peterborough	M. John de Thoresby*, clerk [RoP] F. Gilbert de Aslokby [Aslackby], monk of abbey	Peterborough, 26 March 1340
23/1107	John [of Heslington], abbot of Selby	F. Geoffrey de Gaddesby*, monk of abbey D. Thomas de Brayton*, clerk [CoP] [RoP]	Selby, 20 March 1340

23/1108	Thomas [de Henle], abbot of Westminster	John de Schordich [Shoreditch]*, knight F. Richard de Winton [Winchester], monk of abbey	Piriford [Pyrford], 24 March 1340
23/1109	[Richard Tours], abbot of Leicester	M. Ralph Turvile [Thurvill] F. Ralph de Thurleston [Thurlaston]*, monk [canon] of abbey	Leicester, feast of the Annunciation [25 March] 1340
23/1110	William [de Chiriton], abbot of Evesham	F. Robert de Bray, monk and cellarer of abbey D. Thomas de Evesham*, clerk [RoP]	Evesham, Sunday after feast of the Annunciation [26 March] 1340
23/1111	Thomas [Poucyn], abbot of St Augustine's, Canterbury	F. John de Ripple, monk of abbey John de Polteneye [Pulteney]* William Faunt*	Canterbury, 26 March 1340
23/1112	Michael [of Mentmore], abbot of St Albans	F. Adam de Wyttenham [Wittenham], monk of abbey D. John de Langeton [Langton], clerk	Tynemuth [Tynemouth], 19 March 1340

GREAT COUNCIL AT WESTMINSTER, 2 OCTOBER 1340

1/16	[Simon of Eye], abbot of Ramsey (to Edward, son of the king, duke of Cornwall, earl of Chester and guardian of the realm) [F]	*No proctors named*	Ramsey, 10 Oct. 1340

PARLIAMENT AT WESTMINSTER, 23 APRIL 1341

23/1113	Clergy of York diocese	M. Thomas de Harpham*, advocate of the court of York M. Richard de Santon, advocate of the court of York	York, 16 April 1341
23/1114	Walter [Fifehead], abbot of Hyde near Winchester [LP]	F. John Blanncchynal [Blanccchmal], monk of abbey D. Robert de Keleseye [Kelsey]*, clerk [RoP]	Hyde, Saturday before feast of St George [21 April] 1341
23/1115	William [de Chiriton], abbot of Evesham	F. William de Hampton, monk and cellarer of abbey D. Thomas de Evesham*, clerk [RoP] D. John de Stok [Stoke]*, clerk	Evesham, Thursday before feast of St George, martyr [19 April] 1341
23/1116	[Roger of Thame], abbot of Abingdon	F. William Sarum [Salisbury], monk of abbey [D.] William de Stokes [Stoke]*, clerk	Abingdon, 21 April 1341
23/1117	David [Dafydd ap Bleddyn], bishop of St Asaph	D. Thomas de Capenhurst*, canon of St Asaph	St Asaph, 22 Feb. [sic] 1341
23/1118	John [of Tintern], abbot of Malmesbury	D. Thomas de Evesham*, clerk [RoP] John de Duffeld [Duffield], clerk	Malmesbury, 22 April 1341
23/1119	Henry [of Morcott], abbot of Peterborough	[F.] Gilbert de Aslakby [Aslackby], monk of abbey D. Thomas de Sibthorp*, clerk John de Burgh	Peterborough, [Damaged] after feast of St Alphegus [April] 1341
23/1120	Anthony [Bek], bishop of Norwich	M. Henry [Damaged – Chaddesden]*, archdeacon of Stow D. William de Culpo [Culpho]	Thornegge, 15 April 1341
23/1121	John [de Eclescliff], bishop of Llandaff	D. Gilbert de Wygeton [Wigton]*, treasurer of Llandaff M. John de Karleton [Carlton]*, canon of Wells	Lank, 17 April 1341

23/1122	Thomas [of Moulton], abbot of St Mary's, York	F. John de Eyveryngton [Everington], monk of abbey D. John de Pokelington [Pocklington]*, clerk D. John de Mansegh [Mansergh], clerk	York, 18 April 1341
23/1123	[Richard Tours], abbot of Leicester	F. William de Hexham, monk of abbey F. Ralph de Thurleston [Thurlaston]*, monk of abbey	In the monastery, 20 April 1341
23/1124	John [of Heslington], abbot of Selby	F. Geoffrey de Gaddesby*, monk of abbey D. Thomas de Brayton*, clerk [CoP]	Selby, 14 April 1341
23/1125	Matthew [of Englefield], bishop of Bangor	D. Hywel ap Goronwy, dean of Bangor D. Thomas de Capenhurst*, canon of St Asaph	Gogerth [Gogarth], 13 April [damaged]
23/1126	John [de Breynton], abbot of Glastonbury	F. John de Cantia [Canterbury], monk of abbey M. Nicholas de Bathon [Bath] Nicholas de Herleston [Harlaston]	Glastonbury, 19 April 1341
23/1127	William [Hereward], abbot of Cirencester	D. Thomas de Evesham* [RoP] [D.] Walter de Cirencester* Richard de Leye	Cirencester, Tuesday after the octave of Easter [17 April] 1341
23/1128	John [of Aylsham], abbot of St Benet of Hulme	Thomas de Cotyngham [Cottingham]*, clerk Ralph de Welyngham [Wellingham], clerk	St Benet of Hulme, 17 April 1341
23/1129	John [of Wymondham], abbot of St John's, Colchester	M. Gilbert de Meleford [Melford]	Colchester, Sunday the Quindene of Easter [22 April] 1341

PARLIAMENT AT WESTMINSTER, 16 OCTOBER 1342

23/1131	John [of Aylsham], abbot of St Benet of Hulme	D. Thomas de Cotyngham [Cottingham]*, clerk D. Ralph de Wolyngham [Wellingham], clerk	St Benet of Hulme, 9 Oct. 1342
23/1131A	William [Fifehead], abbot of Hyde near Winchester [LP]	John de Aulton [Alton]*	Hyde, 12 Oct. 1342

GREAT COUNCIL AT WESTMINSTER, 10 SEPTEMBER 1343

23/1132	David [Dafydd ap Bleddyn], bishop of St Asaph	M. Anias de Monte Alto [Enion de Mohaut], canon of St Asaph	St Asaph, 2 Sept. 1343
23/1133	Ralph [of Shrewsbury], bishop of Bath and Wells	John de [illegible] [M.] John de Carleton [Carlton]*	[Illegible], 5 Sept. 1343
23/1134	Anthony [Bek], bishop of Norwich	M. John de Fenton*, archdeacon of Suffolk D. William de Culpho, rector of Ocle [Acle]	Norwich, 6 Sept. 1343

PARLIAMENT AT WESTMINSTER, 18 APRIL 1344

23/1135	William [de la Zouche], archbishop of York	M. John de Thoresby*, canon of Lincoln M. Robert de Askeby [Asby]*, rector of Wessyngton [Wessington], Durham diocese, clerk	Burton near Beverl[ey], 10 April 1344

23/1136	Richard [de Bury], bishop of Durham	M. Thomas de Bradewardyn [Bradwardine]*, doctor of theology M. Richard de Kilvyngton [Kilvington]*, doctor of theology M. Stephen de Kettelbery [Kettleburgh]*, doctor of civil law D. William de Emeldon*, clerk D. William de Hemyngton [Hemington], clerk	Houedon [Howden], 10 April 1344
23/1137	Richard [of Hertford], abbot of Waltham	D. Richard de Wyndesor [Windsor] Bartholomew de Langerich*	Waltham, 18 April 1344
23/1138	Wulstan [of Bransford], bishop of Worcester	M. John de Thoresby* M. John de Seilleye [Severley]* D. John de Stoke*	Hartlebury [Hartlebury], 13 April 1344
23/1139	William [de Bernham], abbot of Bury St Edmunds	D. William de Cotton*, rector of Redgrave	Redgrave Manor, 16 April 1344
23/1140	David [Dafydd ap Bleddyn], bishop of St Asaph	D. Thomas de Capenhurst*, canon of St Asaph	St Asaph, 6 April 1344
23/1141	Matthew [of Englefield], bishop of Bangor	D. Thomas de Cappenhurst [Capenhurst]*, canon of St Asaph D. Henry de Ecclesalle [Eccleshall], rector of Lannbeblic [Llanbeblig], Bangor diocese	Gogerth [Gogarth], 12 April 1344
23/1142	[Henry of Appleford], abbot of Reading	William Lound [London]*, clerk John Frelond [Freeland]*	Reading, 16 April 1344

155

| 23/1143 | William [de Chiriton], abbot of Evesham | F. William de Boys*, monk of abbey
D. William de Newenham*, clerk | Evesham, 10 April 1344 |
| 23/1144 | William [of Throwley], abbot of St Augustine's, Canterbury | F. John de Ripple, monk of abbey
William Waure* | Canterbury, 17 April 1344 |

PARLIAMENT AT WESTMINSTER, 17 JUNE 1344

23/1145	John [Grandisson], bishop of Exeter	M. Robert Hereward*, canon of Exeter M. John de Northwode [Northwood]*, canon of Exeter M. Thomas Crosse [Cross]*, canon of collegiate church of Crediton [Crediton]	Clyst, 26 May 1344
23/1146	Chapter of York [LP]	M. John Gyffard [Giffard]* M. Thomas Sampson* D. John de Wodehouse* D. John de Wynewyk [Winwick]*	York, 23 May 1344
23/1147	Chapter of York	M. John Gyffard [Giffard]* M. Thomas Sampson* D. John de Wodehouse* D. John de Wynewyk [Winwick]*	York, 23 May 1344
23/1148	Geoffrey [de Gaddesby], abbot of Selby	F. Walter de Haldanby [Haldenby], monk of abbey D. Thomas de Brayton*, clerk	Selby, 30 May 1344

24/1151	[Damaged, but context suggests abbot of St Peter's, Gloucester]	[Damaged – William] de Newenham*, clerk William de Cheltenham*	[Damaged], 1344
24/1152	[Henry of Morcott], abbot of Peterborough	John de Burgo [Burgh] [Damaged]	Peterborough, 5 June, 1[damaged]
24/1153	Wulstan [of Bransford], bishop of Worcester	M. John de Thoresby* M. John de Severleye [Severley]* M. John de Stok [Stoke]*	Blockley (Glokkeleye), 26 May 1344
24/1154	Clergy of Carlisle city and diocese [LP]	D. Roger de Crumwell [Cromwell], rector of Melmorby [Melmerby] M. Thomas de Dalston, perpetual vicar of Crosseby [Crosby], Carlisle diocese	Carlisle, 31 May 1344
24/1155	John [of Tintern], abbot of Malmesbury	F. Nicholas de Cirencester, monk of abbey [D.] William de Newenham*, clerk	Malmesbury, 3 June 1344
24/1156	Michael [of Mentmore], abbot of St Albans	F. Adam de Wittenham, monk of abbey F. John de Bynham, monk of abbey	Our priory of Belvoir, Saturday before feast of St Barnabas, apostle [5 June] 1344
24/1157	Prior of Carlisle [LP]	D. Thomas de Pardisow [Pardishowe]* [D.] William de Sandeforth* [Sandford]	Carlisle Chapter House, 28 May 1344
24/1158	[Roger of Thame], abbot of Abingdon	D. John de Sancto Paulo [St Pol]*, clerk [RoP] D. William de Stoke*, clerk	Abingdon, Sunday before St Barnabas, apostle [6 June] 1344

24/1159	John [de Eclescliff], bishop of Llandaff	M. John de Carleton [Carlton]*, canon of Wells M. Richard de Haversham*, canon of Llandaff	Worleton, 20 May, 1344
24/1160	Clergy of Durham archdeaconry [LP]	Walter de Langcester [Lanchester], clerk [Damaged]	[Undated]
24/1162	[Damaged]	Thomas de la Mare, clerk [Damaged]	London, 29 April 1344
24/1163	[John of Wymondham], abbot of St John's, Colchester	D. John de Marton* [Damaged]	[Damaged], 1344
24/1165	[Damaged, probably bishop of Bangor]	[Damaged], canon of St Asaph Gervase ap Ph', rector of L[damaged - Llangian]	Gogerth [Gogarth], morrow of Pentecost [24 May] 1344
24/1166	[Dafydd ap Bleddyn], bishop of St Asaph	[Damaged – Thomas de] Capenhurst*, canon of St Asaph [RoP]	[Damaged], 1344
24/1167	William [de Chiriton], abbot of Evesham	[Damaged – William de] Boys*, monk of abbey D. William de Newenham*, clerk	Evesham, Thursday after feast of the Holy Trinity [3 June] 1344
24/1168	[Richard of Bury], bishop of Durham	M. Thomas de Bradwardyn [Bradwardine]*, doctor of theology M. Richard de Kylvyngton [Kilvington]*, doctor of theology M. Stephen de Ketelbury [Kettleburgh]*, doctor of civil law D. William [Damaged], clerk	Welhall [Wheel Hall, Ricall], 28 May 1344

158

24/1169	Dean and Chapter of Bangor	M. Thomas de Cappenhurst [Capenhurst]*, canon of St Asaph [RoP] M. Jervase [Gervase], rector of Lanngian [Llangian], Bangor diocese	Bangor; morrow of Po[*damaged*], 1344
24/1170	[Thomas of Moulton], abbot of St Mary's, York	F. William de Seyn [Seynesbury], monk of abbey D. David de Wollore* D. John de Mansergh	York, 28 May 1344
24/1171	William [de Bernham], abbot of Bury St Edmunds	D. William de Cotton*, rector of Redgrave	Chevyngton [Chevington] Manor, 6 June 1344
24/1172	Richard [Tours], abbot of Leicester	F. Ralph de Thurleston [Thurlaston]*, monk [canon] of abbey D. Richard de Kersyngton [Cassington] Adam de Cradeleye [Cradley]	Leicester, 6 June 1344
24/1173	William [de la Zouche], archbishop of York	M. John de Thoresby*, canon of Lincoln M. Robert de Askeby [Asby]*, rector of Wessington, Durham diocese, 'our household clerk'	Suthwell [Southwell], 4 June 1344
24/1174	Roger [Barrow], abbot of Bardney [*LP*]	D. Thomas de Sibthorp*, clerk [RoP] William de Saundeby [Saundby], clerk	Bardney, Monday after feast of the Holy Trinity [31 May] 1344
24/1175	[William Hereward], abbot of Cirencester	F. Adam de Astcote, monk of abbey F. Henry de Morton, monk of abbey Walter de Cyrcestre [Cirencester]	Cirencester, Friday in Pentecost week [28 May] 1344

24/1176	Clergy of Northumberland archdeaconry [LP]	
	M. Gilbert de Halughton [Halghton], rector of Ovyngham [Ovingham]	Durham, 21 May 1344
24/1177	William [of Sherborne], abbot of Winchcombe	
	M. William de Adelnynton [Admington], clerk	Winchcombe, 4 June 1344

PARLIAMENT AT WESTMINSTER, 3 FEBRUARY 1346

24/1178	Matthew [of Englefield], bishop of Bangor	
	D. Thomas de Cappenhurst [Capenhurst]*, canon of St Asaph	Gogerth [Gogarth], Thursday the morrow of the Conversion of St Paul [26 Jan.] 1346
	M. Roger de Ecclessalle [Eccleshall], rector of Lanndeiniolen [Llanddeiniolen], Bangor diocese	
24/1179	Wulstan [of Bransford], bishop of Worcester	
	John de [Damaged]erleye [Severley]*	[Illegible], Jan. 1346
	John de Stoke*	
24/1180	William [de la Zouche], archbishop of York (to king or custodian of the realm)	
	M. Gilbert de Welton, professor of civil law	Laumy, 5 Jan. 1346
	D. David de Wollou [Wollore]*, clerk	
	D. William de Burgh*, clerk	
	Peter de Richemund [Richmond]	

GREAT COUNCIL AT WESTMINSTER, 3 MARCH 1347

24/1182	John [of Wymondham], abbot of St John's, Colchester	
	M. John de Marton*	
	M. Richard de Warmyngton [Warmington]	Colchester, 1 March 1347

24/1183	[Walter Fifehead], abbot of Hyde near Winchester	D. Robert de Kelseye [Kesley]*, clerk Nicholas de Kynham, clerk	Hyde, Monday after feast of St Matthias, apostle [25 Feb.] 1347
24/1184	Adam [of Staunton], abbot of St Peter's, Gloucester	D. William de Newenham*, clerk Michael de Aissh [Ash]*	Gloucester, 28 Feb. 1347
24/1185	[Roger of Thame], abbot of Abingdon	D. John de Sancto Paulo [St Pol]*, clerk D. John Scarle*, clerk	Abingdon, Wednesday after feast of St Matthias, apostle [27 Feb.] 1347

PARLIAMENT AT WESTMINSTER, 14 JANUARY 1348

24/1186	[John of Tintern], abbot of Malmesbury (to king)	John C[damaged]	Malmesbury, 9 Jan. 1348
24/1187	Robert [of Aylsham], abbot of St Benet of Hulme	D. John de Codyngton [Coddington]*, clerk John de Berneye* William de Wychyngham [Witchingham]*	St Benet of Hulme, Wednesday after feast of the Epiphany [9 Jan.] 1348
24/1188	William [Cloune], abbot of Leicester [LP]	F. Roger de Repyndon [Repingdon], monk of abbey William de Duffeld [Duffield], clerk	Our abbey of Leicester, 10 Jan. 1348
24/1189	[William of Haddon], abbot of Thorney	M. William de Wittlesey [Whittlesey]*, archdeacon of Huntingdon F. John de Burgh, monk of abbey John de Harrowede [Harrowden]*	Thorney, morrow of the Epiphany [7 Jan.] 1348

24/1190	William of Sherborne], abbot of Winchcombe	M. Henry de Cokham [Cookham]*, clerk D. William de Newynham [Newenham]*, clerk	Winchcombe, Friday before feast of St Hilary [11 Jan.] 1348
24/1191	Dean and Chapter of Bangor	M. David Goch, canon of Bangor	Bangor, Thursday before feast of the Epiphany [3 Jan.] 1348
24/1192	William [Hereward], abbot of Cirencester	F. Henry de Mortone [Morton], monk of abbey M. John de Usk*, clerk D. William de Newenham*, clerk	Cirencester, Sunday the feast of the Epiphany [6 Jan.] 1348
24/1193	Matthew [of Englefield], bishop of Bangor	M. David Goch, canon of Bangor	Gogerth [Gogarth], Thursday before feast of the Epiphany [3 Jan.] 1348
24/1194	[Robert of Nassington], abbot of Ramsey	F. John de Brampton, monk of abbey D. Edmund de Grimesby [Grimsby]*, clerk D. Roger de Elyngton [Ellington], clerk	Ramsey, 11 Jan. 1348
24/1195	William [Boys], abbot of Evesham	D. William de Newenham*, clerk John atte Wode [Atwood]	Evesham, 10 Jan. 1348
24/1196	[Henry of Appleford], abbot of Reading	William de Lound [London]*, clerk Alexander de Chelseye [Chelsea]	Reading, 13 Jan. 1348
24/1197	Robert [Wyvil], bishop of Salisbury [LP]	D. Edmund de Grymmesby [Grimsby]*, clerk D. William de Herleston [Harlaston]*, clerk	Our Park of Ramsbury, 10 Jan. 1348

24/1198	Henry [of Morcott], abbot of Peterborough	D. Robert de Wylesford [Wilford], clerk John de Burgh	Peterborough, Thursday after feast of the Epiphany [10 Jan.] 1348
24/1199	William [de la Zouche], archbishop of York	D. John de Sancto Paulo [St Pol]*, canon of York and Beverley M. Ralph Turvill [Thurvill], canon of York and Beverley M. Gilbert de Welton*, canon of York and Beverley	Ripon, 4 Jan. 1348
24/1200	Clergy of Carlisle diocese [LP]	John de Fletham [Fleetham] Adam de Karleton [Carlton]*	Carlisle, 23 Dec. 1347
25/1201	John [of Wymondham], abbot of St John's, Colchester	D. John de Marton* M. Richard de Warmyngton [Warmington]	Colchester, Thursday after feast of the Epiphany [10 Jan.] 1348
25/1202	Chapter of Worcester	F. Robert de Weston, monk and cellarer of Worcester D. John de Stoke*, rector of Teyneburi [Tenbury Wells]	Worcester Chapter House, 7 Jan. 1348
25/1203	[John of Evesham], prior of Worcester	F. Robert de Weston, monk and cellarer of Worcester D. John de Stoke*, rector of Teyneburi [Tenbury Wells]	Worcester, 7 Jan. 1348
25/1204	Simon [de Bercheston], abbot of Westminster	F. Benedict de Certseye [Chertsey] M. William de Bampton, clerk	Kadygan [Cardigan], 31 Dec. 1347
25/1205	Walter [Fifehead], abbot of Hyde near Winchester [LP]	D. Robert de Keleseye [Kelsey]*, clerk John de Bradelegh	Hyde, Saturday before feast of St Hilary [5 Jan.] 1348

25/1206	John [of Tintern], abbot of Malmesbury	D. William de Newenham*, clerk William Dersham	Malmesbury, Friday after feast of the Epiphany [11 Jan.] 1348
25/1207	Geoffrey [de Gaddesby], abbot of Selby	F. Walter de Haldanby [Haldenby], monk D. Thomas de Brayton*, clerk	Selby, 7 Jan. 1348
25/1208	Chapter of York [LP]	D. John de Sancto Paulo [St Pol]* D.John de Wodehous [Wodehouse]* M. John Berenger*	York, 12 Dec. 1347
25/1209	Roger [Barrow], abbot of Bardney [LP]	F. Geoffrey de Spalding, monk William de Saundeby [Saundby]	Bardney, Thursday after feast of St Hilary [17 Jan.] 1348
25/1210	[Roger of Thame], abbot of Abingdon	D.John de Sancto Paulo [St Pol]*, clerk D. William de Nolas, clerk	Abingdon, 7 Jan. 1348
25/1211	Thomas [of Moulton], abbot of St Mary's, York	F. William de Seynesbury, monk D.John de Pokelyngton [Pocklington]*, clerk	York, 6 Jan. 1348
25/1212	Ralph [of Shrewsbury], bishop of Bath and Wells	John de Sancto Paulo [St Pol]*	Wyvelescombe [Wivelis-combe], 30 Dec. 1347
25/1213	Adam [of Staunton], abbot of St Peter's, Gloucester	D. William de Newenham*, clerk William de Cheltenham*	Gloucester, 1 Jan. 1348

| 25/1214 | Wulstan [of Bransford], bishop of Worcester | M. John de Severleye [Severley]*, 'our chancellor'
 D. William de Saluwarp [Salwarp], 'steward of our household' | Hartlebury, 7 Jan. 1348 |
| 25/1215 | Roger [Northburgh], bishop of Coventry and Lichfield *[LP]* | M. Henry de Chaddesden*, archdeacon of Leicester
 D. Thomas de Clopton*, canon of Lichfield | Heywas, 8 Jan. 1348 |

PARLIAMENT AT WESTMINSTER, 31 MARCH 1348

24/1200A	Chapter of York	D. John de Sancto Paulo [St Pol]*, canon of York M. Gilbert de Welton*, doctor of civil law, canon of York D. John de Wynewyk [Winwick]*, canon of York	York, 20 March 1348
25/1216	[Henry of Appleford], abbot of Reading	William Lound [London]*, clerk Alexander de Chelseye [Chelsea]	Reading, 29 March 1348
25/1217	Simon [de Bercheston], abbot of Westminster	*[Damaged –* Benedict] de Chertsey, monk M. William de Bampton	Kardigan [Cardigan], 10 March 1348
25/1218	John [Trilleck], bishop of Hereford *[LP]*	M. Thomas de Bredewardyn [Bradwardine]*, doctor of sacred theology and canon of Lincoln M. John de Leich [Leech]*, doctor of canon law and canon of Hereford M. John de Sancto Paulo [St Pol]*, canon of York M. Edmund de Grymmesby [Grimsby]* M. Adam de Houton [Houghton]*, doctor of civil law Thomas de Eywls	Golthull, 30 March 1348

165

25/1219	Ralph [of Shrewsbury], bishop of Bath and Wells	D.John de Sancto Paulo [St Pol]* D.John of Wynewyk [Winwick]*, canon of Wells	Wyvelescombe [Wiveliscombe], 22 March 1348
25/1220	William [Hereward], abbot of Cirencester	M.John de Usk*, clerk D. William de Newenham*, clerk	Cirencester, St Gregory [12 March] 1348
25/1221	William [Boys], abbot of Evesham	D. William de Newenham* John atte Wode [Atwood]	Evesham, 25 March 1348
25/1222	William [Cloune], abbot of Leicester [LP]	John de Horsley Geoffrey de Chaddesden*	Leicester, 29 March 1348

PARLIAMENT AT WESTMINSTER, 9 FEBRUARY 1351

25/1223	Robert [Wyvil], bishop of Salisbury [LP]	D. William de [illegible] D.John Gogh*, clerk	[Illegible], 1351
25/1224	Matthew [of Englefield], bishop of Bangor	D. Howel ap Gronwy [Hywel ap Gronow]*, archdeacon of Anglesey D. Gervase ap David, archdeacon of Bangor	Gogerth [Gogarth], Thursday the morrow of the Purification of the Blessed Mary [3 Feb.] 1351
25/1225	[Roger of Thame], abbot of Abingdon	M. Godfrey Fromond* [D.] William de Shiltwode [Shiltwood]	Abingdon, 4 Feb. 1351

25/1226	[William of Haddon], abbot of Thorney	[Damaged] John de Harndon [Harrowden]*	Thorney, 6 Feb. 1351
25/1227	Subprior and Chapter of Worcester	John de Wotthyn	Worcester Chapter House, 5 Feb. 1351
25/1228	Roger [Barrow], abbot of Bardney [LP]	D. Henry de Ingilby [Ingleby]* D. [Damaged] M. William de Burton	Bardney, 6 Feb. 1351
25/1229	William [of Haddiscoe], abbot of St Benet of Hulme	D. Richard de Norwico [Norwich]*, clerk D. Richard de Thursby*, clerk D. William de Bergh [Burgh]*, clerk William de Wychyngham [Witchingham]*	St Benet of Hulme, Thursday the morrow of the Purification of the Blessed Virgin [3 Feb.] 1351
25/1230	William [Boys], abbot of Evesham	D. William de Newenham*, clerk D. Philip de Alycestre [Alcester], clerk John M[damaged] Nicholas de la Rook	Evesham, [Damaged] 1351
25/1231	Dean and Chapter of Bangor	[Damaged]	Bangor, Friday after feast of the Purification of the Blessed Mary [4 Feb.] 1351
25/1232	Henry [of Morcott], abbot of Peterborough	John de Harewedon [Harrowden]* D. Robert de Willeford [Wilford]*	Peterborough, Saturday after feast of the Purification of the Blessed Mary [5 Feb.] 1351

167

PARLIAMENT AT WESTMINSTER, 13 JANUARY 1352

25/1233	[Simon of Blyton], abbot of St John's, Colchester	[D.] Edmund de Grymesby [Grimsby]* M. Richard de Wermyngton [Warmington]	Colchester, Sunday after feast of the Epiphany [7 Jan.] 1352
25/1234	[William Cloune], abbot of Leicester	F. Ralph de [*illegible*], monk Geoffrey de la Launde, rector [*recte* vicar] of Farnynghe [Farthinghoe] Adam de Rothele [Rothley], clerk	Leicester, 7 Jan. 1352
25/1235	Clergy of York diocese [*LP*]	[*Illegible, something of*] St Peter's, York Robert de Hakthorp [Hackthorpe]*, rector of Syengesby [Slingby]	York, 7 Jan. 1352
25/1236	Thomas [Hatfield], bishop of Durham	D. Henry de Ingilby [Ingleby]* M. Robert de Chikwele [Chigwell]* John de [*illegible*] [*Illegible*] de Wyndesore [Windsor] [D.] William de Emildon [Emeldon]*	Aukeland [Bishop Auckland], 6 Jan. 1352
25/1237	Dean and Chapter of Bangor	M. Gervase fitzDavid [ap David], archdeacon of Bangor	Bangor, 7 March [*sic*] 1352
25/1238	Roger [of Thame], abbot of Abingdon	William Harleston, clerk [D.] William Sheltwode [Shiltwood], clerk	Abingdon, 11 Jan. 1352
25/1239	[John of Evesham], prior of Worcester	F. Robert de Weston, monk D. John de Stoke*, rector of Seynebury [Saintbury]	Worcester, morrow of the Epiphany [7 Jan.] 1352

25/1240	Clergy of Bangor diocese	M. Gervase fitz David [ap David], archdeacon of Bangor D. Richard de Estun	Gogerth [Gogarth], 7 Jan. 1352
25/1241	Geoffrey [de Gaddesby], abbot of Selby	D. Thomas de Brayton*, clerk Illard de Usflett [Ousefleet]*	Selby, 3 Jan. 1352
25/1242	Henry [of Morcott], abbot of Peterborough	John de Harnghdon [Harrowden]* D. Robert de Willeford [Wilford]*, clerk	Peterborough, feast of the Epiphany [6 Jan.] 1352
25/1243	Roger [Barrow], abbot of Bardney [LP]	[Illegible - Henry] de Ingelby [Ingleby]*, clerk D. William de Blaunkenay [Blaunkney], clerk William de Saundeby [Saundby], clerk	Bardney, Monday after feast of the Epiphany [8 Jan.] 1352
25/1244	Thomas [of Moulton], abbot of St Mary's, York	F. William de Seynesbury, monk D. John de Pokelyngton [Pocklington] *, clerk	York, 4 Jan. 1352
25/1245	Thomas [de Colwell], abbot of St Augustine's, Canterbury	M. Michael de Northburgh*, doctor of civil law F. Thomas Bregge [Burgh], monk	Canterbury, 3 Jan. 1352
25/1246	Thomas [de la Mare], abbot of St Albans	F. Adam de Wyttenham [Wittenham], prior of St Albans D. John Skarle [Scarle]*, clerk	St Albans, 9 Jan. 1352
25/1247	William [Boys], abbot of Evesham	[D.] William de Newenham*, clerk [D.] John de Stoke*, clerk John Mussard [Mussard]*	Evesham, 5 Jan. 1352

25/1248	Chapter of Worcester	F. Robert de Weston, monk D. John de Stoke*, rector of Seynebury [Saintbury]	Worcester, morrow of the Epiphany [7 Jan.] 1352
25/1249	William de Routhebury [Roth-bury], archdeacon of Carlisle [LP]	D. William de Sandeford [Sandford]*, rector of Musgrave Thomas Daunay*, clerk	Carlisle, morrow of the Epiphany [7 Jan.] 1352
25/1250	Prior of Carlisle [LP]	Robert de Sandfford [Sandford], clerk	Carlisle, Sunday 8 Jan. 1352
26/1251	Matthew [of Englefield], bishop of Bangor	M. Gervase fitz David [ap David], archdeacon of Bangor	Gogerth [Gogarth], 5 Jan. 1352
26/1252	Chapter of York Cathedral [LP]	M. Gilbert de Welton*, doctor of civil law D. Henry de Ingelby [Ingleby]*	York, 10 Jan. 1352
26/1253	William [of Haddiscoe], abbot of St Benet of Hulme	[D.] Richard de Norwico [Norwich]*, clerk William de Bergh [Burgh]*, clerk William de Wychyngham [Witchingham]*	St Benet of Hulme, Monday after feast of the Epiphany [9 Jan.] 1352
26/1254	[Ralph of Shrewsbury], bishop of Bath and Wells	D. William de Stywenham	Banewell [Banwell], 8 Jan. 1352
26/1255	William [de Bernham], abbot of Bury St Edmunds	D. Elias de Grymisby [Grimsby]* M. [sic – recte F.] William de Wyvelingham [Wellingham] [M.] John de Eya [Eye]	Redgrave, 2 Jan. 1352

26/1256	Simon [de Aumeney], abbot of Malmesbury	[D.] William de Newenham*, clerk Richard de Ammeneye [Ampney], clerk Henry Percihay [Percy]*, clerk Thomas Drew, clerk Richard de Urdelegh [Urdeleigh]*	Malmesbury, Saturday the morrow of the Epiphany [7 Jan.] 1352
26/1257	Henry [of Appleford], abbot of Reading [LP]	D. Gilbert de London*, clerk Geoffrey de Astone [Aston]*, clerk	Reading, Saturday after feast of the Epiphany [7 Jan.] 1352
26/1258	Walter [de Monyton], abbot of Glastonbury	D. William de Nywenham [Newenham]*, clerk M. Thomas le Yong [Young]*, clerk	Glastonbury; 12 Jan. 1352
26/1259	[Richard of Shenington], abbot of Ramsey	Nicholas de Styuecle [Styuecle]* Richard Albert of Jakelee [Yaxley]*	Ramsey, 7 Jan. 1352
26/1260	William [Hereward], abbot of Cirencester	M. John de Lameleye [Lambley]*	Cirencester; feast of the Circumcision of the Lord [1 Jan.] 1352
26/1261	Clergy of Carlisle diocese [LP]	Nicholas de Whitryg [Whitrig], rector of Caldebek [Caldbeck] Thomas de Salkeld, rector of Clyfton [Clifton]	Carlisle, Tuesday after feast of the Epiphany [10 Jan.] 1352

GREAT COUNCIL AT WESTMINSTER, 16 AUGUST 1352

26/1262	John [Kirkby], bishop of Carlisle [LP]	D. Henry de Graystok [Greystoke]*	Appelby [Appleby], vigil of St Laurence [9 Aug.] 1352
26/1263	John [Paschal], bishop of Llandaff	Thomas de [Damaged and illegible]	[Damaged] Aug. 1352
26/1264	Ralph [of Shrewsbury], bishop of Bath and Wells	M. Thomas de Bokton [Buxton]*, clerk	Wyvelescomb [Wivelis-combe], 8 Aug. 1352

PARLIAMENT AT WESTMINSTER, 23 SEPTEMBER 1353

26/1265	[Robert of Ipwell], abbot of Winchcombe	M. John de Clipstone F. William de Gloucester, cellarer of Winchcombe	[Undated]
26/1266	Thomas [de la Mare], abbot of St Albans	F. Adam de Wyttenham [Wittenham], prior of St Albans D. John Skarle [Scarle]*, clerk	St Albans, [Damaged] Sept. 135[damaged] 1353
26/1267	Robert [of Ipwell], abbot of Winchcombe	D. William Wakefeld [Wakefield] D. Thomas de Wynchemul	Winchcombe, feast of St Lambert, bishop, [17 Sept.] 1353
26/1268	John [Trilleck], bishop of Hereford	Thomas Hakelind [Hacluit]*, chancellor of Hereford Nicholas de Kaerwent [Caerwent], canon of Hereford	Whyl [Capel Whyl], 18 Sept. 1353
C 49/46/28	William [de Bernham], abbot of Bury St Edmunds	D. Elias de Grymmesby [Grimsby]* M. John de Eye, rector of parish church of St Redgrave, clerk	Culford, 10 Sept. 1353

C 49/46/29	William [Boys], abbot of Evesham	D. William de Newnham [Newenham]*, clerk William de Willerseye [Willersey], clerk	Evesham, 16 Sept. 1353
C 49/46/30	Thomas [de Colwell], abbot of St Augustine's, Canterbury	M. Michael de Northburgh*, doctor of civil law F. Thomas Burgo [Burgh], monk of abbey	Canterbury, 8 Sept. 1353
C 49/46/31	Simon [de Aumeney], abbot of Malmesbury	D. William de Newenham*, clerk Henry Percehay [Percy]* Thomas de Coubrigge [Cowbridge]	Malmesbury, 20 Sept. 1353
C 49/46/32	[Richard of Shenington], abbot of Ramsey	D. Michael de Ravenesdale [Ravendale]* Robert de Haysand*	Ramsey, 22 Sept. 1353
C 49/46/33	Ralph [of Eastcott], abbot of Cirencester	M. John de Lech [Leech]*, doctor of both laws	Cirencester, feast of the Exaltation of the Holy Cross [14 Sept.] 1353
C 49/46/34	Walter [de Monyton], abbot of Glastonbury	D. William de Nywenham [Newenham]*, clerk D. William de Tylneye [Tilney], clerk	Glastonbury, Wednesday before feast of St Matthew, apostle [18 Sept.] 1353
C 49/46/35	William [of Haddiscoe], abbot of St Benet of Hulme	D. Richard de Norwyco [Norwich], clerk D. John de Codyngton [Coddington]*, clerk	St Benet of Hulme, Tuesday after feast of the Exaltation of the Holy Cross [17 Sept.] 1353
C 49/46/36	Robert [of Ramsey], abbot of Peterborough	D. Roger de Chestirfeld [Chesterfield]*, clerk William de Irtelingburgh [Irthlingborough], marshal of the lord archbishop of York	Peterborough, Saturday the feast of St Matthew, apostle [21 Sept.] 1353

C 49/46/37	[William of Haddon], abbot of Thorney	F. Thomas de [Illegible] M. William de Bradle [Bradley], clerk M. Richard de Wodelond [Woodlands], clerk	[Illegible]
C 49/46/38	Roger [Barrow], abbot of Bardney	M. John de Langtoft*, clerk D. Henry de Ingelby [Ingleby]*, clerk D. William de Blaunkeney [Blankney], clerk F. Thomas de Welton, monk of abbey	Bardney, feast of St Matthew, apostle [21 Sept.] 1353
C 49/46/39	Thomas [sic – should be John Sheppey], bishop of Rochester	M. Laurence Fastolf, canon of London, clerk D. William de Tilneye [Tilney], clerk	Clive [Trottiscliffe], Rochester diocese, Friday after feast of the Exaltation of the Holy Cross [20 Sept.] 1353
C 49/46/40	Geoffrey [de Gaddesby], abbot of Selby	F. John de Goldale, monk of abbey D. Thomas de Brayton*, clerk [Damaged]	Selby, Monday after feast of the Exaltation of the Holy Cross [16 Sept.] 1353
C 49/46/41	Thomas [of Moulton], abbot of St Mary's, York	F. William de Seynesbury, monk of abbey D. John de Pokelyngton [Pocklington], clerk	In the monastery, [illegible] Sept. 1353

PARLIAMENT AT WESTMINSTER, 28 APRIL 1354

26/1269	[John of Horncastle], prior of Carlisle [LP]	D. Henry de Graystok [Greystoke]*, rector of Rouley [Rowley]	Carlisle, 8 April 1354

26/1270	Subdean and Chapter of Lincoln [LP]	D. Richard de Whitewell	Lincoln, 22 April 1354
26/1271	Chapter of York [LP]	D. John de Wynewyk [Winwick]*, treasurer of York D. Henry de Ingelby [Ingleby]*	York, 23 April 1354
26/1272	[John of Horncastle], prior and Chapter of Carlisle [LP]	D. Henry de Graystok [Greystoke]*, rector of Rouley [Rowley] D. Adam de Hotum [Houghton]*, rector of Warsopp [Warsop]	Carlisle Chapter House, 8 April 1354
26/1273	Ralph [of Shrewsbury], bishop of Bath and Wells	John de Wyniwyk [Winwick]*, canon of Wells	Wyveliscomb [Wiveliscombe], 22 April 1354
26/1274	Thomas [de Colwell], abbot of St Augustine's, Canterbury	M. Michael de Northburgh*, doctor of civil law F. Thomas Breggte [Burgh], monk	[Illegible] April 1354
26/1275	[Robert of Ipwell], abbot of Winchcombe	F. John de Gloucester, monk D. William de Tyryngtone [Terrington]*	Winchcombe, 24 April 1354
26/1276	[Roger of Thame], abbot of Abingdon	D. William de Shiltwode [Shiltwood], clerk Robert de Wyghthull [Wythall]*, clerk	Abingdon, St George [23 April] 1354
26/1277	Thomas [de Horton], abbot of St Peter's, Gloucester	D. William de Newenham*, clerk D. Richard de Nortwyco [Norwich]*, clerk Robert Palet*	Gloucester, Wednesday the feast of St George, martyr [23 April] 1354

26/1278	Ralph [of Shrewsbury], bishop of Bath and Wells	D. William de Nywenham [Newenham]*, clerk	Wyveliscomb [Wivelis-combe], 22 April 1354
26/1279	Thomas [Fastolf], bishop of St Davids	D. John Gough [Gogh]*, clerk D. William de Tylneye [Tilney], clerk	Clyve [Trottiscliffe] in Rochester diocese, Saturday the morrow of feast of St Mark, evangelist [26 April] 1354
26/1280	Geoffrey [de Gaddesby], abbot of Selby	D. Thomas de Brayton*, clerk Illard de Usflet [Ousefleet]*	Selby, 17 April 1354
26/1281	Thomas [de la Mare], abbot of St Albans	D. [sic – recte F.] John Mote, monk D. [sic – recte F.] Richard de Rokeston, monk	St Albans, 20 April 1354
26/1282	Thomas [of Moulton], abbot of St Mary's, York	F. William de Seynesbury, monk D. John de Pokelyngton [Pocklington], clerk	In the monastery, 23 April 1354
26/1283	Simon [de Aumeney], abbot of Malmesbury	D. William Nywenham [Newenham]*, clerk Henry Porcehay [Percy]* Thomas Drew Thomas de Coubrigge [Cowbridge]	Malmesbury, Friday the feast of St Mark, evangelist [25 April] 1354
26/1284	Henry [of Appleford], abbot of Reading [LP]	D. William de London*, clerk Geoffrey de Astone [Aston]*, clerk	Reading, 20 April 1354
26/1285	William [of Haddiscoe], abbot of St Benet of Hulme	D. William de Bergh [Burgh]*, clerk William de Wychyngham [Witchingham]*	St Benet of Hulme, 24 April 1354

26/1286	Roger [of Barrow], abbot of Bardney [LP]	D. Henry de Ingilby [Ingleby]*, clerk D. William de Blankenay [Blankney] F. Thomas de Stapilton [Stapelton]*, monk	Bardney, 16 April 1354
26/1287	Ralph [of Eastcott], abbot of Cirencester	M. John de Lech [Leech]*, doctor of canon law D. William Newenham*	Cirencester, 12 April 1354
26/1289	William [de Bernham], abbot of Bury St Edmunds	D. Elias de Grymesby [Grimsby]*, clerk D. William de Scheltwode [Shiltwood], clerk	Bury St Edmunds, 18 April 1354
26/1291	[Richard of Shenington], abbot of Ramsey	D. Michael de Ravenesdale [Ravendale]*, rector of Mepershale [Meppershall]	Ramsey, Saturday the morrow of St Mark, evangelist [26 April] 1354
26/1292	Walter [de Monyton], abbot of Glastonbury	D. William de Nywenham [Newenham]*, clerk D. William de Tylneye [Tilney], clerk	Glastonbury, 20 April 1354
26/1293	Dean and Chapter of Bangor	Blediumus fitz Howel [Bledyn ap Hywel], rector of Dervel [Derfel], St Asaph diocese	Bangor, 20 April 1354
26/1294	Walter [Fifehead], abbot of Hyde near Winchester [LP]	M. John Wolvesle [Wolvesley], canon of Salisbury D. William [Chuert, Chuvere], rector of Werplesdon [Worplesdon]	Hyde, 22 April 1354

PARLIAMENT AT WESTMINSTER, 23 NOVEMBER 1355

26/1295	Clergy of Carlisle diocese [LP]	M. John de Welton, clerk M. William de Ragenhill [Ragnall], clerk	Carlisle, 6 Nov. 1355
26/1296	Dean and Chapter of Bangor Cathedral	D. Howel fitz Goronwy [Hywel ap Gronow]*, archdeacon of Anglesey	Bangor, 25 Oct. 1355
26/1297	Roger [of Thame], abbot of Abingdon	Hugh de Aston*, clerk Thomas Churchull [Churchill], clerk [D.] William Shiltwode [Shiltwood], clerk	Abingdon, 14 Nov. 1355
26/1298	Matthew [of Englefield], bishop of Bangor	D. Howel fitz Goronwy [Hywel ap Gronow]*, archdeacon of Anglesey	Gogerth [Gogarth], 4 Nov. 1355
26/1299	Thomas [Percy], bishop of Norwich	M. Adam de Houtene [Houghton]*, advocate in the court of Canterbury D. William de Swyneflet [Swinefleet]*, rector of Elsyngg [Elsing]	Semere [Semer], 6 Nov. 1355
26/1300	William, abbot of [Damaged, possibly Bury St Edmunds]	D. Elias de Grymmesby [Grimsby]* William de Wychingham [Witchingham]*	Elmeswell [Elmswell], 12 Nov. 1355
27/1301	Thomas [de Horton], abbot of St Peter's, Gloucester	D. William de Newenham* Robert Palet*	Gloucester, 8 Nov. 1355
27/1302	Henry [of Appleford], abbot of Reading [LP]	D. William de London*, clerk	Reading, 20 Nov. 1355

27/1303	William [Boys], abbot of Evesham	F. John de Ambresleye [Ombersley]*, monk of abbey D. William de Neuwenham [Newenham]*, clerk D. John de Stoke*, clerk	Evesham, 16 Nov. 1355
27/1304	Robert [of Ipwell], abbot of Winchcombe	F. John de Gloucestria [Gloucester], monk of abbey D. William de Tyryngtone [Terrington]*, clerk	Winchcombe, Friday the feast of St Edmund, king and martyr [20 Nov.] 1355
27/1305	Robert [Stratford], bishop of Chichester	M. John de Letth [Leech]*, doctor of both laws	Aldyngbourne [Aldingbourne], 21 Nov. 1355
27/1306	Ralph [of Shrewsbury], bishop of Bath and Wells *[LP]*	M. John de Carleton [Carlton]*, dean of Wells D. John de Wynewyk [Winwick]* D. Henry Ingelby [Ingleby]* D. William de Nywenham [Newenham]*	Banewell [Banwell], 16 Nov. 1355
27/1307	Walter [de Monyton], abbot of Glastonbury	D. William de Nywenham [Newenham]*, clerk D. William de Tilneye [Tilney], clerk	Domerham [Damerham], 20 Nov. 1355
27/1308	Robert [of Ramsey], abbot of Peterborough	D. Roger de Chestirfeld [Chesterfield]*, clerk John de Hariwedon [Harrowden]* Roger de Wakirle [Wakerley]*	Peterborough, Wednesday the feast of St Martin [11 Nov.] 1355
27/1309	[William of Haddon], abbot of Thorney	M. William de Wyttleseye [Whittlesey]*, archdeacon of Huntingdon John de Harndon [Harrowden]*	Thorney, 17 Nov. 1355

27/1310	[Thomas de la Mare], abbot of St Albans	F. John Mote, monk of abbey D. John Skarle [Scarle]*, clerk	St Albans, [damaged] 1355
27/1311	Simon [de Aumeney], abbot of Malmesbury	D. William de Nywenham [Newenham]* Henry Pichay [Percy]* Richard de Urdeleye [Urdeleigh]*	Malmesbury, Monday the feast of St Edmund, bishop and confessor [16 Nov.] 1355
27/1312	Chapter of York [LP]	D. John de Wynwyk [Winwick]*, treasurer of York [M.] Andrew Offord* D. David de Wellore [Wollore]*, canon of York D. Henry de Ingelby [Ingleby]*, canon of York	York, 17 Nov. 1355
27/1313	Thomas [of Moulton], abbot of St Mary's, York	F. John de Marton, monk of abbey D. John de Pokelyngton [Pocklington]*	In the monastery, 12 Nov. 1355
27/1314	Thomas [de Colwell], abbot of St Augustine's, Canterbury	D. William de Newenham* F. Thomas Bregge [Burgh], monk of abbey	Canterbury, 20 Nov. 1355
27/1315	Chapter of Worcester	F. Walter de Wynfreton [Winforton]*, monk of priory M. John de Branketre [Braintree]*, clerk D. John de Stok [Stoke]*, clerk	Worcester Chapter House, 18 Nov. 1355
27/1316	[Ralph of Eastcott], abbot of Cirencester	M. John de Lech [Leech]*, doctor of both laws M. John de Lameleye [Lambley]*	Cirencester, feast of St Martin [11 Nov.] 1355

PARLIAMENT AT WESTMINSTER, 17 APRIL 1357

27/1318	William [de Bernham], abbot of Bury St Edmunds	D. Elias de Grymmesby [Grimsby]*, rector of Norton Robert de Charwelton*, clerk William de Wychingham [Witchingham]*	Culforde [Culford], 13 April 1357
27/1319	Clergy of Carlisle diocese [LP]	M. John de Welton, clerk M. William de Ragenhill [Ragnall], clerk	Carlisle, 3 April 1357
27/1320	John [Fossor], prior of Durham and the Chapter [LP]	D. [sic – recte F.] William de Masham, monk of priory D. Hugh de Brandon, clerk	Durham Chapter House, 8 April 1357
27/1321	Chapter of Carlisle [LP]	D. Thomas Dounay [Daunay]*	Carlisle, 5 April 1357
27/1322	Chapter of Worcester	F. Walter de Wynferton [Winforton]*, monk and cellarer of abbey M. Robert de Nettleton, clerk M. John de Branketre [Braintree]*, clerk M. John de Stoke*, clerk	Worcester, 16 April 1357
27/1323	Dean and Chapter of Bangor	D. Gruffydd Tresgoet, canon of Bangor D. William ap Madog, clerk	Bangor, 4 April 1357
27/1324	[Robert of Ramsey], abbot of Peterborough	D. William de London* D. Robert de Wylford [Wilford]*	Peterborough. 10 April 1357

27/1325	Chapter of York [LP]	D. John de Wynewyk [Winwick]*, treasurer of York D. Henry de Ingilby [Ingleby]*, canon of York D. David de Wellore [Wollore]*, canon of York	York, 2 April 1357
27/1326	Walter [Fifehead], abbot of Hyde near Winchester	M. Thomas Enham, clerk M. William Cherne, clerk	Hyde, 1 April 1357
27/1327	John [Thoresby], archbishop of York	D. Henry de Ingelby [Ingleby]*, canon of York D. David de Wellore [Wollore]*, canon of York M. Thomas de Bucton [Buxton]*, official in the court of York [D.] Henry de Barton*, clerk	Cawode [Cawood], 12 April 1357
27/1328	Thomas [of Moulton], abbot of St Mary's, York	F. William de Seynesbury, monk of abbey D. John de Pokelyngton [Pocklington]*, clerk	In the monastery, 6 April 1357
27/1329	Ralph [of Eastcott], abbot of Cirencester	M. John de Leth [Leech]*, doctor of both laws M. John de Lameleye [Lambley]*	Cirencester, Tuesday the feast of St Benedict, abbot [21 March] 1357
27/1330	Thomas [of Stapelton], abbot of Bardney [LP]	D. Henry de Ingelby [Ingleby]*, clerk M. John de Branketre [Braintree]*, clerk William de Saundeby [Saundby], clerk	Bardney, Wednesday in Easter Week [12 April] 1357
27/1331	Robert [Stratford], bishop of Chichester	M. John de Letth [Leech]*, doctor of both laws	Aldyngbourne [Aldingbourne], 14 April 1357
27/1332	Thomas [de Horton], abbot of St Peter's, Gloucester	D. William de Newenham*	Gloucester, 2 April 1357

27/1333	Ralph [of Shrewsbury], bishop of Bath and Wells [LP]	D. William de Newenham*	Wyveliscombe [Wivelis-combe], 6 April 1357
27/1334	Henry [of Appleford], abbot of Reading [LP]	D. William de London, clerk; Geoffrey de Astone [Aston]*, clerk	Reading, 8 April 1357
27/1335	[Roger of Thame], abbot of Abingdon	F: Thomas de Weston, monk of abbey; Robert de Wyghthull [Wythall]*, clerk; [D.] William de Shiltwode [Shiltwood], clerk	Abingdon, 16 April 1357
27/1336	Walter [de Monyton], abbot of Glastonbury	[Damaged] [D.] William de Tilneye [Tilney], clerk	Glastonbury, 12 April 1357
27/1337	John [Trilleck], bishop of Hereford	M. [Illegible] D. Nicholas de Kaerwent [Caerwent], canon of Hereford	Prestebury [Prestbury], 12 April 1357
27/1338	[Thomas Fastolf], bishop of St Davids	D. [Illegible – John] Gogh*, archdeacon of St Davids; M. Adam de Hoton [Houghton]*, canon of St Davids	Lantefey [Lamphey], 10 April 1357
27/1339	Prior of Carlisle [LP]	Richard de Hoton [Houghton]	Carlisle, 5 April 1357
27/1340	[William of Haddiscoe], abbot of St Benet of Hulme	D. Thomas de Brayton*, clerk; John de Berneye*	St Benet of Hulme, 10 April 1357
27/1341	Robert [of Ipwell], abbot of Winchcombe	D. William de Newenham*, clerk; D. William de Tyryntone [Terrington]*, clerk; D. John de Stoke*, clerk	Winchcombe, 14 April 1357

27/1342	Henry [of Casewick], abbot of Crowland	M. John de Lameleye [Lambley]*, rector of Toft [Toft-with-Newton], clerk D. Nicholas de Stamford*, clerk	Crowland, Easter Day [9 April] 1357
27/1343	Geoffrey [de Gaddesby], abbot of Selby	D. Thomas de Brayton*, clerk D. William de [Damaged], clerk	Selby, 6 April 1357
27/1344	John [Paschal], bishop of Llandaff	M. Richard de Bermyngham [Birmingham], canon of Llandaff M. William de Honyngton [Honington], advocate in the court of Canterbury	Marthu [Mathern], 4 April 1357
27/1345	[Richard of Shenington], abbot of Ramsey	F. John de Claxton, monk of abbey D. Michael de Ravensdale [Ravendale]*, clerk	Ramsey, 12 April 1357

PARLIAMENT AT WESTMINSTER, 5 FEBRUARY 1358

5/228	[John of Horncastle], prior of Carlisle [LP]	Thomas Dounay [Daunay]	Carlisle, Sunday before feast of the Conversion of St Paul [21 Jan.] 1358
27/1346	John [Trilleck], bishop of Hereford	M. Thomas de Trillek [Trilleck]*, dean of Hereford D. John de Wyndlesore [Windsor], rector of Clyve [Clive], Worcester diocese	Sevenhampton, 25 Jan. 1358

27/1347	Roger [of Thame], abbot of Abingdon	[F.] Thomas de Westone [Weston], monk of abbey Robert de Wyghthull [Wythall]*, clerk [D.] William de Shiltwode [Shiltwood], clerk	Abingdon, 1 Feb. 1358
27/1348	[Richard of Shenington], abbot of Ramsey	Nicholas de Styuecle* D. John de Ditton*, rector of Ripton Abbatus [Abbots Ripton]	Ramsey, Monday after feast of the Conversion of St Paul [29 Jan.] 1358
27/1349	Ralph [of Eastcott], abbot of Cirencester	D. [sic – recte F.] Nicholas de Ameneye [Ampney]*, monk of abbey M. John de Lameleye [Lambley]*	Cirencester, Sunday the morrow of St Hilary [14 Jan.] 1358
27/1350	Roger [Northburgh], bishop of Coventry and Lichfield [LP]	D. John de Wynwyk [Winwick]*, canon of Lichfield	Wybbenbury [Wynbunbury], 24 Jan. 1358
28/1351	Subprior and Chapter of Carlisle [LP]	D. Henry de Ingilby [Ingleby]*, canon of Carlisle D. Walter Power*, canon of Carlisle	Carlisle Chapter House, 26 Jan. 1358
28/1352	William [of Dunstable], prior of Coventry	F. William de Greneburgh*	Coventry, morrow of the Purification of the Blessed Mary [3 Feb.] 1358
28/1353	[Henry of Appleford], abbot of Reading	D. William de London*, clerk Edmund de Chelseye [Chelsea]* John de Stratfeld [Stratfield]*	Reading, 20 Jan. 1358
28/1354	Henry [of Casewick], abbot of Crowland	M. John de Lameleye [Lambley]*, clerk D. Nicholas de Stamford*, clerk	Crowland, 23 Jan. 1358

28/1355	John [Grandisson], bishop of Exeter	D. Edmund Darundell [de Arundel]* D. Otto de Grauntsoun [Grandisson]* D. Thomas de [Damaged] M. John Wylie[damaged] [Wyliot]*, chancellor of Exeter D. Thomas Caignes [Keynes], canon of [Damaged – Exeter] D. David Wollouere [Wollore]*, canon of [Damaged]	Chuddelegh [Chudleigh], 24 Jan. 1358
28/1356	Clergy of Carlisle diocese [LP]	M. John de Welton M. William de Ragenhill [Ragnall]	Carlisle, 24 Jan. 1358
28/1357	William [of Haddiscoe], abbot of St Benet of Hulme	D. John de Ludham*, clerk	St Benet of Hulme, Tuesday after feast of the Conversion of St Paul [30 Jan.] 1358
28/1358	Geoffrey [de Gaddesby], abbot of Selby	F. John de Goldale, monk of abbey D. Thomas de Brayton*, clerk Illard de Usflet [Ousefleet]*	Selby, Monday the feast of St Vincent, martyr [22 Jan.] 1358
28/1359	William de Ruthebery [Rothbury], archdeacon of Carlisle [LP]	M. William de Ragenhill [Ragnall], clerk D. Peter de Morland, perpetual vicar of Torpeunowe [Torpenhow], Carlisle diocese	Carlisle, 24 Jan. 1358
28/1360	Subprior and Chapter of Worcester	F. Walter de Wynforton [Winforton]*, monk of priory M. John de Branketre [Braintree]*, clerk [D.] John de Stoke*, clerk	Worcester Chapter House, 28 Jan. 1358

186

28/1361	Thomas [of Moulton], abbot of St Mary's, York	F. John de Gaytrigg, monk of abbey D. John de Pokelyngton [Pocklington]*, clerk Thomas de Ingelby [Ingleby]*	In the monastery, 24 Jan. 1358
28/1362	Chapter of York [LP]	D. John de Wynwk [Winwick]*, treasurer of York [D.] Henry de Ingelby [Ingleby]*, canon of York [D.] David de Wollore*, canon of York	York, 30 Jan. 1358

PARLIAMENT AT WESTMINSTER, 15 MAY 1360

28/1363	Thomas [de Horton], abbot of St Peter's, Gloucester	D. William de Newenham*	Gloucester, 8 May 1360
28/1364	Robert [of Ipwell], abbot of Winchcombe	D. William de Newenham*, clerk D. Richard de Pyrytone [Pirton]*, clerk	Winchcombe, 12 May 1360
28/1365	[John of Horncastle], prior of Carlisle [LP]	Thomas Daunay*	Carlisle, 6 May 1360

PARLIAMENT AT WESTMINSTER, 24 JANUARY 1361

28/1366	[Roger of Thame], abbot of Abingdon	[F.] Thomas de Westone [Weston], monk of abbey Robert de Wyghthull [Wythull]*, clerk [Damaged], clerk	Abingdon, 20 Jan. 1361

28/1367	Thomas [de Ringstead], bishop of Bangor	D. Robert Sye[damaged]	Northampton, 18 Jan. [damaged]
28/1368	Thomas [Barnack], abbot of Crowland	F. Henry de Irtelynburgh [Irthlingborough], monk of abbey [Damaged – Nicholas] de Stamford, clerk [Damaged], clerk	Crowland, 19 Jan. 1361
28/1369	[Thomas Fastolf], bishop of St Davids	D. John Gogh*, archdeacon of St Davids D. Richard de Piriton [Pirton]*, canon of St Davids [Damaged] de Sancto Claro [St Clares], precentor of collegiate church of Abergwili [Abergwili], St Davids diocese	L[damaged] Manor, 1361
28/1370	[John Thoresby], archbishop of York	[Damaged] [D.] David de Wollore*, canon of York [D.] Richard de Ravenser* [Damaged - Henry] de Barton*, clerk	Cawode [Cawood], [Damaged], 1361
28/1371	William [de Bernham], abbot of Bury St Edmunds	D. Edmund de Grymesby [Grimsby]*, rector of Norton, Norwich diocese William de Wethyngham [Wellingham], monk of abbey	Culford, 18 Jan. [damaged –1361]
28/1372	Geoffrey [de Gaddesby], abbot of Selby	F. John de Goldale, monk of abbey [D.] Thomas de Brayton*, clerk	[Damaged], Jan. 1361

PARLIAMENT AT WESTMINSTER, 13 OCTOBER 1362

28/1373	Gilbert [Welton], bishop of Carlisle	D. Henry de Graystok, [Greystoke]*, clerk D. Richard de Tissyngton [Tissington]*, clerk Thomas de Sandford*	Rosa [Rose] Manor, 3 Oct. [*no year*]
28/1374	[William of Haddon], abbot of Thorney	John de Harndon [Harrowden]* Oliver de Lufwyk [Lowick]	Thorney, 5 Oct. 1362
28/1375	John [Thoresby], archbishop of York	M. Thomas de Bucton [Buxton]*, doctor of law D. Henry de Barton*, canon of York	Cawode [Cawood], 5 Oct. 1362
28/1376	Thomas [de la Mare], abbot of St Albans	F. John Mote, monk of abbey Robert de Segynton [Seckington], clerk	Belueru', 9 Oct. 1362
28/1377	Henry [of Overton], abbot of Peterborough	D. Richard de Treton [Tretton]* D. Robert de Wilford*	Peterborough, 20 Sept. 1362
28/1378	John [of Evesham], prior of Worcester	D. William de Hulle [Hull], clerk John de Dunclent, clerk	Worcester, 6 Oct. 1362
28/1379	Walter [de Monyton], abbot of Glastonbury	M. Thomas le Jonge [Young], clerk M. Hugh de Penebrigg [Pembridge]*, clerk	Glastonbury, 10 Oct. 1362
28/1380	Clergy of Durham diocese [*LP*]	M. William Legat, rector of Brauncepath [Brancepeth] M. William de Fakeman [Fakenham], notary	Durham, 1 Oct. 1362

28/1381	[John of Horncastle], prior of Carlisle [LP]	Thomas Dawnay [Daunay]*	Carlisle, feast of St Michael, archangel [29 Sept.] 1362
28/1382	Thomas [de Colwell], abbot of St Augustine's, Canterbury	F. Thomas Shulleford [Shelford], monk of abbey James Palmere [Palmer]*, clerk	Canterbury, 12 Oct. 1362
28/1383	William [Marreys], abbot of St Mary's, York	[D.] David de Wollore* [D.] William de Haukesworth [Hawksworth]*	In the monastery, 8 Oct. 1362
28/1384	Thomas [of Stapelton], abbot of Bardney [LP]	F. Thomas de Welton, monk of abbey	Bardney, 11 Oct. 1362
28/1385	Walter [of Winforton], abbot of Winchcombe	M. William de Thynghulle [Thinghull]*, dean of the Arches D. William de Hulle [Hull], rector of Marteleye [Martley]	Winchcombe, 8 Oct. 1362
28/1386	Thomas [de Horton], abbot of St Peter's, Gloucester	M. William de Thynghull [Thinghull]*, dean of the Arches D. Thomas Moynge [Moigne]*, knight Robert Palet*	Gloucester, 29 Sept. 1362
28/1387	Richard de Castrobuard [Bernard Castle], archdeacon of Northumberland, Durham diocese [LP]	Henry Graspays, canon and prebend in the collegiate church of Aukland [Bishop Auckland] M. William Fakenham	Durham, 1 Oct. 1362
28/1388	William [of Dumbleton], abbot of Reading [LP]	F. John de Hodesdone [Hoddesdon], monk of abbey [D.] William de London*, clerk	Reading, 14 Oct. 1362

190

28/1389	William [de Greneburgh], prior of Coventry	D. William Burstall*, clerk F. Roger de Wentebrigge [Wentbridge], monk of priory	Coventry, 10 Oct. 1362
28/1390	Clergy of Carlisle diocese *[LP]*	D. Richard de Tissyngton ['Tissington]*, clerk D.John de Bow[*illegible*]d [Bowland]*, clerk	Carlisle, 26 Sept. 1362
28/1391	Geoffrey [de Gaddesby], abbot of Selby	F.John de Goldale, monk of abbey Illard de Usflete [Ousefleet]*	Selby, 6 Oct. 1362
28/1392	John [Grandisson], bishop of Exeter	D. Simon [Islip], archbishop of Canterbury and primate of all England	Chuddelegh [Chudleigh], 3 Oct. 1362
28/1393	William [of Haddiscoe], abbot of St Benet of Hulme	F. William de Methelwolde [Methwold]*, monk of abbey D. Walter de Bergh [Burgh]	St Benet of Hulme, Sunday after feast of St Fidis, Virgin [9 Oct.] [*illegible*]
28/1394	Subprior and Chapter of Worcester	D. William de Hulle [Hull], clerk John de Dunclent, clerk	Worcester Chapter House, 6 Oct. 1362
28/1395	Prior [John Fossor] and Chapter of Durham *[LP]*	Roger de Fulthorp* [D.] Hugh de Brandon	Durham Chapter House, 1 Oct. 1362
28/1396	Thomas [Barnack], abbot of Crowland	F. Henry de Irtelyngburgh [Irthlingborough], monk of abbey D. Nicholas de Stamford* D.John de Merys of Kyrketon [Kirkton]	Crowland, 9 Oct. 1362
30/1456	William de Westelee [Westle], archdeacon of Durham	John de H[e]rlee, rector of Segfeld [Sedgefield] M. William de Fakenham, clerk, notary public	Durham, 4 Oct. 1362

PARLIAMENT AT WESTMINSTER, 6 OCTOBER 1363

28/1397	Thomas [Barnack], abbot of Crowland	F. Henry de Irtlingburgh [Irthlingborough], monk of abbey D. Nicholas de Stamford*, clerk D. Robert de Wilforth [Wilford], clerk	Crowland, feast of St Matthew, apostle [21 Sept.] 1363
28/1398	[Richard of Shenington], abbot of Ramsey	M. John de Carlton*, canon of Lincoln Nicholas de Stiuecle [Styuecle]* [D.] Michael de Ravendale*, clerk	Ramsey, 2 Oct. 1363
28/1399	[William of Haddon], abbot of Thorney	D. Thomas de Thorp, rector of [Damaged] [Damaged], rector of Helpestoun [Helpston]	[Undated]
28/1400	Prior and Chapter of Ely [LP]	M. John de Norton*, chancellor of Salisbury F. Thomas de Thetford, monk of priory	Ely, 1 Oct. 1363
29/1401	Chapter of York [LP]	D. William de Wykeham*, canon of York D. David de Wollore*, canon of York M. Thomas de Bucton [Buxton]*, canon of York	York, 14 Sept. 1363
29/1402	Richard de [Damaged – Bernard Castle], archdeacon of Northumberland, Durham diocese [LP]	M. William de Fakenham, notary and bishop of Durham's clerk	Durham, 6 Sept. 1363
29/1403	Chapter of Lincoln [LP]	M. William de Askeby*, canon of Lincoln M. John de Carleton [Carlton]*, canon of Lincoln D. Walter Power*, canon of Lincoln D. Adam de Lymbergh*, canon of Lincoln	Lincoln, 3 Oct. 1363

192

29/1404	William [Marreys], abbot of St Mary's, York	D. David de Wolloure [Wollore]* D. William de Haukesworth [Hawksworth]*	In the monastery, 30 Sept. 1363
29/1405	Geoffrey [de Gaddesby], abbot of Selby	F. John de Goldale, monk of abbey D. William de Mirfeld [Mirfield]*, clerk	Selby, 24 Sept. 1363
29/1406	Walter [of Winforton], abbot of Winchcombe	D. William Hulle [Hull], clerk D. Thomas Thelewall [Thelwall], clerk	Winchcombe, Tuesday after feast of St Michael [3 Oct.] 1363
29/1407	John [Grandisson], bishop of Exeter	D. William de Monte Acuto [Montague], earl of Salisbury D. John de Monte Acuto [Montague], knight M. John Wyliet [Wyliot]*, canon of Exeter M. Robert de Wycford [Wickford]*, canon of Exeter M. Nicholas de Braibrok [Braybrook]*, canon of Exeter	Chuddelegh [Chudleigh], 28 Sept. 1363
29/1408	Clergy of Coventry and Lichfield diocese [LP]	M. John de Longedon [Longden]*, clerk M. Thomas de Rippeley [Ripley]*, clerk	Lichfield, 29 Sept. 1363
29/1409	Chapter of Lichfield [LP]	M. Thomas de Ryppeley [Ripley]*, clerk	Lichfield, 29 Sept. 1363
29/1410	Thomas [of Stapelton], abbot of Bardney [LP]	F. Thomas de Welleton [Welton], monk of abbey D. Peter de Barton*, clerk	Bardney, 2 Oct. 1363
29/1411	John [Buckingham], bishop of Lincoln	M. William de Thyngehull [Thinghull]*, doctor of both laws, bishop's official D. Walter Power*, canon of Lincoln D. John de Thorp, canon of St Paul's, London	Lydyngton [Lyddington], 21 Sept. 1363

29/1412	William de Westle, archdeacon of Durham [LP]	M. William de Facneham [Fakenham], clerk D. John de Grantham, rector of Northcotes, Norwich diocese [sic]	Esyngton [Easington], Thursday the feast of St Matthew, apostle [21 Sept.] 1363
29/1413	John [Thoresby], archbishop of York	M. Thomas de Bucton [Buxton]*, doctor of law D. Henry de Barton*, canon of York	Thorp by York [Bishopthorpe], 2 Oct. 1363
29/1414	Walter [de Monyton], abbot of Glastonbury	M. Thomas le Yonge [Young]*, clerk [M.] Hugh de Penbrigg [Pembridge]*, clerk	Glastonbury, 1 Oct. 1363
29/1415	Thomas [Pethy], abbot of Hyde near Winchester	F. Walter de Sperkeford [Sparkford], monk of abbey	Hyde, 25 Sept. 1363
29/1416	Subprior and Chapter of Coventry [LP]	D. William Burstall*, clerk F. Roger de Wentebrigg [Wentbridge], monk of priory	Coventry Chapter House, Tuesday after St Michael [3 Oct.] 1363
29/1417	William [of Haddiscoe], abbot of St Benet of Hulme	F. William de Mothelw[damaged – Methwold]*	St Benet of Hulme, Monday after feast of [damaged] 1363
29/1418	[Henry of Overton], abbot of Peterborough	D. Richard de Treton [Tretton]*, clerk D. Robert de Wylford [Wilford]*, clerk	Peterborough, 27 Sept. 1363
29/1419	William [of Dumbleton], abbot of Reading	F. John de Hodesdon [Hoddesdon] D. William de London*, clerk	Reading, 3 Oct. 1363

194

29/1420	William [de Greneburgh], prior of Coventry	D. William Burstall*, clerk F. Roger de Wentebrigg [Wentbridge], monk of abbey	Coventry, 3 Oct. 1363
29/1421	[Richard of Shenington], abbot of Ramsey	M. John de Carlton*, doctor of civil law Nicholas de Styuecle* M. [Damaged]	Ramsey, 2 Oct. 1363

PARLIAMENT AT WESTMINSTER, 20 JANUARY 1365

29/1422A	Thomas [Pethy], abbot of Hyde near Winchester	F. Richard de Rutherfeld [Rotherfield]	Hyde, 17 Jan. 1365
29/1422B	The abbots, priors, rectors, vicars and other clergy of the diocese of Carlisle [LP]	M. William de Hall John de Bowland*, archdeacon of Carlisle, rector of Arthuret D. Robert de Derham	Carlisle, Monday after feast of St Hilary [20 Jan.] 1365

PARLIAMENT AT WESTMINSTER, 4 MAY 1366

29/1423	Thomas [de la Mare], abbot of St Albans	[F.] John Mote, monk and prior of abbey Robert Muskham*, clerk	St Albans, 26 April 1366

ASSEMBLY AT WESTMINSTER, 10 JANUARY 1370[1]

29/1424	Thomas [Trilleck], bishop of Rochester [LP]	M. John de Brankotre [Braintree]; Thomas Eboracen [York]; D. William Durraunt, rector of St Michael ad ripam regine [St Michael Queenhithe], London	Trottesclyve [Trottiscliffe], 2 Jan 1370
29/1425	Walter [Camme], abbot of Malmesbury	Thomas Maxham, monk of abbey; Robert de Charlton*; John Colyngbourne [Collingbourne]*	Malmesbury, 4 Jan. 1370

PARLIAMENT AT WESTMINSTER, 24 FEBRUARY 1371

29/1426	William de Feriby [Ferriby] [the elder], archdeacon of Cleveland, York diocese [LP]	D. John Carpe [Carp]*, rector of Ekyngton [Eckington], Lichfield diocese; D. John de Popelton [Poppleton], rector of Wygyngton [Wiggington], York diocese; D. William de Feriby [Ferriby, the younger]*	York, 12 Feb. 1371
29/1427	Clergy of Winchester diocese [LP]	M. Robert Wyckford [Wickford]*, clerk; M. John Karw [Carew], clerk	Potenham [Puttenham], 20 Feb. 1371

1 These two letters refer to an assembly (neither calls it a parliament) at Westminster on the Thursday after Epiphany. It is possible that it was a great council, although this meeting is otherwise unknown.

29/1428	[Roger Cradock], bishop of Llandaff *[LP]*	[M.] John de Brangtre [Braintree]*, treasurer of York [*Illegible* – Thomas de Braundeston]*, chancellor of Llandaff	Mathne [Mathern], Quinquagesima Sunday [16 Feb.] 1371
29/1429	Nicholas de Neuton, archdeacon of Cornwall, Exeter diocese *[LP]*	M. John Blanchard [Blaunchard]*, advocate in the court of Canterbury	Exeter, 5 Feb. 1371
29/1430	Clergy of Exeter diocese *[LP]*	M. Robert Wykfforde [Wickford]*, doctor of laws [M.] William Bede [Byde]*, doctor of laws	Exeter, 15 Feb. 1371
29/1431	Clergy of Winchester diocese *[LP]*	M. Robert Wycford [Wickford]* Richard Wycton [Witton] [M.] John de Karues [Carew], rector of Bedyngton [Beddington]	Winchester, 17 Feb. 1371
29/1432	John [Thoresby], archbishop of York	D. Richard de Ravenser*, archdeacon of Lincoln D. Henry de Barton*, canon of York	Thorp by York [Bishopthorpe], 14 Feb. 1371
29/1433	William [Courtenay], bishop of Hereford	Simon [Sudbury], bishop of London John [Barnet], bishop of Ely M. John Codeford [Codford *alias* Silvester]*, archdeacon of Wiltshire, Salisbury diocese, doctor of civil law M. John Barnet*, inceptor in laws	Tiverton, 18 Feb. 1371
29/1434	Robert [Stretton], bishop of Coventry and Lichfield *[LP]*	M. Nicholas de Chaddesden*, canon of Lichfield M. John Schepey [Sheppey]*, canon of Lichfield	Heywode [Heywood, Lancashire], 6 Feb. 1371

29/1435	John [of Sutton], abbot of Reading	F. John de Speresholt [Sparsholt], monk of abbey Nicholas Spayn [Spaigne]*, clerk	Reading, 20 Feb. 1371
29/1436	Thomas [de la Mare], abbot of St Albans	[F.] John Mote, monk and prior of abbey John Whittewell [Whitwell]	St Albans, 23 Feb. 1371
29/1437	Henry [of Overton], abbot of Peterborough	M. William de Askeby*, clerk F. John de Rameseie [Ramsey], monk of abbey	Peterborough, 1 Feb. 1371
29/1438	Chapter of [St Paul's] London	D. Amandus Fittelyng [Fitlyng]*, canon of London D. John Wade*, canon of London	London Chapter House, 23 Feb. 1371
29/1439	[Walter de Legh], prior of Worcester	[M.] John de Brancetre [Braintree]*, clerk [Illegible – William] de la Hulle [Hull], clerk	Worcester, 22 Feb. 1371
29/1440	Chapter of York [LP]	Richard de [Illegible] [D.] Michael de Ravendale*, clerk [M.] Robert de Wykford [Wickford]*	York, 14 Feb. 1371
29/1441	Robert [Wyvil], bishop of Salisbury [LP]	M. John Blanchard [Blaunchard]*, clerk M. John Silvestre [Silvester alias Codford]*, clerk	Sonning, 22 Feb. 1371
29/1442	Thomas [Trilleck], bishop of Rochester	No proctors named	Trottesclyve [Trottiscliffe], 20 Feb. 1371
29/1443	Walter [de Monyton], abbot of Glastonbury	M. Hugh de Penebrugge [Pembridge]*, clerk D. Walter Broun, clerk	Glastonbury, 12 Feb. 1371

29/1444	Thomas [Pethy], abbot of Hyde near Winchester	Walter Brutford [Britford], monk of abbey	Hyde, 18 Feb. 1371
29/1445	Thomas [Trilleck], bishop of Rochester [LP]	John de [illegible] Thomas [illegible] D. William Durraunt, rector of St Michael in ripam regine [St Michael, Queenhithe], London	Trottesclyve [Trottiscliffe], 20 Feb. 1371
29/1446	John [of Ombersley], abbot of Evesham	Thomas de Newenham*, rector of Neubury [Newbury] John Blake William Clerk	Evesham, 16 Feb. 1371
29/1447	John [of Sherburn], abbot of Selby	D. William de Mirfeld [Mirfield]*, clerk D. Elias de Sutton, clerk James de Raygate [Reigate]	Selby, 14 Feb. 1371
29/1448	Walter [of Winforton], abbot of Winchcombe	M. John de Branketre [Braintree]*, clerk	Winchcombe, 20 Feb. 1371
29/1449	William [Methwold], abbot of St Benet of Hulme	John de Herlyngg [Harling]* George de Felbrygg [Felbridge]*	St Benet of Hulme, Tuesday after feast of St Valentine, martyr [18 Feb.] 1371
29/1450	[Richard of Shenington], abbot of Ramsey	Nicholas de Styuecle* D. Michael de Ravendale*, clerk [F] Robert Waryn	Ramsey, 17 Feb. [no year]

199

30/1451	[John Deeping], abbot of Thorney	Nicholas Styuecle* F: Geoffrey de Brunne, monk of abbey	Thorney, 18 Feb. 1371
30/1452	[Simon Sudbury], archbishop of Canterbury	William [Courtenay]*, bishop of London [William Lenn]*, bishop of Worcester Adam [Houghton], bishop of St Davids	[Undated]
30/1453	[Simon Sudbury], archbishop of Canterbury	[William Courtenay]*, bishop of London [William Lenn]*, bishop of Worcester [Adam Houghton]*, bishop of St Davids	Lambeth, 16 March 1371

PARLIAMENT AT WESTMINSTER, 28 SEPTEMBER 1371

30/1454	Walter [de Camme], abbot of Malmesbury	Robert de Cherlton [Charlton]* John Colyngbourne [Collingbourne]* Richard Urdele [Urdeleigh]* John Bryg [Robert atte Bregg of Lambeth], rector of St Nicholas Aken [Acon], London	Malmesbury, 24 Sept. 1371
30/1455	John [Thoresby], archbishop of York	[D.] Richard de Ravenser*, archdeacon of Lincoln [D.] Henry de Barton*, canon of York	Thorp [Bishopthorpe], 24 Sept. 1371

30/1457	[Thomas of Stapelton], abbot of Bardney	[D.] Peter de Barton*, clerk Robert Beverag [Beverage] of Badburgham	Bardney, 24 Sept. 1372
30/1458	Robert [Wyvil], bishop of Salisbury	M.John Blanchard [Blaunchard]*, archdeacon of Worcester	Poterne [Potterne], 8 Oct. 1372
30/1459	Thomas [Hatfield], bishop of Durham	Reginald de Hilling, canon and prebendary of St Stephen's chapel, Westminster Walter de Beverle [Beverley], canon and prebendary of St Stephen's chapel, Westminster Hugh de Westwik [Westwick], rector of Eggesclif [Egglescliffe], Durham diocese	Aukland [Bishop Auckland], 30 Sept. 1372
30/1460	Thomas [Brantingham], bishop of Exeter	M.John Wyliot [Wyliot]*, chancellor of Exeter Cathedral [M.] William Byde*, the bishop's official	[Bishop's] Clyst Manor, 4 Sept. 1372
30/1461	Walter [Camme], abbot of Malmesbury	John Colyngbourne [Collingbourne]* Robert de Cherlton [Charlton]* Richard Urdele [Urdeleigh]*	Malmesbury, 6 Oct. 1372
30/1462	Chapter of Worcester Cathedral	M.John de Branktre [Braintree]*, clerk William Mulso*, clerk M.John Blanchard [Blaunchard]*, clerk	Worcester Chapter House, 27 Oct. 1372

30/1463	Chapter of Lincoln Cathedral	M. John de Belvoir*, canon of Lincoln John de Selby, canon of Lincoln	Lincoln, 5 Oct. 1372
30/1464	[Richard of Shenington], abbot of Ramsey	Nicholas de Styuecle* [D.] Michael de Ravensdale [Ravendale]*, clerk	Ramsey, 13 Oct. 1372
30/1465	[John of Sutton], abbot of Reading	F. John de Spersholt [Sparsholt], monk of abbey and 'our chamberlain' [Illegible]	Reading, 31 Oct. 1372
30/1466	Walter [de Monyton(e)], abbot of Glastonbury	M. Robert Wycforde [Wickford]* M. Robert Crosse [Cross]	Glastonbury, 9 Oct. 1372
30/1467	William de Ferriby [the elder], archdeacon of Cleveland, York [diocese]	[D.] Henry de Barton*, canon of York [D.] Michael de Ravendale*, canon of York	York, 16 Oct. 1372
30/1468	John [Thoresby], archbishop of York, primate of England and legate of the Holy See	D. Richard de Ravenser*, archdeacon of Lincoln D. Henry de Barton*, canon of York	Thurpe by York [Bishopthorpe], 15 Oct. 1372
30/1469	[John Deeping], abbot of Thorney	Nicholas de Styuecle* F. John de Raundes [Raunds]*, monk of abbey Oliver de Lufwyk [Lowick]	Thorney, Feast of SS Simon and Jude [28 Oct.] 1372
30/1470	John [of Sherburn], abbot of Selby	[D.] William de Mirfield*, clerk and canon of Lincoln [D.] Henry de Barton*, clerk and canon of Lincoln	Selby, 9 Oct. 1372

30/1471	Thomas [de la Mare], abbot of St Albans	F. John Mote, monk and prior of St Albans John Whytewell [Whitwell]	St Albans, 1 Nov. 1372
30/1472	Chapter of York	[D.] Henry de Barton* [D.] Michael de Ravendale*	York, 15 Oct. 1372
30/1473	Henry [of Overton], abbot of Peterborough	[D.] Richard de Tretton*, clerk F. Thomas de Bury, monk of Peterborough	Peterborough, 31 Oct.1372
30/1474	[William Methwold], abbot of St Benet of Hulme	John de Herlyngg [Harling]* George de Felbrygg [Felbridge]*	St Benet of Hulme, Saturday after SS Simon and Jude [30 Oct.]
30/1475	Thomas [de Horton], abbot of St Peter's, Gloucester	John Clyfford [Clifford], vicar of Gloucester	Gloucester, 10 Nov. 1372
30/1476	[Walter of Winforton], abbot of Winchcombe	[D.] Richard de Piriton [Pirton]*, clerk	Winchcombe, 26 Oct. 1372
30/1477	William [Marreys], abbot of St Mary's, York	F. Richard de Appilton [Appleton], monk of St Mary's [D.] William de Sandford* [D.] Michael de Ravendale*	York, 27 Oct. 1372
30/1478	John [of Ombersley], abbot of Evesham	[M.] John de Shepey [Sheppey]* Thomas de Newenham*	Evesham, Monday after SS Simon and Jude [1 Nov.]
30/1479	[Nicholas Ampney], abbot of Cirencester	Robert de Cherlton [Charlton]* Gilbert de Sutton*	Cirencester, 19 Oct 1372

203

| 30/1480 | Humphrey Cherlton, archdeacon of Richmond, York diocese | Walter Power*, rector of Warton | York, 24 Oct 1372 |
| 30/1481 | Walter [de Legh], prior of Worcester | M. John de Branktre [Braintree]*, clerk
William de Mulso*, clerk
M. John Blanchard [Blaunchard]*, clerk | Worcester, 27 Oct 1372 |

PARLIAMENT AT WESTMINSTER, 21 NOVEMBER 1373

30/1483	Chapter of Worcester Cathedral	M. John Blanchard [Blaunchard]*, archdeacon of Worcester William Hulle [Hull], clerk	Worcester, 17 Nov. 1373
30/1484	Robert [Stretton], bishop of Coventry & Lichfield	M. Richard de Bermyngham [Birmingham], canon of Lichfield M. Nicholas de Chaddesdon [Chaddesden]*, canon of Lichfield M. John de Schillingford [Shillingford]*, advocate of the court of Canterbury	Heywode [Haywood], 12 Nov. 1373
30/1485	John [Bukton], prior of Ely and the Chapter	M. John de Dunwich*, doctor of canon law M. Roger de Sutton*, doctor of civil law	Ely Chapter House, 16 Nov. 1373
30/1486	Robert [Wyvil], bishop of Salisbury	M. John Blanchard [Blaunchard]*, archdeacon of Worcester, doctor of laws Roger Cloun [Clun]*, archdeacon of Salisbury	Poterne [Potterne], 16 Oct. 1373

30/1487	Henry [Despenser], bishop of Norwich	[D.] William de Swynflet [Swinefleet]*, archdeacon of Norwich M. John de Shillyngford [Shillingford]*, clerk, advocate of the court of Canterbury M. Thomas de Shirford [Shereford]*, clerk, advocate of the court of Canterbury [Arches]	Hoxne, 16 Nov. 1373
30/1488	Walter [Camme], abbot of Malmesbury	John Colyngbourne [Collingbourne]* Robert Cherlton [Charlton]* Richard Urdele [Urdeleigh]*	Malmesbury, Sunday after St Martin [13 Nov.] 1373
30/1489	Chapter of York Minster	M. Humphrey de Cheriton [Charlton]*, archdeacon of Richmond, canon of York [D.] Richard de Ravenser*, archdeacon of Lincoln, canon of York Henry de Wakefield*, canon of York	York, 9 Nov. 1373
30/1490	Thomas [Brantingham], bishop of Exeter	M. William Byde*, the bishop's official [M.] John de Shillingford*, doctor of laws Walter Aldebury [Alderby], canon of St Paul's, London	[Bishop's] Clyst Manor, 4 Nov. 1373
30/1491	[John of Ombersley], abbot of Evesham	M. John Blanchard [Blaunchard]*, archdeacon of Worcester, clerk Thomas de Newenham*, clerk	Evesham, 15 Nov. 1373
30/1492	Adam [Houghton], bishop of St Davids	M. John David*, chancellor of St Davids Cathedral Henry Snayth [Snaith]*, canon of St Davids	Lawadeyn [Llawhaden] Castle, 30 Oct. 1373

30/1493	[William Methwold], abbot of St Benet of Hulme	John de Herlyngg [Harling]* John de Holkham	In the monastery, 6 Nov. 1373
30/1494	Subdean and Chapter of Lincoln	M. John de Belvoir*	Lincoln Chapter House, 17 Nov. 1373
30/1495	[Thomas Pethy], abbot of Hyde near Winchester	F. John Chaworth, monk of abbey	Hyde, Friday in the octave of Martinmas [18 Nov.] 1373
30/1496	John [of Sherburn], abbot of Selby	[D.] Henry de Barton*, canon of Lincoln [D.] William de Mirfeld [Mirfield]*, canon of Lincoln	Selby, 26 Oct. 1373
30/1497	[Walter de Monyton(e)], abbot of Glastonbury	M. John Blanchard [Blaunchard]*, clerk [D.] Walter Broun, clerk	Glastonbury, 14 Nov. 1373
30/1498	Thomas [of Stapelton], abbot of Bardney	F. Thomas de Welton, monk of abbey [D.] Peter de Barton*, clerk	Bardney, 16 Nov. 1373
30/1499	[Richard of Shenington], abbot of Ramsey	Nicholas de Stuecle [Styuecle]* [D.] Michael de Ravendale*, clerk F. Robert Waryn, monk of abbey	Ramsey, 17 Nov. 1373
30/1500	[Thomas Barnack], abbot of Crowland	M. Simon de Milton [Multon]* John de Folkyngham [Folkingham]*	Croyland [Crowland], 10 Nov. 1373
31/1501	John [Buckingham], bishop of Lincoln	M. John Belvoir*, canon of Lincoln [M.] John Barnet*, bishop's official	Lidington [Lyddington], 17 Nov. 1373

31/1502	William [Marreys], abbot of St Mary's York	[D.] Michael de Ravendale* F. Richard de Appilton [Appleton], monk of abbey Robert de Wyclif*	In the monastery, 17 Nov. 1373
31/1503	Nicholas [Ampney], abbot of Cirencester	Robert de Cherlton [Charlton]* Gilbert de Sutton*, clerk	Cirencester, 3 Nov. 1373
31/1504	Walter [of Winforton], abbot of Winchcombe	M. John Appelby [Appleby]*, dean of St Paul's [D.] Richard de Pyriton [Pirton]*, canon of St Paul's	Winchcombe, 15 Nov. 1373
31/1505	[John Deeping], abbot of Thorney	Nicholas Stuecle [Styuecle]* John Harlington*	Thorney, feast of St Martin [11 Nov.] 1373
31/1506	Thomas [de la Mare], abbot of St Albans	F. Robert Chestan, monk of abbey John Whittewell [Whitwell]	St Albans, 20 Nov. 1373
31/1507	Walter [de Legh], prior of Worcester	M. John Blanchard [Blaunchard]*, archdeacon of Worcester William Halle [Hall], clerk	Worcester, 17 Nov. 1373
31/1508	William de Feriby [Ferriby] [the elder], archdeacon of Cleveland [LP]	[D.] Michael de Ravendale*, canon of York [D.] John Carp*, rector of Stokesley, York diocese [D.] William de Feriby [Ferriby]* the younger	York, 10 Nov. 1373
31/1509	John [of Sutton], abbot of Reading	M. William Bide [Byde]*, doctor of laws Nicholas Spaigne*, clerk	Reading, 19 Nov. 1373

| 31/1510 | [Henry of Overton], abbot of Peterborough | [D.] Richard de Tretton*, clerk
F. Thomas de Bury, monk of abbey
John de Harwedon [Harrowden]* | In the monastery, 15 Nov. 1373 |

PARLIAMENT AT WESTMINSTER, 28 APRIL 1376

31/1513	William Gynewell, archdeacon of Buckingham [LP]	M.John de Bannebury [Banbury]*, rector of Horton, Lincoln diocese Thomas Bodewyn, rector of Northkellyseye [North Kelsey], Lincoln diocese	Buckingham, 26 April 137[damaged]
31/1514	Subdean and Chapter of [Damaged – Wells]	[Damaged]	Wells, 22 April 1 [Damaged] and 50 Edward III [1376]
31/1517	Chapter of York [LP]	[D.] Richard de Ravenser*, archdeacon of Lincoln William de Gunthorpe*, canon of York John de Fordeham [Fordham]*, canon of York [D.] Michael de Ravendale*, canon of York M. Adam de Thorp, canon of York	York Chapter House, 1 April 1376
31/1518	Walter [de Camme], abbot of Malmesbury	Robert Cherlton [Charlton]* John Colyngbourne [Collingbourne]*	Malmesbury, Thursday the morrow of St George [24 April] 1376

31/1519	Robert [Stretton], bishop of Coventry and Lichfield [LP]	M. Richard de Bermyngham [Birmingham], bishop's official M. John de Shylyngford [Shillingford]*, doctor of laws D. John de Moreton, rector of Checkeleye [Checkley], Coventry and Lichfield diocese	Heywode [Haywood], 13 April 1376
31/1520	John [of Sutton], abbot of Reading	[D.] Peter de Barton*, clerk Thomas Seynt Alban [St Albans]*	Reading, 21 April 1376
31/1521	[John Deeping], abbot of Thorney	F. Geoffrey de Brune [Brunne], monk of abbey John Harwedon [Harrowden]* John de Harlyngton [Harlington]*	Thorney, St Mark, evangelist [25 April] 1376
31/1522	Thomas [Pethy], abbot of Hyde near Winchester	F. John Chaworth, monk of abbey Thomas Marnham*, clerk	Hyde, [damaged] St George [April] 1376
31/1523	[Nicholas Ampney], abbot of Circencester	Gilbert de Sutton*, clerk John de Wardon, clerk	Cirencester, 23 Jan. 1376
31/1524	John [of Sherburn], abbot of Selby	Robert de Crull [Crowle]*, clerk Adam de Chesterfield*, clerk	Selby, 2 March 1376
31/1525	[William Marreys], abbot of St Mary's, York	F. Richard de Appilton [Appleton], monk of abbey [D.] Michael de Ravendale*	In the monastery, 15 April 1376

31/1526	[Henry of Overton], abbot of [Peterborough]	[D.] Richard de Tretton*, clerk [F.] Thomas de Bury, monk of abbey John de Harughdon [Harrowden]*	In the monastery, Friday the feast of St Mark, evangelist [25 April] 1376
31/1527	William [Methwold], abbot of St Benet of Hulme	John de Herlyngg [Harling]*	St Benet of Hulme, 20 April 1376
31/1528	[Richard of Shenington], abbot of Ramsey	Nicholas de Stuecle [Styuecle]* [D.] Michael de Ravendale*, clerk [F.] Robert Waryn	Ramsey, 24 April 1376
31/1529	Thomas [Barnack], abbot of Crowland	[D.] Richard de Tretton*, clerk John de Folkyngham [Folkingham]*, clerk F. John de Grantham, monk of abbey	[Illegible], [Illegible] kalends May 1376
31/1530	John [of Omberseley], abbot of Evesham	John Newenham*, clerk Robert de Faryngton [Farrington]*, clerk	[Damaged], [Damaged] April 137 [damaged]
31/1531	John [Chynnok alias Wynchestre], abbot of Glastonbury	M. John Blanchard [Blaunchard]*, clerk M. Robert Cross, clerk	Glastonbury, 21 April 1376
31/1532	Walter [of Winforton], abbot of Winchcombe	M. John Appilby [Appleby]*, dean of St Paul's, London [D.] Richard de Pyriton [Pirton]*, canon of St Paul's, London	Winchcombe, 25 April [damaged]

210

PARLIAMENT AT WESTMINSTER, 27 JANUARY 1377

31/1512	Chapter of York	[D.] Richard de Ravenser*, canon of York M. Walter de Skyrlaw [Skirlaw]*, canon of York M. John de Waltham*, canon of York	Chapter House, 14 Jan. 1377
31/1515	Subprior and Chapter of Bath	[Damaged] [M.] Thomas Spert*, doctor of laws	Bath Chapter House, 22 [Damaged]
31/1533	Thomas [Appleby], bishop of Carlisle	M. Walter Skirlawe [Skirlaw]*, clerk John Marshall*, clerk John de Kirkby* Thomas de Skelton William de Stirkeland [Strickland]*	[Damaged – Rose, 8] Jan. 1377
31/1534	John [of Omberseley], abbot of Evesham	M. Thomas Stowe*, doctor of laws Robert de Faryngton [Farrington]*	Evesham, 12 Jan. 1377
31/1535	William [of Methwold], abbot of St Benet of Hulme	John de Herlyng [Harling]* John de Holkham	In the monastery, 22 Jan. 1377
31/1536	Thomas [de la Mare], abbot of St Albans	F. Robert Chestan, monk of abbey Robert Flaunville	St Albans, 6 Jan. 1377
31/1537	[Richard of Shenington], abbot of Ramsey	[D.] Michael de Ravendale* Nicholas Green	Ramsey, 25 Jan. 1377

31/1538	Roger de Freton, dean of Chichester Cathedral	John Bishopeston [Bishopstone]*, chancellor of Chichester John de Freton*, archdeacon of Norfolk	Chichester, 23 Jan. 1377
31/1539	William [Marreys], abbot of St Mary's, York	[F] Richard de Appilton [Appleton], monk of abbey [D] Michael de Ravendale*	In the monastery, 20 Jan. 1377
31/1540	Thomas [of Barnack], abbot of Crowland	[D.] Richard de Tretton*, clerk John Folkingham*, clerk F. John de Grantham, monk of abbey	Crowland, 21 Jan. 1377
31/1541	John [of Brinkley], abbot of Bury St Edmunds	F. John de Lakyngheth [Lakenheath], monk of abbey [D] Peter de Barton*, clerk	Elmeswell [Elmswell], 21 Jan. 1377
31/1542	John [of Sherburn], abbot of Selby	Robert de Crull [Crowle]*, clerk Adam de Chesterfield*, clerk	Selby, 10 Jan. 1377
31/1543	Robert [Stretton], bishop of Coventry and Lichfield [LP]	M. Richard de Bermingham [Birmingham], canon of Lichfield [M.] John de Shillingford*, advocate in the court of Canterbury [D.] John de Moreton, rector of Chekkeley [Checkley], Lichfield diocese	Heywode [Haywood], 22 Jan. 1377
31/1544	[Henry of Overton], abbot of Peterborough	[D.] Richard de Tretton*, clerk F. Thomas de Bury, monk of abbey John de Harwedon [Harrowden]*	In the monastery, 24 Jan. 1377

31/1545	Peter [of Hanney], abbot of Abingdon	F: Robert Frileford [Frilford], monk of abbey Thomas de Hanneye [Hanney], rector of Longeworth [Longworth] [D.] William de Shiltewode [Shiltwood], rector of Chelrey [Childrey]	Abingdon, 22 Jan. 1377
31/1546	[John Deeping], abbot of Thorney	F: Geoffrey de Brunne, monk of abbey John de Harondon [Harrowden]* John Harlington*	Thorney, 23 Jan. 1377
31/1547	[Thomas of Stapelton], abbot of Bardney [LP]	[D.] Peter de Barton* Robert Beverage	Bardney, feast of SS Fabian and Sebastian [20 Jan.] 1377
31/1548	Walter [Camme], abbot of Malmesbury	Robert Cherlton [Charlton]* John Colingbourne [Collingbourne]*	Malmesbury, 18 Jan. 1377
31/1549	Thomas [Pethy], abbot of Hyde near Winchester	F: John Eynsham*, monk of abbey [D.] Peter de Barton* Thomas de Grymesby [Grimsby]*	Hyde, 11 Jan. 1377
31/1550	William de Feriby [Ferriby] [the elder], archdeacon of Cliveland [Cleveland]	M. John de Waltham*, canon of York [D.] John Carp*, canon of York M. John Percehay [Percy], skilled in law	York, 16 Jan. 1377
32/1551	Nicholas [de Ampney], abbot of Cirencester	John de Wardon Richard [Damaged]ynn	Cirencester, feast of St Maurus, abbot [15 Jan.] 1377

32/1552	John de Appilby [Appleby], archdeacon of Carlisle	John de Kirkeby [Kirkby]* Robert de Thorley Laurence de Stapelton [Stapleton]	Carlisle, 8 Jan. 1377
32/1553	John [Chynnock *alias* Wynchestre], abbot of Glastonbury	M. John de Shillingford*, clerk M. John Blanchard [Blaunchard]*, clerk [D.] Walter Broun, clerk	Glastonbury, 22 Jan. 1377
32/1554	William [de Greneburgh], prior of Coventry	F. Roger de Wentebrigg [Wentbridge], monk of abbey Robert de Melton*, clerk	Coventry, 6 Jan. 1377
32/1555	Thomas [Brantingham], bishop of Exeter	M. William de Byde*, bishop's official [M.] John Shillingford*, doctor of laws [M.] Ralph Tregresiowe*, doctor of laws	Clist [Clyst Gabriel] Manor, 22 Jan. 1377
32/1556	Chapter of Chichester [LP]	John Bishopeston [Bishopstone]*, chancellor of Chichester John Vincent, canon of Chichester	Chapter House, 20 Jan. 1377
32/1557	Clergy of Carlisle diocese [LP]	Matthew de Wygton [Wigton] Robert de Karlell [Carlisle]	Carlisle, 19 Jan. 1377
32/1559A	John [de Sutton], abbot of Reading	F. John de Spersolt [Sparsholt], monk of abbey [D.] Peter de Barton*, clerk	Reading, 15 Jan. 1377
51/2529	Robert [Berrington of Walworth], prior of Durham Cathedral [LP]	John Dent William Lampard Gilbert de Elvette [Elvet]	Durham, 12 Jan. [*illegible*]

214

Misfiled Letters in SC 10

1/40	Letter, in French, from Edward II to the bishop of Rochester concerning arrangements for Edward I's body, dated 1 September 1307.
2/98	Letter from Richard Swinfield, bishop of Hereford, certifying that he has executed the *praemunientes* clause for the parliament of March 1313 at Westminster. Dated at Bosbury, 13 March 1313.
14/687	Election return for two burgesses from Bristol for the parliament of 26 November 1330.
27/1317	Letter from John Grandisson, bishop of Exeter, appointing Henry Percehay*, John Tremayn, Nicholas Whityng and Robert de Kyrkham [Kirkham] as his proctors. The text of this letter simply refers to the king's letter of 18 August and explains that the bishop cannot personally attend on the day and in the place there named. There is no corresponding writ on the close rolls. However, there is a writ of 8 November, 1356, in which John Grandisson is summoned 'before the king and his council on the octave of Hilary next, to show cause why the king should not visit his free chapel of Bosham and exercise the jurisdiction of visitation there as in his other free chapels' (*CCR, 1354–1360,* p. 288). This could be a second summons following the bishop's failure to appear earlier. Significantly, Grandisson styles himself in 27/1317 as 'bishop of Exeter and chaplain of your ancient royal free chapel of Bosham', suggesting that this letter refers to a dispute between king and bishop over this issue, and that Grandisson was appointing proctors for legal rather than parliamentary purposes.

Letters of Unknown Date

The following letters are those within the fifty-one files of clerical proctors in SC 10 which cannot be assigned to a parliament. In most cases, this is because they are damaged, fragmentary or illegible, although some are complete and legible but lack a dating clause and internal evidence which would permit a date to be inferred. The dates of 51/2524 and 51/2542 can be guessed but not stated with absolute confidence. The proctors named in many of the letters from file 51 indicate that they date from the reigns of Edward II and Edward III.

1/7	[Damaged – abbot of Ramsey?]	F. William de Gumecestre [Godmanchester], 'our sacristan'	[Addressed to King Henry (III)]
1/11	Thomas, abbot of [Illegible]	F. Ralph, monk of Leicester	[Illegible]
1/25	John, abbot of St Peter's, Gloucester [LP]	Laurence de [Illegible]	Gloucester, [Illegible]
2/52	Walter [de Wickwane?], abbot of Winchcombe	John [Damaged]	[Damaged]
2/60B	[Damaged]	[Damaged]	[Damaged]

Ref			
2/82	Walter [de Wickwane?], abbot of Winchcombe	M. William de B[illegible]	[Illegible] 6 Edward II [1312–13]
3/119	David [Damaged – bishop of St Davids?]	D. Matthew de Shireford [Sherford]	Lante[damaged – Lamphey?]
11/531	[Damaged] [LP]	[The right-hand half of this document is missing]	London, 12 September [Damaged]
21/1003	This letter no longer exists. A note dated 26/11/[19]32 has been inserted, reading 'No. 1003 has been attached to 1031 (in this file) of which it was a fragment.'		
23/1130	Abbot of Cirencester (to John, archbishop of Canterbury)	F. R [damaged] [This letter seems to refer to a convocation rather than a parliament, as it mentions a meeting of all the clergy of the province of Canterbury at St Paul's under the archbishop.]	[Undated]
Between 23/1131A and 23/1132	At this point, there is a badly damaged letter inserted between 23/1131A and 23/1132, without a number, but with a handwritten note that it was 'From Chancery, Assorted Miscellanea, 26 April 1923'. It is to the king, and is the sixteenth year of his reign in England, so presumably Edward III, for a parliament at Westminster, but no other names or dating evidence survives.		
23/1149	[Robert of Nassington], abbot of Ramsey		[Damaged], 18 & 5 Edward III [1344–5]
23/1150	[Damaged]		[Damaged] 1344
24/1161	[Damaged]		[Damaged]

218

24/1164	[Damaged]		[Damaged]
24/1181	[Illegible]		[Illegible]
Between 24/1182 and 24/1183	*Between 1182 and 1183 a document has been inserted, without a number, with a note 'From Chancery, Assorted Miscellanea, 26 April, 1923'. The letter is stained and in bad condition, and only a very few words are legible under UV light.*		
26/1290	[Damaged]		[Damaged]
31/1511	John [Harewell], bishop of Bath and Wells	[M.] John de Shillingford*, doctor of laws / Peter de Barton*	[Damaged], 1385 and 19th year of bishop's consecration
31/1516	Robert [Damaged]	Alan de Billyngham [Billingham] / Robert Lambard / [Damaged – at least one additional name lost]	Durham, [Damaged] 1376
32/1559B	[Damaged]	[Illegible]	[Illegible], feast of St Chad, bishop [2 March] [Damaged]
34/1663	[Illegible]	[Illegible]	
35/1745	[Illegible]	[Illegible]	
35/1750B	[Adam Houghton?], bishop of St. Davids	[Illegible]	[Illegible] 138[:illegible]

219

36/1764	[Illegible]		[Illegible]
36/1795A	Abbot of Shrewsbury [LP]		[Illegible]
50/2478A	[Illegible]		[Illegible]
50/2478B	Richard [Wykke, bishop of Norwich]	[Illegible]	Hoxne Manor, [Illegible]
51/2524	Dean and chapter of York [LP]	Henry de Clyff [Cliff]*, canon of York / John Gyffard [Giffard]*, canon of York	York, 1 Sept. [illegible]
51/2525	Walter [de Monyton], abbot of Glastonbury	M. Thomas Yonge [Young]*, clerk / M. Hugh de Penebrigg [Pembridge]*, clerk	Glastonbury, 23 April [Damaged]
51/2526	Abbot of Abingdon	D. [Illegible], clerk / D. John de Sancto Paulo [St Pol]*, clerk	Abingdon, feast of St Matthew, apostle [Illegible]
51/2527	Abbot of Abingdon	D. Thomas de Evesham*	Abingdon, 11 Jan. [no year]
51/2528	Abbot of Colchester	[Illegible], Norwich diocese, clerk / Richard de [Illegible], clerk	Colchester, 23 [Illegible]
51/2530	William, abbot of Thornton	M. John de [Damaged]	[Damaged]
51/2531	[Illegible]	[Illegible]	[Illegible] Jan. [Illegible]

51/2532	William, abbot of Thornton	[Damaged], monk of abbey Alan de [Damaged]	Thornton, [Damaged]7
51/2533	John, abbot of Reading	[Damaged]	Reading, viii kal. [Damaged]
51/2534	W[damaged], abbot of Evesham	[Damaged] [Damaged] de Stoke, 'my clerk'	Evesham, Thursday before feast of [Damaged]
51/2535	Chapter of St Davids [LP]	[Damaged], precentor of St Davids	St Davids, 10 May [Damaged]
51/2536	Archbishop of York [F]	No proctors named	Cawode [Cawood], 24 Feb. [no year]
51/2537	John, bishop of Lincoln [F]	No proctors named	Stow Park, 5 Jan. [no year]
51/2538	John, abbot of Battle	F. Peter de Willoughby, monk of abbey	[Undated]
51/2539	Abbot of Malmesbury	D. Thomas de Evesham [C] [Damaged]	Malmesbury, [Damaged]
51/2540	Abbot of [Illegible]	Thomas de Geryngton Walter de [Illegible] Thomas de [Illegible] Thomas de [Damaged]	[Illegible]
51/2541	[Illegible]	[Damaged]	[Illegible]

221

51/2542	John, prior of Coventry [*This is addressed to Henry VIII and for parliament in London on 15 April, possibly that of 1523*]	Abbot of Winchcombe Thomas, monk of priory Ralph Swillington, recorder of Coventry Roger Wigston, gentleman	Coventry, [*Damaged*]
51/2546	[*Illegible*]	[*Damaged*]	[*Illegible*]

Letters from the *Vetus Codex*

There are no surviving documents in SC 10 relating to the parliament which met at Carlisle on 20 January 1307. However, a list of those sending proxies and the names of their proctors survives in the transcript of the parliament's proceedings contained in the Vetus Codex (TNA C 153/1, membranes 130–1). These are transcribed in PW, I.ii, 185–6, with the entries for the lower clergy calendared in Denton and Dooley, Representatives of the Lower Clergy, pp. 104–6. A modern transcription and translation is included in the material for the January 1307 parliament in PROME.

Thomas [Bitton], bishop of Exeter	Henry de Pynkenee [Pinkeny], rector of Honyton [Honiton]
John [Dalderby], bishop of Lincoln	Hugh de Normanton*, canon of Lincoln Robert de Askeby [Asby]*, rector of Hale [Great Hale]
Walter [Haselshaw], bishop of Bath and Wells	William de Cherelton [Charlton]*, canon of Wells
S[imon of Ghent], bishop of Salisbury	Thomas Chaumpeneys, rector of Westhildeslee [West Ilsey]
Robert [Orford], bishop of Ely	M. Geoffrey de Pakenham*, clerk M. Richard de Denford, clerk

Henry [Woodlock], bishop of Winchester [R]	M. Philip de Barton, archdeacon of Surrey [*appointed his own proctor*] M. Gilbert de Middleton, clerk M. John de Bleyho [Bloyho]*, clerk M. Richard Wodelok [Woodlock]*, clerk
Richard [Swinfield], bishop of Hereford	Adam de Herwynton [Harvington]*, rector of Aure [Awre] Walter de Lugwardyn [Lugwardine], rector of Monesle [Munsley]
D[avid Martin], bishop of St Davids	M. John Bussh [Bush]*, canon of St Davids Warin Martyn*, knight
L[lywelyn de Bromfield], bishop of St Asaph	M. Matthew Ruffim M. Howel ap Ithel [Hywel ap Ithel]
Gervase [de Seez], archdeacon of Chichester	Nicholas de Dynnesleye [Dinsley], vicar of Boseham [Bosham]
Dean and chapter of Wells	M. Thomas de Luggore*, canon of Wells M. William de Cherleton [Charlton]*, canon of Wells
[Thomas de Charlton], archdeacon of Wells	Henry de Pynkene [Pinkeny], rector of Honyton [Honiton]
Chapter of Worcester Cathedral	F. John de Sancto Brevello [St Briavels], monk of priory William de Thorntoft*, clerk
Subprior and chapter of Rochester	Robert, rector of Hoo
Chapter of Lincoln	M. Robert de Pykering [Pickering], canon of Lincoln M. Hugh de Normanton*, canon of Lincoln

[Francis Neapoleonis], archdeacon of Worcester	[F.] John de Sancto Briavello [St Briavels] Ingelard de Warle [Warley]*, clerk
Chapter of Exeter	Henry de Pynkeneie [Pinkeny], rector of Honynton [Honiton]
Chapter of Chichester	Clement de Peccham [Patcham], canon of Chichester
Ralph [de Fodringhey], archdeacon of Ely	M. Geoffrey de Pakenham*, clerk M. Richard de Conyngton [Conington]*, clerk M. Adam Elyot [Eliot]*, clerk
[William de Berges], archdeacon of Berkshire	M. William Bukkestanes [Buckstone]*
Chapter of Salisbury	M. John de Tarenta [Tarrant], clerk M. William de Buckestanes [Buckstone]*, clerk
Thomas [Wychampton], archdeacon of Salisbury	M. John de Tarenta [Tarrant]
Dean [William de Hambleton] and Chapter of York	Adam de Osgodby*, canon of York
[Henry of Lakenham], prior of Norwich	M. Hugh de Swafham [Swaffham]* M. Thomas de Fuldon M. William de Tutington [Tuttington]
Prior [Nicholas de Tarente] and convent of Winchester	M. Richard de Dene [Dean], clerk Eudo Thornetonstiward [Thornton Steward], clerk
Chapter of Ely	M. Richard de Dene [Dean], clerk

J[ohn], archdeacon of St Davids — John Boish [Bush]*, canon of St Davids
Henry de Lutegarshale [Ludgarshall]
Warin Martyn *

[Henry de Bradenham], archdeacon of Sudbury — M. John Hardy, rector of Thrillowe [Thurlow]

[William de Knapton], archdeacon of Norwich — M. Hugh de Swafham [Swaffham]*

[Henry de Shorne], archdeacon of Hereford — Walter de Lugwardyn [Lugwardine]

Chapter of Norwich — M. Hugh de Swafham [Swaffham] *
M. Thomas de Fuldon
M. William de Tutington [Tuttington]

[Richard de Bernard], archdeacon of Shropshire — Walter de Lugwardyn [Lugwardine]

Chapter of Hereford — Walter de Lugwardyn [Lugwardine], clerk
John Craft, clerk

Chapter of St Asaph — Madoc Goch, canon of St Aspah
Howel [Hywel], rector of Lanarmon [Llanarmon]

A., dean of St Asaph and L[lywellyn ap Hwfa], archdeacon of St Asaph — Madoc Goch, canon of St Aspah
Howel [Hywel], rector of Lanarmon [Llanarmon]

Viceregent of the dean of St Paul's, London and the chapter — M. John de Bedeford [Bedford]*

Roger [de Wesenham], archdeacon of Rochester	M. John Bussh [Bush]*, clerk John de Colon [Cologne]*, clerk
W[alter de Burdon], archdeacon of Gloucester	M. John de Wakerle [Wakerley] [*appointed a substitute*]
Philip [de Barton], archdeacon of Surrey	John de Brantingham
William de la More, master of the Order of the Temple in England	F. William de Grafton
Archdeacon of Norfolk	M. Hugh de Swafham [Swaffham]* M. Alan de Swafham [Swaffham]
Chapter of Rochester	Robert de Brok [Brooke], clerk
John de Greenstreet], prior of Rochester	Peter de Fangefosse [Fangfoss], clerk
[Thomas Wouldham], bishop of Rochester	M. John Bussh [Bush], rector of Beggenham [Beckenham] D. Peter de Fangefosse [Fangfoss], perpetual vicar of Eldyng [Yalding]
[Thomas de Fyndon], abbot of St Augustine's, Canterbury	William de Ayremynne [Airmyn]*, clerk
John of Brockhampton], abbot of Evesham	Simon de Saultford [Saltford], monk of abbey
[William of Badminton], abbot of Malmesbury	John le Bray*, clerk William Cotspore
John de Wyke], prior of Worcester	John de Sancto Brevello [St Briavels], monk of priory Adam de Herwynton [Harvington], clerk

[Philip of Bedwyn], abbot of Waverley	Subprior of Waverley
[John de Maryns], abbot of St Albans [*The text notes that the king has excused the abbot, but he nevertheless sent the two named proctors*]	Adam de Redbourn, monk of abbey Ralph de Dalton*, clerk
[John de Greenstreet], prior of Rochester	Robert Moslee [Moseley]
[Bartholomew of Winchester], abbot of Chertsey	John de Bray*, clerk
[Geoffrey Fromond], abbot of Glastonbury	Robert de Stapelbrugg [Staplebridge]
[?Adam of Arundel], abbot of Quarr	Geoffrey de Worthe [Worth], monk of abbey
Abbot of Netley	James de Bichley, monk of abbey
[Geoffrey de Feringges], abbot of Hyde near Winchester	William Fyanmur
Abbot of Combe	*No proctor appointed*
[William], abbot of Vaudey	Richard de Hatherle [Hatherley], clerk
[Walter of Wenlock], abbot of Westminster	William de Chalk, monk of abbey
Abbot of Swineshead	F. Robert, monk of abbey
[Nicholas of Whaplode], abbot of Reading	F. John de Sutton, monk of abbey F. Jordan de Sutton, monk of abbey
Abbot of Jervaulx	F. John de Donesford [Dunsforth], monk of abbey

[John of Sawtry], abbot of Ramsey	F. William de Grafham, monk of abbey
[Thomas of Tottington], abbot of Bury St Edmunds	F. John de Eversdon [Eversden], monk of abbey M. Ralph de Torny*, clerk
Abbot of Tupholme	F. Alan, canon of Neuhus [Newhouse]
[Richard of Sutton], abbot of Barlings	F. John de Fornle
[Walter de Wickwane], abbot of Winchcombe	F. Walter de Apperleye [Apperley]
[Thomas of Hedon], abbot of Newhouse	F. Alan de Middelton [Middleton]
[John Thoky], abbot of St Peter's, Gloucester	Roger de Assherugg [Ashridge]*, clerk Ralph de Eyton, clerk
[John of Gilling], abbot of St Mary's, York	F. William de Tanefeld [Tanfield], monk of abbey
[William], abbot of St Radegund near Dover	*No proctor appointed*
[William of Over], abbot of Croxden	F. William de Shepesh [Shepshed], monk of abbey
[Simon of Luffenham], abbot of Crowland	Robert de Schulthorp [Sculthorpe]
Subprior and convent of Durham	F. Hugh de Monte Alto [Mohaut] F. Thomas de Killington
Clergy of Lincoln diocese	Peter de Medeburn [Medbourne], rector of Ingoldeby [Ingoldsby] John de Horkestowe [Horkstow], rector of Herington [Harrington]

229

Clergy of Worcester archdeaconry	Reginald le Porter, rector of Bourton [?Bourton on Dunsmore?]
Clergy of Exeter diocese	M. Thomas Crabbe, clerk M. Ralph de Stok [Stoke]*, clerk
Clergy of Bath and Wells diocese	M. Hugh de Walmesford*, clerk M. Henry de Moneketon [Monkton], clerk
Clergy of Rochester diocese	Robert, rector of Hoo Peter [de Fangfoss], vicar of Ealdyng [Yalding]
Clergy of Chichester archdeaconry	Nicholas de Dynneslee [Dinsley], vicar of Boseham [Bosham]
Clergy of Ely diocese	M. Richard de Conyngton [Conington]*, clerk M. Adam Eliot, clerk*
Clergy of Durham diocese	M. Adam de Morpath [Morpeth], clerk John de Pampesworth [Pampisford], clerk
Clergy of York diocese	M. John Fraunceis [Francis], rector of Queldryk [Wheldrake] William de Bergh [Burgh]*, rector of Thornton
Clergy of Salisbury diocese	M. William de Buckestanes [Buckstone]*, clerk John de Trenta [Tarrant], clerk
Clergy of Surrey archdeaconry	M. Richard de Barton, clerk Hugh de Tychwell [Titchwell], clerk [appointed a substitute]

Clergy of Winchester archdeaconry — M. Richard Wodeloc [Woodlock]*, clerk; Hugh de Tychewell [Titchwell], clerk

Clergy of London diocese — M. William de Melford; Roger de Arewold [Harrold], chaplain

Clergy of Lewes archdeaconry — M. William de Malmesbur [Malmesbury]

Clergy of Suffolk and Sudbury archdeaconry — M. John Hardy, rector of Trillawe [Thurlow]

Clergy of Norwich and Norfolk archdeaconry — M. Hugh de Swafham [Swaffham]*

Clergy of Shropshire archdeaconry — William, rector of Silveton; Walter de Lugwardyn [Lugwardine], rector of Museleye [Munsley]

Clergy of Carlisle diocese — M. John de Boghes [Bowes]; M. William de Goseford [Gosforth]; M. Robert de Suthayk*; M. Adam de Appelby [Appleby]*

Clergy of St Asaph diocese — Madoc Goch, canon of St Asaph; Howel [Hywel], rector of Lanarmon [Llanarmon]

Clergy of Gloucester archdeaconry, Worcester diocese — M. John de Wakerle [Wakerley] [appointed a substitute]

Abbot of Furness — F. John, subprior of abbey

[Roger of Driffield], abbot of Meaux

Abbot of Alnwick

[John de Southber], abbot of Stanley

[Richard of Bishops Cleve], abbot of Abingdon

John de Wakerley, proctor of the clergy of Gloucester archdeaconry

Hugh de Tichewell [Titchwell], proctor of the clergy of Surrey archdeaconry

Abbot of St Agatha

Abbot of Byland

F. John de Wandeford, monk of abbey
Gilbert de Kelleshull [Kelshall], clerk

F. John de Coldigham [Coldingham], monk of abbey

D. William de Raseney

Robert de Offinton [Uffington]

John de Bray*, clerk

John de Brantingham

F. Alan de Middelton [Middleton]

F. Peter de Wiluby [Willoughby], monk of abbey

Biographical Details for Proctors

This list gives brief additional details for those proctors marked in the main text with an asterisk, but makes no pretence to be exhaustive; we have tried merely to indicate the types of background from which the proctors were drawn. In seeking to identify individuals we have erred on the side of caution, especially in respect of laymen. Some surnames were too common to be useful in identification, while in many families the same Christian name might be used in several generations, or in different branches of the family. Widely divergent alternative spellings are indicated in brackets, and problematic identifications in *italics*.

In addition to the volumes listed below in the abbreviations, the following sources have been consulted: *Calendar of Close Rolls*; *Calendar of Patent Rolls*; J. H. Baker, *The Order of Serjeants at Law*, Selden Society, supplementary series 5 (1984); *The Medieval Court of Arches*, ed. F. Donald Logan, C&Y 95 (2005); *Officers of the Exchequer*, compiled by J. C. Sainty, List & Index Society, special series 18 (1983); *Return of the Name of Every Member of the Lower House of the Parliaments of England, Scotland and Ireland*, vol. I (1878); Sir John Sainty, *The Judges of England 1272–1990*, Selden Society, supplementary series 10 (1993); Nigel Saul, *Knights and Esquires: The Gloucestershire Gentry in the Fourteenth Century* (Oxford, 1981); David M. Smith & Vera C. M. London, *The Heads of Religious Houses: England & Wales, II.1216–1377* (Cambridge, 2001); T. F. Tout, *Chapters in the Administrative History of Mediaeval England*, 6 vols. (Manchester, 1920–33); John Grassi, 'Royal Clerks in the Diocese of York in the Fourteenth Century', *Northern History* 5 (1970), 12–33; John le Neve, *Fasti Ecclesie Anglicanae 1300–1541*, 12 volumes (revised edition: London, 1962–7); *Discovery*, the online catalogue of The National Archives; and the card index of chancery clerks in the map room of TNA.

The following abbreviations are used.

E   A biography appears in A. B. Emden, *A Biographical Register of the University of Oxford to A.D. 1500*, 3 vols. (Oxford, 1957–9).

E:Ca   A biography appears in A. B. Emden, *A Biographical Register of the University of Cambridge to 1500* (Oxford, 1963).

O   A biography appears in the *Oxford Dictionary of National Biography*.

W   Chancery clerk for whom a career summary appears in B. Wilkinson, *The Chancery under Edward III* (Manchester, 1929).

Acton, John   E.

Acton, Nicholas   King's clerk; chamberlain and escheator of North
                            Wales, 1329–30; chamberlain of the exchequer,
                            1330–7.

Airmyn, Adam   Chancery clerk; archdeacon of Norfolk, 1327–35.

Airmyn, Richard   Chancery clerk; keeper of the rolls, 1324–5; keeper of
                            the privy seal, 1327–8; keeper of the Domus Conver-
                            sorum, 1327–39; O.

Airmyn, William   Chancery clerk; keeper of the rolls, 1316–24; keeper
                            of the Domus Conversorum, 1316–25; keeper of
                            the privy seal, 1324–5; bishop-elect of Carlisle, 1325;
                            bishop of Norwich, 1325–36; treasurer, 1331–2; O.

Albert, Richard   Commissioner to keep the Statute of Labourers,
                            1355.

Altestowe, John   MP for Cornwall, Mar. 1330, Nov. 1330, Mar. 1332,
                            Sept. 1336 and July 1338.

Alton, John   Escheator of Hants. and six other counties, occ. April
                            1340; sheriff of Berks., 1341; MP for Hants., Sept.
                            1334 (Aulton, Aultone).

Ampney, Nicholas   Abbot of Cirencester, 1363–93.

Appleby, Adam   Official of Carlisle, occ. 1311–19, 1325–32.

Appleby, John   Dean of St Paul's, 1364–89; E.

Arundel, Edmund   Prebendary of Husthwaite, York Minster,
                            1340–6; treasurer of Chichester Cathedral, ?–1349
                            (Darundell).

Asby, Robert   Chancery clerk (Askeby).

Ash, Michael   MP for Glos., June 1344.

Ashridge, Hugh   King's clerk.

Askeby, William   E (*alias* Scoter).

Astley, Thomas   E.

Aston, Geoffrey   King's clerk.

Aston, Hugh   Clerk of common pleas, occ. 1359.

Aston, Robert   Steward of Cirencester Abbey estates, occ. 1321.

Aston, Roger   E.

Aylestone, Robert   King's clerk; keeper of the rolls of the common
                            bench, 1322–?; keeper of the privy seal, 1323–4 and
                            1334; baron of the exchequer, 1324–32; archdeacon
                            of Wilts., 1326–31; archdeacon of Berks., 1331–4;
                            treasurer, 1332–4; E.

Badew, Richard   Chancellor of the University of Cambridge, 1326–9;
                            E.

Badminton, John   King's clerk; E.

Baldock, Richard   E.

Baldock, Robert   Keeper of the privy seal, 1320–3; controller of the

	wardrobe, 1320–3; keeper of the great seal, 1323–36; archdeacon of Middlesex, ?–1326; E.
Bamburgh, Thomas	Chancery clerk; keeper of the great seal, 1331, 1334, and 1338–9; greater clerk of chancery, 1332–40; O; W.
Banbury, John	E.
Bardelby, Hugh	Chancery clerk.
Bardelby, Robert	Chancery clerk; keeper of the great seal, 1310, 1311–12, 1313, 1315, 1316, 1317, 1318, 1319, 1320 and 1321.
Bardelby, William	Chancery clerk; keeper of the rolls of Ireland, 1334–7.
Barnet, John	Archdeacon of London, 1356–62; bishop of Worcester, 1362–3; bishop of Bath and Wells, 1363–6; treasurer, 1363–9; bishop of Ely, 1366–73; E; O.
Barton, Henry	King's clerk.
Barton, Peter	Chancery clerk; greater clerk of chancery, 1376–95; W.
Battle, Richard	E (de la Bataylle).
Beche, Edmund	Archdeacon of Berks., 1334–?; keeper of the great wardrobe, 1334–5; controller of the wardrobe, 1335–7; keeper of the wardrobe, 1337–8.
Bedford, John	Archdeacon of London, ?–1308.
Belvoir, John	E.
Benniworth, Henry	E (Benyngworth).
Berenger, John	King's clerk.
Berneye, John	Attorney for the citizens of Norwich, 1326–31; MP for Norwich, May 1335; MP for Norfolk, Sept. 1346, Jan. 1348, April 1357 and May 1368.
Billoun, John	MP for Bodmin, May 1322; MP for Cornwall, Oct. 1324, Jan. 1327, Feb. 1329 and Feb. 1351; MP for Helston, March 1337 and Jan. 1352.
Bintworth, Richard	Keeper of the privy seal, 1337–8; bishop of London, 1338–9; chancellor, 1338–9; E; O.
Birland, Richard	Chancery clerk.
Birston, William	Archdeacon of Gloucester, 1308–17; E.
Bishopstone, John	Chancellor of Chichester, 1371–84.
Blaston, Geoffrey	Prebendary of Bishopshull, 1304–11, Lichfield Cathedral; archdeacon of Derby 1311–28.
Blaunchard, John	Archdeacon of Worcester, 1371–83; E.
Blewbury, John	Chancery clerk; greater clerk of chancery, 1332–8; E; W.
Bleyho, John	E (Bloyou).
Blyth, Walter	King's clerk.

Bolingbroke, Richard	Attorney of Ebulo le Strange, 1334, 1340.
Borden, William	King's clerk.
Bourn, William	Justice of Common pleas, occ. 1309.
Bowland, John	King's clerk.
Boys, William	E.
Boys, William	Abbot of Evesham, 1345–67.
Brabazon, John	E (le Brabazon).
Bradwardine, Thomas	Archbishop of Canterbury, 1349; E; O.
Bradwell, William	MP for Worcs., May 1322, Oct. 1324, Mar. 1332 and Jan. 1333; MP for Glos., Feb. 1324, Sept. 1331, Mar. 1332 and Jan. 1333; steward of Cirencester Abbey estates, occ. 1319.
Braintree, John	Chancery clerk; greater clerk of chancery, 1355–75; clerk of the Black Prince; W (Branketre).
Braundeston, Thomas	Chancellor of Llandaff, occ. 1367–72; precentor of Llandaff, 1372–?.
Bray, John	Chancery clerk.
Bray, Thomas	E.
Braybroke, Nicholas	Archdeacon of Cornwall, 1381–97; E.
Brayton, Thomas	Chancery clerk; greater clerk of chancery, 1332–61; clerk of parliament, Mar. 1340, 1341, 1343, 1344 and 1346; keeper of the great seal, 1340–1, 1343, 1349 and 1351; W.
Brenchley, Richard	Examiner general of the Court of Arches, 1313 (Brinchesleye); Archdeacon of Huntington, 1329–37 (Brinchesle); prebendary of Consumpta-Per-Mare, St. Paul's, London, 1327–37 (Brencheslee).
Bridgwater, John	Chancery clerk.
Bristol, Simon	Chancellor of Wells Cathedral, 1337–*c*.1343.
Brocklesby, William	Exchequer clerk, fl. 1322–52; remembrancer of the exchequer, 1326–41; baron of the exchequer, 1341–51; E.
Brune, John	Deputy sheriff of Worcs., occ. Nov. 1335.
Bruton, Laurence	Benefactor to Hailes Abbey, 1333.
Buckstone, William	E.
Burgh, Hugh	Chancery clerk.
Burgh, William	Chancery clerk.
Burstall, William	Chancery clerk, fl, 1338–88; greater clerk of chancery, 1370–81; keeper of the rolls, 1371–81; keeper of the Domus Conversorum, 1371–81; keeper of the great seal, 1371 and 1377; W.
Burton, Richard	King's clerk.
Burton, William	King's clerk.
Bush, John	King's clerk; notary.

Buxton, Thomas	E (Bucton).
Byde, William	E.
Caldbeck, Thomas	Archdeacon of Carlisle, 1318–20.
Cambridge, Nicholas	E:Ca.
Capenhurst, Thomas	Chancery clerk, 1328; greater clerk of chancery, 1344–7; W.
Carlton, Adam	King's clerk.
Carlton, Henry	King's clerk (Carleton).
Carlton, John	E (Carleton).
Carlton, John	Dean of Wells, 1350–61; E (Carleton).
Carlton, John	Archdeacon of Suffolk, 1359–67; E (Carleton).
Carp, John	King's clerk; cofferer of the wardrobe, 1376–90; keeper of the wardrobe, 1390–9.
Caunton, Gruffudd	Archdeacon of Carmarthen, 1335–55; archdeacon of Cardigan, occ. 1355, 1360.
Cave, Thomas	E.
Chaddesden, Geoffrey	King's clerk
Chaddesden, Henry	King's clerk; archdeacon of Leicester, 1347–54; keeper of the regent's seal, 1347.
Chaddesden, Nicholas	Advocate of the court of Arches; E.
Chaddesley, Richard	E.
Chamberlain, Simon le	Knight; MP for Lincs., Jan. 1316 and May 1322 (Chamberlayn).
Chapel, John	MP for Carlisle, Jan. 1324, Nov. 1325, Sept. 1327 and Feb. 1328 (Capella).
Charlton, Humphrey	Archdeacon of Richmond, 1359–83; E.
Charlton, Robert	Serjeant at law, 1383; chief justice of common pleas, 1388–95; O.
Charlton, William	Prebendary of Barton St David; E.
Charwelton, Robert	King's clerk.
Cheam, Peter	Prior of Southwark, 1305–27.
Chelsea, Edmund	Serjeant at law, 1354; king's serjeant, 1361–71; justice of king's bench, 1371–2 (Chelrey).
Cheltenham, William	MP for Glos., Nov. 1325, Apr. 1328, Sept. 1331, Sept. 1332, Jan. 1333, Feb. 1334, Sept. 1334, May 1335, Sept. 1336 and July 1338.
Chester, Richard	E.
Chesterfield, Adam	Controller of works, Tower of London and Palace of Westminster, 1355–75.
Chesterfield, John	Clerk of the treasurer, c.1341–52.
Chesterfield, Roger	Chancery clerk; greater clerk of chancery, 1360–7; W.
Chigwell, Robert	Chancery clerk; clerk of Queen Philippa, c.1336–c.1345; greater clerk of chancery, 1340; W.

Chiriton, William	Abbot of Evesham, 1316–44.
Chisbridge, Richard	MP for Devon, Oct. 1319, May 1319, July 1321, May 1322, Nov. 1322, Feb. 1324, Oct. 1324 and Nov. 1325.
Cirencester, Walter	MP for Glos., Nov. 1325; escheator of Glos., before Jan. 1335.
Claver, John	Serjeant at law, 1305–1330s; justice of assize to 1335.
Cliff, Thomas	King's clerk.
Cliff, William	King's clerk.
Cliffe, Henry	Chancery clerk; greater clerk of chancery, ?–1333; keeper of the privy seal, 1325; keeper of the rolls, 1325–33; keeper of the great seal, 1328, 1329, 1331 and 1332; E; O.
Clopton, Thomas	King's clerk; keeper of the wardrobe, 1347–9.
Clun, Roger	King's clerk; archdeacon of Salisbury, 1361–?.
Coddington, John	Chancery clerk; greater clerk of chancery, 1350–69; clerk of parliament, 1352. W. *One of two chancery clerks of this name, 'not always distinguishable' (Grassi).*
Codford, John	Archdeacon of Wiltshire, 1361–?; E.
Coleshill, John	E (Coleshulle).
Coleshill, William	Occ. as attorney, 1324.
Collingbourne, John	Chancery clerk (Colyngbourne).
Cologne, John	King's clerk (Colonia).
Conington, Richard	E:Ca (Conyngton).
Cophath, John	MP for Reading, April 1341.
Cotes, William	MP for Canterbury, May 1319.
Cookham, Henry	Chancellor of Chichester, *c.*1343–*c.*1365; E (Cokham).
Cottingham, Robert	King's clerk; controller of the wardrobe, 1305–7.
Cottingham, Thomas	Chancery clerk; greater clerk of chancery, 1337–50; keeper of the great seal, 1349; W.
Cotton, William	King's clerk.
Courtenay, William	Chancellor of the University of Oxford, 1367–9; bishop of Hereford, 1369–75; bishop of London, 1375–81; archbishop of Canterbury, 1381–96; chancellor, 1381; E; O.
Crompe, Simon	Prior of Worcester, 1339–40.
Crosby, John	Chancery clerk.
Cross, Thomas	Keeper of the great wardrobe, 1337–44; chamberlain of the exchequer, 1347–9; E.
Crowle, Robert	King's clerk.
Dalton, Ralph	King's clerk.
Daunay, Thomas	MP for Appleby, Sept. 1346 and Feb. 1351 (Dounay).
David, John	Chancellor of St Davids Cathedral, 1361–1407.
Dene, William	Archdeacon of Rochester, 1323–59.

Ditton, John	Chancery clerk.
Donet, Stephen	Receiver of many local commissions, 1341–66. *There were two men of this name, but there is no inquisition post mortem by which to distinguish them.*
Dunwich, John	E:Ca (Donewich).
Eastcote, Ralph	Abbot of Cirencester, 1352–8.
Edenham, Geoffrey	King's clerk.
Edwinstowe, Henry	Chancery clerk, fl. 1313–50; greater clerk of chancery, 1329–*c*.1348; clerk of parliament, Nov. 1330, Sept. 1331, Mar. 1332 and Jan. 1333; keeper of the great seal, 1331, 1332 and 1334; W.
Eglesfield, Adam	King's clerk.
Ellerker, John	Chamberlain and escheator of North Wales, 1338–40. *One of two brothers of that name, probably 'the younger'.*
Eliot, Adam	E:Ca (Elyot).
Emeldon, William	Chancery clerk; greater clerk of chancery, 1337–60/61; W.
Enderby, John	Chancery clerk.
Enderby, Richard	Chancery clerk; E:Ca.
Englefield, Matthew	Bishop of Bangor, 1328–57; E.
English, William	MP for Westmorland, May 1319, July 1321, Jan. 1327, Sept. 1327, July 1328, Feb. 1329, Mar. 1330, Sept. 1331, Mar. 1332, Sept. 1332, Jan. 1333, Feb. 1334, Sept. 1334, May 1335, Mar. 1336, Sept. 1337, Apr. 1341, June 1344 and Mar. 1348; MP for Cumberland, Sept. 1334 (Lengleys, le Engleys).
Escrick, Thomas	Chancery clerk.
Everdon, John	Dean of St Paul's Cathedral, 1322–35; E.
Evesham, Simon	King's clerk.
Evesham, Thomas	Chancery clerk; greater clerk of chancery, 1332–43; keeper of the great seal, 1340–1; keeper of the rolls, 1341; W.
Eye, Simon	Abbot of Ramsey, 1316–42.
Eynsham, John	Abbot of Hyde near Winchester, 1381–94.
Fastolf, Laurence	E:Ca.
Farrington, Robert	Chancery clerk, fl. 1379 – 1404.
Faunt, William	Justice of king's bench, occ. 1338.
Faversham, Thomas	Keeper of the Cinque Ports, 1322, 1330.
Felbridge, George	King's yeoman, 1361; king's esquire, 1367.
Fenton, John	Archdeacon of Suffolk, 1331–47; E.
Ferriby, William (*the younger*)	King's clerk; notary of Richard II, fl. 1370–1400.
Fincham, Adam	King's clerk: king's attorney.
Fitzwarren, Peter	MP for Northants., Sept. 1331 and Sept. 1336 (Fitzwarin).

Fitlyng, Amandus	King's clerk; official of London and keeper of the spiritualities of the diocese of London, *sede vacante*, 1375.
Folkingham, John	Chancery clerk.
Fordham, John	Keeper of the privy seal, 1377–81; dean of Wells Cathedral, 1379–81; archdeacon of Canterbury, 1380–1; bishop of Durham, 1381–8; treasurer, 1386; bishop of Ely, 1388–1425; O.
Foxcote, Richard	Sheriff of Glos., 1332–8 and 1351–2.
Foxton, Robert	King's clerk; chirographer of King's Bench, 1312–34.
Foxton, Thomas	E:Ca.
Fraunceys, David	Chancellor of St. David's Cathedral, occ. 1326, 1328; archdeacon of St. Davids, occ. 1333 (Franceys).
Fraunceys, John	Chancery clerk.
Freeland, John	MP for Oxon., April 1341.
Freton, John	Chancery clerk; archdeacon of Norfolk, 1375–85; greater clerk of chancery, 1376–?; W.
Fromond, Godfrey	E.
Fulthorp, Roger	Serjeant at law, 1371–4; justice of common pleas, 1374–88.
Gaddesby, Geoffrey	Abbot of Selby, 1342–68.
Garland, Henry	Chancellor of Chichester, *c.*1305–18; dean of Chichester, 1318–*c.*1340.
Geraud, John	Prebendary of Blewbury, Salisbury Cathedral, 1336–?, and of Longdon, Lichfield Cathedral, 1336–9.
Giffard, John	Notary and steward of Queen Isabella.
Glinton, Simon	Rector of Hilgay (Glynton).
Gogh, John	Chancery clerk; greater clerk of chancery, 1350–60; archdeacon of St Davids, 1349–?1362; W.
Grandisson, Otto	MP for Kent, Jan. 1333, Sept. 1337, June 1344, Jan. 1348, March 1348, Feb. 1351, Jan. 1352, April 1354, Aug. 1354 and Feb. 1358.
Green, Nicholas	MP for Rutland, Feb. 1371, Oct. 1372 and Jan. 1377.
Greneburgh, William	Prior of Coventry, 1361–90.
Grete, Peter	MP for Worcs., Apr. 1328, Feb. 1329, Jan. 1333, Feb. 1334, Sept. 1334, May 1335, Sept. 1336, Feb. 1338 and July 1338.
Greystoke, Henry	Baron of the exchequer, 1356–65.
Grimsby, Edmund	Chancery clerk, fl. 1319–54; keeper of the rolls of Ireland, 1333–4; greater clerk of chancery, *c.*1337–52/53; W.
Grimsby, Elias	Chancery clerk; greater clerk of chancery, 1340–60/61; W.
Grimsby, Thomas	Clerk.

Gronow, Hywel ap	Archdeacon of Anglesey, ?–1368; bishop of Bangor, 1371–2.
Gunthorpe, William	Keeper of the wardrobe, 1366–8; treasurer of Calais, 1368–73; exchequer baron, 1373–87.
Gynwell, John	Steward of the earl of Lancaster, 1343–5; attorney general of the earl of Lancaster, occ. 1345; bishop of Lincoln, 1347–62; O (Kynwell).
Hackthorpe, John	Notary.
Hacluit, Thomas	Chancellor of Hereford Cathedral, 1349–75.
Hale, Richard	MP for Glos., Feb. 1334.
Halnatheby, John	Chancery clerk.
Harclay, Michael	Brother of Andrew Harclay, earl of Carlisle; canon lawyer; official of the archdeacon of Richmond, 1312–17, 1318–23.
Harlaston, William	Chancery clerk; archdeacon of Norfolk, 1326–7; keeper of the great seal, 1328 and 1329.
Harling, John	King's esquire; usher of the king's chamber, 1375 (Herlyng).
Harling, Richard	E:Ca.
Harlington, John	MP for Hunts., Jan. 1377, Nov. 1384, Jan. 1394, Jan. 1395, Oct. 1399.
Harpham, Thomas	E.
Harrowden, John	Escheator in Cambs. & Hunts., 1355–6; Sheriff of Cambs. , 1356; MP for Hunts, June 1344, Jan. 1348, March 1348, Nov. 1355 and Jan. 1377.
Harvington, Adam	King's clerk; chief Baron of the exchequer of Ireland, 1324–7; chancellor of the exchequer of Ireland, 1326–7; chancellor of the exchequer, 1327–30.
Haselbech, Adam	E. (Haselbeche)
Havering, Richard	Constable of Bordeaux, 1307–8; archdeacon of Chester, 1315–41; E.
Haversham, Richard	E.
Hawkeslowe, Richard	MP for Worcs., May 1322, Feb. 1324, Jan. 1327, Feb. 1328, Apr. 1328, Sept. 1331 and Mar. 1332.
Hawksworth, William	Chancery clerk (Haukesworth).
Hay, John	MP for Herts., Sept. 1314, May 1319, May 1322, Nov. 1322, Sept. 1331 and March 1332; sheriff of Essex & Herts. 1311–12 and 1332–3.
Haydock, Henry	Chancery clerk; greater clerk of chancery, 1353–?1361; chancellor of the county of Lancaster, occ. 1353; W.
Haysand, Robert	MP for Huntingdon, April 1354, Nov. 1356, May 1360.
Hemmingburgh, Robert	Chancery clerk, 1324; keeper of the rolls of Ireland, 1337–46.

Henley, James	Prebendary of Hampton, Hereford Cathedral, ? 1306–30
Hereward, Robert	E.
Hereward, William	Abbot of Cirencester, 1335–52.
Hethe, Hamo	Prior of Rochester, 1314–17; bishop of Rochester, 1317–52; O.
Hildesley, John	Baron of the exchequer, 1332–4; chancellor of the exchequer, 1334–41; E.
Hillary, Roger	Chief justice of Irish court of common pleas, 1329–37; justice of common pleas, 1337–41; chief justice of common pleas, 1341–2 and 1354–6; O.
Hoicton, John	King's clerk.
Holbeach, Ralph	E:Ca.
Hotham, Alan	King's clerk; E:Ca (Hothum).
Houghton, Adam	Bishop of St Davids, 1361–89; E; O.
Houton, John	Cofferer of the wardrobe, 1328–31 and 1335–7; chamberlain of the exchequer, 1337–*c.*1340 and 1344–7; baron of the exchequer, 1347–56.
Hull, Hugh	MP for Hereford, July 1321, Nov. 1322, Sept. 1327, Feb. 1328, April 1328 and July 1328 (Hulle).
Hull, Walter	Archdeacon of Bath, 1342–53 (Hulle).
Hungate, Nicholas	Cofferer of the wardrobe, 1314–15; controller of the wardrobe, 1326–8.
Husthwayt, John	King's clerk.
Icklesham, Robert	Prebendary of Hunderton, Hereford Cathedral, 1313–22.
Ingleby, Henry	Chancery clerk; keeper of the Domus Conversorum, 1350–71.
Ingleby, Thomas	MP for Yorks., March. 1348.
Ipwell, Robert	Abbot of Winchcombe, 1352–60.
Islip, John	Steward of Thorney Abbey.
Islip, Simon	Archdeacon of Stow, 1332–3; archdeacon of Canterbury, 1343–8; keeper of the privy seal, 1347–50; archbishop of Canterbury, 1349–66; O.
Kelsey, Robert	Chancery clerk; greater clerk of chancery, 1341–?1349; W.
Kelshall, Richard	MP for Herts., Feb. 1334; MP for Essex, Sept. 1334 and Mar. 1336; serjeant at law, 1329; justice of Common Pleas, 1341–54; still living, June 1357.
Kendal, William	Archdeacon of Carlisle, occ. 1322, 1340.
Kettleburgh, Stephen	E.
Kilkenny, Philip	E.
Kilsby, William	Receiver of the chamber, 1335–8; keeper of the privy seal, 1338–42; O.

Kilvington, Richard	Dean of St Paul's Cathedral, 1354–61; E.
Kirkby, John	MP for Westmorland, Oct. 1382.
Kirkby, William	King's clerk.
Kirkby, William	Prior of Belvoir (Lincs.), 1315–6
Lambley, John	Advocate of the court of Arches; E.
Langerich, Bartholomew	MP for Essex, Sept. 1337.
Langtoft, John	Chancery clerk; greater clerk of chancery, 1333–?1360; E; W.
Langtoft, Thomas	Chancery clerk.
Ledbury, Stephen	E.
Leech, John	Chancellor of the University of Oxford, 1338–9; official of the court of Arches; E (Lecche).
Leicester, William	Chancery clerk.
Lenn, William	Dean of Chichester Cathedral, 1349–62; bishop of Chichester, 1362–8; bishop of Worcester, 1368–73; O.
Leominster, Hugh	Prebendary of Church Withington, Hereford Cathedral, 1317–27
Lincoln, Thomas	Serjeant at law, cr. 1329; d. 1364.
Llywelyn ap Madoc ab Ellis	Archdeacon of St Asaph, c.1331–?; dean of St Asaph, ?–1357; bishop of St Asaph, 1357–75.
London, Gilbert	King's clerk.
London, Thomas	King's clerk.
London, William	Chancery clerk.
Longden, John	E.
Lovel, Gilbert	E.
Lowick, John	MP for Hunts., May 1335, Mar. 1337, Sept. 1337, Feb. 1338, July 1338, Feb. 1339, Oct. 1339 (Luffwyk).
Luddenham, William	Bishops' clerk; subdean of Salisbury Cathedral, 1329–30 (Lobenham, Lubbenham).
Luddington, Peter	King's clerk; keeper of the writs and rolls of Commons Pleas, occ. 1327, 1337.
Lude, John	E (de la Lowe).
Ludham, John	King's clerk.
Luggore, Thomas	King's clerk; E (Lugoure)
Lymbergh, Adam	Chancery clerk.
Markenfield, John	King's clerk.
Marnham, Thomas	King's clerk.
Marshall, John	King's clerk.
Marton, John	Chancery clerk; greater clerk of chancery, 1341–9; W.
Marton, Richard	King's clerk.
Martyn, Warin	Professional soldier.
Mauley, Stephen	King's clerk; archdeacon of Cleveland, 1289–1317.

Melton, Robert	Chancery clerk.
Merton, John	King's clerk.
Methwold, William	Abbot of St Benet of Hulme, 1365–96.
Mirfield, William	Chancery clerk; greater clerk of chancery, 1362–75; keeper of the great seal, 1371.
Mitford, John	Chancery clerk.
Moigne, Thomas	Knight, MP for Glos., Jan. 1361 and Oct. 1362.
Morcott, Henry	Abbot of Peterborough, 1338–53.
Mortimer, William	Prebendary of Cubington, Herford Cathedral, 1300–11.
Morton, Hugh	E.
Mulso, William	Dean of St Martin-le-Grand, 1364–76; chamberlain of the exchequer, 1365–75; keeper of the king's wardrobe, 1375–6.
Multon, Simon	Chancery clerk; greater clerk of chancery, 1372–6; W.
Murimuth, Adam	'Historian and diplomat'; E; O.
Muskham, Elias	King's clerk.
Muskham, Robert	Chancery clerk.
Muskham, William	E.
Mussard, John	MP for Staffs., April 1354, Jan. 1361; for Worcs., Nov. 1355
Musselwick, Gilbert	Archdeacon of Carmarthen, ?1300–13; E.
Nassington, John	Archdeacon of Barnstaple, 1330–49; E.
Nassington, Robert	E.
Nassington, Robert	Abbot of Ramsey, 1342–9.
Nassington, Thomas	Archdeacon of Exeter, 1331–45; E.
Nassington, William	E.
Newenham, John	Chancery clerk; chamberlain of the exchequer, 1365–9; O.
Newenham, Thomas	Chancery clerk; greater clerk of chancery, 1370–c.1394; keeper of the great seal, 1377; W; O.
Newenham, William	Chancery clerk; greater clerk of chancery, c.1343–?1360; W.
Newhay, Thomas	King's clerk.
Newport, Richard	E.
Normanton, Hugh	Chancery clerk.
Northburgh, Michael	Archdeacon of Suffolk, 1347–53; keeper of the privy seal, 1350–4; bishop of London, 1354–61; O.
Northwood, John	Archdeacon of Exeter, 1329–30; archdeacon of Totnes, 1338–49; chancellor of the University of Oxford, 1345–9; E (Northwode).
Norton, John	Chancery clerk.
Norton, John	Chancellor of Salisbury Cathedral, 1361–1402.

Norwich, Richard	King's clerk.
Offord, Andrew	Chancery clerk; archdeacon of Middlesex, 1349–58; greater clerk of chancery, 1353–8; keeper of the great seal, 1353; E; W; O.
Offord, John	Keeper of the privy seal, 1342–4; dean of Lincoln Cathedral, 1344–8; chancellor 1345–9; abp-elect of Canterbury, 1348–9; O.
Oliver, Ralph	E:Ca (Olyver de Sandon).
Ombersley, John	Abbot of Evesham, 1367–79.
Orleton, Thomas	Chancellor of Salisbury Cathedral, 1322- ?
Osgodby, Adam	Chancery clerk; keeper of the rolls, 1295–1316; keeper of the Domus Conversorum, 1307–16; O.
Oswestry, Richard	Canon of St. Asaph Cathedral, occ. 1345.
Otterhampton, William	King's clerk.
Ottringham, Richard	E:Ca (Oteringham).
Ousefleet, Illard	Serjeant at law, 1354–65.
Pagrave, Ralph	E:Ca.
Pakenham, Geoffrey	Chancellor of the University of Cambridge, 1290–2; E:Ca.
Palet, Robert	MP for Glos., Feb. 1351 and Feb. 1371.
Palmer, James	Clerk of the pipe, 1368–75; E.
Pardinis, Guichard	E.
Pardishowe, Thomas	Chancery clerk; keeper of the great seal, 1341; greater clerk of chancery, *c*.1341; W.
Parles, John	Lawyer; MP for Colchester, July 1313, Oct. 1318, May 1322, Feb. 1328, Sept. 1334, May 1335, Mar. 1336, Sept. 1336, Feb. 1339, Oct. 1339, June 1344 and Jan. 1348.
Paynel, John	King's clerk.
Pembridge, Hugh	E. (Penbrigge).
Percy, Henry	Serjeant at law, 1371; king's serjeant, 1372–7; baron of the exchequer, *c*.1375; justice of common pleas, 1377–80.
Pickering, Robert	Dean of York Minster, 1312–33; E.
Pickering, William	Archdeacon of Nottingham, 1291–1310; dean of York Minster, 1310–12; E.
Pirton, Richard	Chamberlain of the exchequer, 1353–65.
Pocklington, John	Chancery clerk.
Portington, Thomas	Chancery clerk.
Pottersbury, Thomas	E.
Power, Walter	Chancery clerk; greater clerk of chancery, *c*.1341–75; keeper of the great seal, 1371; W.
Pulteney, John	Mayor of London, 1331, 1332, 1334 and 1337; O.

Rasen, Robert	Chancery clerk.
Ravendale, Michael	Chancery clerk; greater clerk of chancery, 1372- ?; W.
Ravendale, William	Keeper of the hanaper, 1339–45.
Ravenser, Richard	Chancery clerk; keeper of the hanaper, 1357–79 ; treasurer of Queen Philippa, 1362–7 ; greater clerk of chancery, 1363–86 ; archdeacon of Lincoln, 1368–86 ; keeper of the great seal, 1377; W ; O.
Raunds, John	Prior of Ravenstone, 1398–1417.
Reculver, William	MP for Canterbury, Sept. 1332.
Ross, Nicholas	King's clerk.
Ripley, Thomas	Advocate of the court of Arches, 1368–74; E:Ca (Rippley).
Rothwell, William	King's clerk.
Sadington, Robert	Chief baron of the exchequer, 1334–43; treasurer, 1340; chancellor, 1343–5; O.
St Albans, Thomas	Attorney (Sancto Albano).
St Pol, John	Chancery clerk; keeper of the great seal, 1334, 1338, 1339–40 and 1349; greater clerk of chancery, 1334–50; keeper of the rolls, 1337–40; keeper of the Domus Conversorum, 1339–50; archdeacon of Cornwall, 1346–9; archbishop of Dublin, 1349–62; chancellor of Ireland, 1350–6; W; O.
Sais, Anian	Archdeacon of Anglesey, ?–1309; bishop of Bangor, 1309–28.
Sampson, Thomas	E.
Sandford, Robert	MP for Westmorland, Oct. 1320, May 1322, Nov. 1322, Feb. 1324, Oct. 1324, Nov. 1325, Feb. 1328, Jul. 1328, Feb. 1329, Nov. 1330, Sept. 1331, Sept. 1332, Jan. 1333, Feb. 1334 and May 1335.
Sandford, Thomas	MP for Appleby, Feb. 1334, Jan. 1339, March 1340 and April 1341; MP for Westmorland, July 1338, Sept. 1346, March 1351, Jan. 1361 and Jan. 1365.
Sandford, William	King's clerk; keeper of the writs in common bench, occ. 1363.
Scarle, John	Chancery clerk.
Segrave, Stephen	Chancellor of the University of Cambridge, 1303–6; dean of Glasgow, 1307–?; archdeacon of Essex, 1315–19; dean of Lichfield Cathedral, 1320–3; archbishop of Armagh, 1323–33; E:Ca; O.
Seles, William	Servant of Glastonbury abbey, occ. 1327.
Selton, William	King's clerk; E.
Sevenhampton, John	MP for Glos., Feb. 1328.
Severley, John	Archdeacon of Worcester, 1349–53; E.
Sheppey, John	E (Shepey).

Shereford, Thomas	E:Ca (Shirford).
Shillingford, John	E (Shillyngford).
Shoreditch, John	E (Shordich).
Shulton, Henry	Rector of Stretton on the Fosse, Warwicks.
Sibthorp, Thomas	Chancery clerk; keeper of the hanaper, 1324–7; greater clerk of chancery, *c.*1338–51; W.
Skirlaw, Walter	Chancery clerk; archdeacon of the East Riding, 1359–85; greater clerk of chancery, 1376–?; keeper of the privy seal, 1382–6; bishop of Coventry and Lichfield, 1385–6; bishop of Bath and Wells, 1386–8; bishop of Durham 1388–1406; W; O.
Skyrne, John	Commissary-general of the court of York, occ. 1318 (Skyren, Skern, Skyrio).
Snainton, John	Benefactor of St. Mary's, York, 1304–5, and 1311–12.
Snaith, Henry	Chancellor of the exchequer, 1371–7.
Southwick, Robert	Official of Carlisle, occ. 1303 (Suthayk).
Spaigne, Nicholas	Chancery clerk; greater clerk of chancery, 1369–74/75; keeper of the great seal, 1371; W.
Spert, Thomas	E.
Spineto, Hugh	Prebendary of Minor Pars Altaris, 1311–13, of Alton Australis, 1313–29, Salisbury Cathedral.
Stanford, John	King's clerk.
Stamford, Nicholas	Chancery clerk.
Stapelton, Thomas	Abbot of Bardney, 1355–79.
Stanek, Simon	E (Stanes).
Staunton, John	King's clerk.
Staunton, Thomas	Prebendary of Grimston, Salisbury Cathedral, 1318–24 (or 34); precentor of Salisbury 1344–7; king's clerk.
Stockton, Nicholas	E (Stokton).
Stoke, John	Almost certainly two men of that name, the earlier one being a chancery clerk, the later Comptroller of the pipe, 1348–*c.*1358; baron of the exchequer, 1365–75.
Stoke, Ralph	King's clerk.
Stoke, William	King's clerk.
Stonegrave, Adam	King's clerk.
Stowe, Thomas	King's clerk.
Stratfield, John	MP for Reading, Jan. 1348.
Stratford, Henry	Chancery clerk; greater clerk of chancery, 1340.
Stratford, John	Dean of the court of the Arches, *c.*1318–23; bishop of Winchester, 1323–33; treasurer, 1326–7; chancellor, 1330–4 and 1340; archbishop of Canterbury, 1333–48; O.

Stratford, Robert	Chancery clerk; greater clerk of chancery, 1330–7; keeper of the great seal, 1331 and 1332; chancellor of the exchequer, 1331–4; dean of Wells, 1334–6; chancellor of the University of Oxford, 1335–8; bishop of Bath and Wells, 1337–62; chancellor, 1338 and 1340; E; O.
Strickland, William	Bishop of Carlisle, 1399–1419; O (Stirkeland).
Styuecle, Nicholas	MP for Huntingdonshire, July 1328, Feb. 1329, July 1338, Sept. 1346, Jan. 1348, March 1348, Feb. 1351, Jan. 1352, Nov. 1355, April 1357, Feb. 1358, May 1360, Jan. 1361, Oct. 1362, Oct. 1363, May 1368, Feb. 1371, June 1371, Oct. 1372, April 1376; escheator in Cambs. & Hunts., 1356–7; sheriff of Cambs. & Hunt., 1356–7. *Two generations were certainly members of Edward III's parliaments, but in the absence of an inquisition post mortem the generations are hard to disentangle. The fact that a Nicholas Styuecle junior, was MP for Hunts in April 1341 suggests that father and son may have overlapped as parliamentarians.*
Surteys, Thomas	MP for Northumberland, Jan. 1361, Oct. 1362, Oct. 1372 (Surtees).
Sutton, Gilbert	Chancery clerk.
Sutton, Roger	Chancery clerk; E:Ca.
Swaffham, Hugh	E:Ca.
Swinefleet, William	Archdeacon of Norfolk, 1361–87.
Tauton, Robert	King's clerk.
Terrington, William	King's clerk (Tyryngtone, Tyryntone).
Thelwall, Thomas	Chancery clerk; master of the rolls of Ireland, 1372–5; greater clerk of chancery, 1376–?; chancellor of the Duchy of Lancaster, 1377–8; W.
Thinghull, William	Examiner general of court of Arches, 1356; Dean of Arches, 1361–5; E:Ca.
Thoresby, John	Chancery clerk; greater clerk of chancery, 1340–9; keeper of the rolls, 1341–5; keeper of the great seal, 1343; keeper of the privy seal, 1345–7; bishop of St Davids, 1347–9; bishop of Worcester, 1349–52; chancellor, 1349–56; archbishop of York, 1352–73; O.
Thorney, Ralph	Attorney; rector of Herringswell (Torney).
Thorntoft, William	King's clerk.
Thorp, Walter	Prebendary of St. Botolph, Lincoln Cathedral, 1303–?
Thriplow, Henry	E:Ca (Triplow).
Thurlaston, Ralph	Prior of Mottisfont, 1352–66; E.
Thursby, Richard	Keeper of the hanaper, 1345–57.
Tintern, John	Abbot of Malmesbury, 1340–9.
Tissington, Richard	Chancery clerk; greater clerk of chancery, 1373–?; W.

Trefor, Matthew	E (Trefaur, Trevaur).
Tregresiowe, Ralph	E (Tregrisiow).
Trehampton, John	Escheator in Lincs., Northants., & Rutland, 1340–1; escheator in Lincs. & Rutland, 1345–8; sheriff of Lincs., 1345–8; MP for Lincs., Oct. 1324, March 1330, Nov. 1330, March 1332, Sept. 1332, Feb. 1334, Feb. 1334.
Tretton, Richard	King's clerk; household clerk of Robert Thorp (chancellor, 1371–2).
Trilleck, Thomas	Dean of Hereford Cathedral, 1353–63; dean of St Paul's Cathedral, 1363–4; bishop of Rochester, 1364–72; O.
Tymparon, Robert	Chancery clerk.
Tyndene, Gilbert	Purveyor for the king's household, occ. 1331.
Tynton, Thomas	King's clerk.
Urdeleigh, Richard	Steward of Cirencester Abbey, occ. 1388.
Usk, John	King's clerk.
Valognes, Robert	King's clerk; precentor, 1317–20, prebendary of Warthill, York Monster, 1323–43 (Waleyns).
Wade, John	King's clerk.
Wakefield, Henry	Archdeacon of Northampton, 1371–2; archdeacon of Canterbury, 1374–5; keeper of the wardrobe, 1369–75; treasurer, 1377; bishop of Worcester 1375–95; O
Wakerley, Roger	Rector of Braybroke, occ. 1350.
Walmesford, Hugh	Prebendary of Buckden, Lincoln Cathedral, 1327–44.
Waltham, John	Keeper of the rolls, 1381–6; keeper of the Domus Conversorum, 1381–6; archdeacon of Richmond, 1385–8; keeper of the privy seal, 1386–9; bishop of Salisbury, 1388–95; treasurer, 1391–5; O.
Waltham, Roger	King's clerk; keeper of the wardrobe, 1322–3; E.
Warley, Ingelard	King's clerk (Warle).
Warmington, Walter	Prebendary Sexaginta Solidorum, Lincoln Cathedral, 1305–11; prebendary of Leighton Manor, Lincoln Cathedral, 1311–? (Wermington).
Wath, Michael	Chancery clerk; greater clerk of chancery, 1334–40; keeper of the rolls, 1334–7; keeper of the great seal, 1339–40; W; O.
Waure, William	MP for Canterbury, May 1335; abbot of St. Augustine's attorney, 1343.
Wawayn, John	Constable of Bordeaux, 1343–7.
Welton, Gilbert	Bishop of Carlisle, 1353–62; E; O.
Westmancote, John	King's clerk.
Whatton, Thomas	Rector of Speldhurst, Kent, occ. 1327.
Whitewell, Hasculf	MP for Rutland, Sept. 1314, Jan, 1315, Nov. 1325, May 1335, Apr. 1343 and June 1344.

Whittlesey, William	Archdeacon of Huntington, 1337–61; bishop of Rochester, 1362–4, bishop of Worcester, 1364–8; archbishop of Canterbury 1368–74; E; O.
Wickford, Robert	Chancery clerk; archdeacon of Winchester, 1361–72; greater clerk of chancery, 1370–?1376; constable of Bordeaux, 1373–5; chancellor of Ireland, 1376–84; archbishop of Dublin, 1376–90; E (Wikeford); W; O.
Wigton, Gilbert	King's clerk.
Wilford, Geoffrey	Chancery clerk (Wyleford).
Wilford, Robert	King's clerk.
Winforton, Walter	Abbot of Winchcombe, 1360–95.
Winwick, John	Keeper of the privy seal, 1355–60; O.
Witchingham, William	Serjeant at law, 1354–65; justice of common pleas, 1365–77.
Wittenham, William	Tenant of Reading Abbey; MP for Reading, Feb. 1328, July 1328; Nov. 1330; Sept. 1331; Feb. 1334; Jan. 1340; March 1340.
Wodehouse, John	Chancery clerk; keeper of the hanaper, 1327–39; W.
Wollore, David	Chancery clerk; greater clerk of chancery, 1344–*c.*1370; keeper of the rolls, 1345–71; keeper of the great seal, 1349, 1351 and 1353; W.
Woodlock, Richard	E (Wodelok).
Woodstock, James	MP for Oxon., Feb. 1328, Dec. 1332, Feb. 1334; MP for Berks., Sept. 1334, Mar. 1336, Sept. 1336.
Worcester, Robert	Archdeacon of Worcester, 1337–49.
Worth, Robert	E.
Wyclif, Robert	Exchequer clerk.
Wykeham, William	Keeper of the privy seal, 1363–7; archdeacon of Huntington, 1363; archdeacon of Lincoln, 1363–7; bishop of Winchester, 1367–1404; chancellor 1367–71; O.
Wyliot, John	Chancellor of Exeter Cathedral, *c.*1351–83; E.
Wythall, Robert	Clerk of king's bench, 1339–61 (Wyghthull).
Young, Thomas	E, vol. III, appendix.
Zouche, William	Keeper of the great wardrobe, 1329–34; archdeacon of Barnstaple, 1329–30; archdeacon of Exeter, 1330–1; controller of the wardrobe, 1334–5; keeper of the privy seal, 1335–7; dean of York Minster, 1336–40; treasurer, 1337–8 and 1338–40; archbishop of York, 1340–52; O.

Sample Letters

There is little variation in the formulae for appointments of proctors. Nearly all were addressed to the king or in his absence the regent, although a few are letters patent which the proctors would perhaps have carried with them as evidence of their authority. Appointments of proctors by spiritual peers nearly always give an excuse for non-attendance, usually ill-health, old age, or pressure of business, but these seem to have been largely conventional. The following letters have been chosen to illustrate such variations as do exist, and represent every element among the clergy called to parliament.

The punctuation has been somewhat modernised, but the capitalisation in the manuscripts retained.

SC 10/1/3

Undated letter from H (probably Henry of Rothley), abbot of Leicester, excusing his absence from a parliament beginning at Westminster on the octave of the Purification (9 February). It is likely that this is one of three letters for the parliament of February 1248, which are the earliest documents in SC 10.

Serenissimo domino suo H[enrico] dei gracia illustri regi Anglie Domino Hibernie Duci Normannie Aquitannie et Comiti Andegavie, suus in omnibus humilis ac devotus clericus Frater H dei permissione abbas Leycestrensis salutem cum omni subieccione reverencia et honore. Variis et immutabilibus prepediti negociis debitis urgentibus multimodo ad mandatum vestrum in octavo purificacionis beate Marie apud Westmonasterium comparere non possumus. Idcirco dominacioni vestre ea qua possumus humilitate supplicamus quatinus si placet absenciam nostram habeatis excusatam quia ad beneplacitum vestrum in omnibus prompti sumus et erimus. Valeat et vigeat dominacio vestra regia per tempora longiora.

SC 10/3/117

Letter from Richard Swinfield, bishop of Hereford, excusing his absence from the parliament beginning at Westminster on 8 July 1313 on grounds of ill-health, and appointing Adam Osgodby, John Gargrave and Stephen Ledbury as his proctors for the assembly. Dated at Bosbury (a manor of the bishops of Hereford), 22 June 1313. Swinfield repeatedly sent proctors during his episcopate rather than attend parliament in person, and this is a typical example of his letters of appointment and those of other bishops of the period.

Excellentissimo principi ac suo domino reverendo Domino Edwardo dei gracia illustrissimo Regi Anglie Domino Hibernie et Duci Aquitannie, Ricardus eiusdem dei permissione Ecclesie Herefordensis Episcopus quicquid potest reverentie et honoris. Quia adversa valitudine et debilitate nostri corporis impediti parliamento vostro tenendo apud Westmonasterium in Quindena Nativitatis Sancti Johannis Baptiste proximo futuro non poterimus personaliter interesse, iccirco in omnibus negociis sive causis nos iura nostra et Ecclesie nostre tangentibus et statum regni vestri de quibus in ipso parliamento vestro ad honorem dei et sancte ecclesie ac Regni vestri utilitatem tractatum haberi contigerit quantum ad nos attinet discretos viros et amicos in Christo dilectos Dominum Adam de Osegodeby et dominum Johannem de Geregrave Canonicos prebendales in ecclesia de Bureford nostre diocesis, ac magistrum Stephanum de Ledebur' iuris civilis professorem nostros procuratores seu attornatos coniunctim et divisim facimus, ordinamus et constituimus per presentes. Ratum habituri et gratum quicquid per predictos procuratores seu attornatos nostros coniunctim, vel duos, aut unum eorum divisim una cum prelatis et proceribus Regni vestri presentibus tunc ibidem factum fuerit in premissis. In cuius rei testimonium sigillum nostrum est appensum. Dat' apud Bosebur' xxii^{mo} die mensis Iunii Anno domini Millesimo Trecentisimo Terciodecimo.

sc 10/8/373

Walter Winter, archdeacon of Carmarthen, excuses his absence from the parliament beginning at York on 2 May 1322 on grounds of business, and appoints David Fraunceys as his proctor. Dated at St Davids, 15 April 1322. Between 1295 and 1340 lower clergy were summoned to parliament indirectly by the praemunientes clause which the archbishops forwarded to the bishop; these reported back to the primate on the execution of this command. This explains why the archdeacon sent his apology and notice of appointment to the archbishop of Canterbury (Walter Reynolds) and not to the king.

Venerabili in Christo patri ac domino, domino Waltero dei gracia Cantuariensis Archiepiscopo totius Anglie primati, Suus humilis et devotus filius Walterus Wynter Archidiaconus de Kaermardyn salutem et debitam obedienciam tanto patri cum omni reverencia et honore: Quia parliamento serenissimi principis ac domini mei domini Edwardi dei gracia Regis Anglie illustris apud Eboracensum a die Pasche proxima futura in tres septimanas deo propicio tenendo interesse non possumus, variis et arduis negociis detentus, et multipliciter et racionabili causa perpeditus, Dilectum michi in Christo Magistrum David Fraunceys Rectorem ecclesie de Villa Johannis in Ros procuratorem meum ordino, facio et constituo per presentes, Dans eidem plenam et sufficientem potestatem nomine meo una vobiscum et suffraganeis vestris ceterisque prelatis ac reliquo clero vestre Cantuariensis provincie, aliis que magnatibus et proceribus Regni Anglie, super diversis et arduis negociis dictum dominum regem ac statum Regni Anglie specialiter tangentibus tractandi suumque consilium impendendi faciendi, ulterius et consenciendi hiis que in dicto parliamento de communi consilio prelatorum, magnatum et procerum ac cleri vestre Cantuariensis provincie predictorum pro statu et utilitate Regis et Regni ac ecclesie Anglicane, divina disponente clemencia salubriter ordinari contigitur super negociis antedictis. Ratum et gratum habituri quicquid dictis procurator meus nomine meo in dicto parliamento in premissis duxerit faciendum. In cuius rei testimonium sigillum meum presentibus est appensum. Dat' apud Menevia' xvii kalendas Maii Anno domini M^{mo} CCC^{mo} vicesimo secundo.

SC 10/23/1141

Matthew of Englefield, bishop of Bangor, excuses his absence from the parliament beginning at Westminster on 8 April 1344 on account of ill-health, and appoints Thomas of Capenhurst and Henry of Eccleshall as his proctors. Dated at Gogarth (a manor of the bishops of Bangor), 12 April 1344. This begins as a standard letter close until – very unusually – it is made a letter patent in the penultimate sentence.

Excellentissimo Domino suo Domino Edwardo Dei Gracia Regi Anglie et Francie illustri Matheus eiusdem permissione Bangorensis Episcopus Salutem in eo per quem reges regnant et principes dominantur. Quia nos, corporis nostri infirmitate prepediti in instanti consilio vestro apud Westmonasterium in quindena pasche proximo futuro personaliter interesse non valemus, Ad comparendum coram vobis tunc ibidem, pro nobis et nomine nostro, et ad tractandum vobiscum et cum ceteris prelatis, proceribus et procuratoribus Regni vestri tunc ibidem convenientibus, Super quibusdam arduis et urgentibus negociis tam honorem dei et Ecclesie Anglicane quam salubrem Regimen Regni vestri ac salvacionem et deffensionem eiusdem summe contingentibus et ad consentiendum hiis que ad honorem dei et utilitatem Ecclesie et Regni vestri tunc ibidem, divina favente clemencia, contigerint ordinari dilectos nobis in Christo dominos Thomam de Cappenhurst Canonicum Assavensis et Henricum de Ecclesalle Rectorem Ecclesie de Lannbeblic nostre diocesis coniunctim et divisim nostros facimus et constituimus procuratores et excusatores, Ratum habentes et gratum habituri quicquid iidem procuratores nostri, aut eorum alter, in premissis et ea concernentibus rationabiliter duxerint seu duxerit faciendum. In cuius rei testimonium has nostras litteras regie maiestati vestre mittimus patentes. Dat' apud Gogerth xii° die mensis Aprilis Anno domini millesimo quadragesimo quarto Et consecracionis nostre sextodecimo.

SC 10/30/1485

Letter patent jointly from John Bukton, prior of Ely, and the chapter of Ely Cathedral, appointing John Dunwich and Roger Sutton as proctors for the parliament beginning at Westminster on 21 November 1373. Dated in Ely Chapter House, 16 November 1373. There are many examples of letters patent, but this document is unusual in explicitly mentioning the business to be discussed in parliament.

Pateat per presentes quod nos Frater Johannes Prior ecclesie cathedralis Eliensis et eiusdem loci Capitulum, ad comparendum nomine nostro in instanti parliamento excellentissimi Principis domini nostri Domini Edwardi dei gracia illustris Regis Anglie apud Westmonasterium in crastino Sancti Edmundi Regis proximo futuro deo auctore tenendo ac etiam ad tractandum super hiis que magnificenciam status eiusdem domini Regis ac utilitatem Regni sui et ecclesie Anglicane, et precipue super his que concernerunt expedicionem guerre seu iura sua et corone in partibus transmarinis cum eodem domino Rege nostro ac prelatis magnatibus et proceribus dicti Regni sui, nec non ad faciendum et plene consenciendum his omnibus et singulis que tunc ibidem de communi consilio, favente domino, ordinari contigerit super negociis antedictis, Dilectos nobis in Christo Magistros Johannem de Dunwich iuris canonici professorem et Rogerum de Sutton iuris civilis professorem coniunctim et divisim et quemlibet eorum in solidum, Ita quod non sit melior condicio occupantis Procuratores nostros ordinamus facimus et constituimus cum plenitudine potestatis ad omnia supradicta faciendum et que qualitas huius negocii exigit et requirit. Ratum habituri et gratum quicquid procuratores nostri, seu eorum alter, nomine nostro duxerint seu duxerit faciendum in premissis. In cuius rei testimonium sigillum commune capituli nostri ad causas presentibus est appensum. Dat' apud Ely in domo nostro capitulari sextodecimo die mensis Novembris anno domini millesimo CCC septuagesimo tercio et Regni eiusdem domini nostri Regis Quadragesimo septimo.

On the dorse: Procuratores pro parliamento Regis.

sc 10/31/1520

Letter of John of Sutton, abbot of Reading, excusing his absence from the parliament beginning at Westminster on 28 April 1376 on grounds of ill-health and for other legitimate reasons, and appointing Peter Barton and Thomas St Albans as his proctors. Dated at Reading, 21 April 1376. This document makes explicit reference to the fact that the proctors would show their letters.

Excellentissimo Principi et domino nostro domino Edwardo dei gracia Regi Anglie et Francie illustri, suus humilis et devotus capellanus Johannes permissione divina abbas monasterii Radyng omnimodam reverenciam et pro salubri statu vestro apud altissimum assiduam per instanciam devotorum. Quia propter invaliditudinem corporis et aliis causis legitimis adeo sumus prepediti quo minus in parliamento vestro apud Westmonasterium die lune proxima post festum sancti Georgii proxima futuri tenendo cum ceteris prelatis magnatibus et proceribus regni vestri super arduis urgentibus negociis vos et statum et defensionem regni vestri Anglie ac ecclesie Anglicane concernentibus trataturi interesse \non/ valemus personaliter, dilectos nobis in Christo dominum Petrum de Barton clericum et Thomam Seynt Alban presencium exhibitores nostros procuratores et excusatores in hac parte ordinamus et facimus per presentes. Ratum habituri et firmum quicquid iidem Petrus et Thomas, seu alter illorum, fecerint vel fecerit in premissis. In cuius rei testimonium sigillum nostrum presentibus duximus apponendum. Dat' apud Redyng xxi die mensis Aprilis anno regni vestri Anglie Quinquagesima.

sc 10/37/1808

Letter patent from the clergy of Cleveland archdeaconry (York diocese), appointing Richard Coniston and Richard Skipsea as proctors for what would become known as the Merciless Parliament in 1388. Dated at Guisborough, 6 January 1388. The senders appear not to have known on which date in February parliament would begin, as a blank is left for the day, although their colleagues in the archdeaconry of York (37/1815) were aware that it would commence on 3 February. According to the text, the letter was sealed with a seal borrowed from the archdeacon of Cleveland's official.

Noverit Universis quod Nos Clerus Archidiaconatus Cliveland ordinamus, facimus et constituimus per presentes dilectos nobis in Christo Reverendos et discretos viros Magistros Ricardum de Conyngeston Officialem curie Eboracensis et Ricardum de Skypsee Rectorem ecclesie \de/ Slaytburn' Inceptorem Iuris Canonicum ad comparendum coram Excellentissimo principe et domino nostro Reverendissimo domino Ricardo dei gracia Rege Anglie et Francie illustri, ceterisque magnatibus et proceribus Regni Anglie in parliamento suo apud Westmonasterium [*blank in ms*] die mensis Februarii proxima futura cum prorogacione dierum subsequencium; Dantes et concedentes eisdem proctoribus nostris plenam et specialem potestatem pro nobis, et nomine nostro, cum ceteris procuratoribus cleri Eboracensis diocesis ad consenciendum nomine nostro hiis que tunc ibidem de communi consilio Regni Anglie divina favente clemencia contigerit salubriter ordinari. Ratum et gratum habendi et habituri sub ypotheca et obligacione bonorum nostrum quicquid procuratores nostri in hac parte nostro nomine duxerint faciendum. In cuius rei testimonium sigillum Reverendi viri domini Archiadiaconi Cliveland .. Offic' presentibus appensum procuravimus. Et nos .. Officialis antedictus ad instantem rogatum Cleri Archidiaconatus predicti sigillum Officii nostri presentibus apposuimus. Dat' apud Gysburn' in Cliveland sexto die mensis Januarii Anno domini millesimo CCC^{mo} octogesimo septimo.

sc 10/41/2003

William of Wykeham, bishop of Winchester, excuses his absence from the parliament beginning at Westminster on 30 September 1402 and appoints John Prophet, Thomas Stanley, Robert Farrington, John Elmer, John Campden and Robert Ketton as his proctors. Dated at Bishop's Waltham, 27 September 1402. This letter demonstrates the tendency towards increasingly verbose letters of appointment in the fifteenth century, as well as the use of increasing numbers of proctors.

Excellentissimo in Christo principi et domino nostro Domino Henrico dei gracia Regi Anglie et Francie et domino Hibernie, Willelmus permissione divina Wyntoniensis Episcopus salutem in eo per quem reges regnant et principes dominantur. Quia nos corporali molestia et infirmitate ad presens perpediti in parliamento apud Westmonasterium in crastino Exultationis sancte Crucis ultimo preterito ordinate et usque ad crastinum sancti Michaelis proxima futura eciam apud Westmonasterium in prorogato interesse personaliter non valemus, Dilectos nobis in Christo Magistros Johannem Prophet, Thomam Stanle, Robertum Faryngton, Johannem Elmer, Johannem Campeden et Robertum Keten clericos coniunctim et divisim et quemlibet eorum in solidum nostros procuratores et attornatos ordinamus, facimus et constituimus per presentes. Dantes et concedentes eisdem nostris procuratoribus et attornatis et eorum cuilibet ut premittitur in solidum potestatem generalem et mandatum specialem pro nobis et nomine nostro in parliamento predicto comparendi absenciam que nostram excusandi allegandi proponendi et si necesse fuerit causis absencie nostre huiusmodi probandi necnon vobiscum cum contumacione et prorogacione dierum tunc sequencium et locorum super omnibus et singulis in vestro brevi de parliamento nobis directo comprehensis statum et utilitatem ecclesie et regni anglie concernentibus tractandi suaque consilia et auxiliae super ipsis nomine nostro et pro nobis impendendi et eciam hiis que ibidem ex vestra aliorum que procerum et magnatum deliberacione communi ad honorem dei et ecclesie sue sancte contigerit concorditer ordinari conscenciendi ulteriusque faciendi et recipiendi in hac parte quod iustum fuerit et negociorum in dicto parliamento tractandorum qualitas et nostre vocacionis effectus exiget et requiret. Ratum et gratum nos perpetus habituri quicquid predicti procuratores et attornati nostri vel eorum aliquis fecerint aut fecerit in premissis vel aliquot premissorum sub ypotheca et obligacione omnium bonorum nostrorum promittimus et exponimus caucionem. Vestram igitur magistatem regiam humiliter deprecamur quatinus nostram huiusmodi absenciam de presenti excusatam haberi dignetur vestra celsitudine racione supradicta quam semper dirigat et conservet in prosperis dextera Regis Regum. In cuius rei testimonium sigillum nostrum fecimus hiis apponi. Dat' apud SuthWaltham vicesimo septimo mensis Septembris Anno domini millesimo quadringentesimo secundo Et nostre consecracionis anno trecesimo quinto.

SC 10/50/2452

Letter from John Litlington, abbot of Crowland, appointing Nicholas Dixon, William Tresham, Thomas Kirkby, John Louth and John Stanlow as his proctors for the parliament beginning at Westminster on 25 January 1442. Dated at Crowland, 13 January 1442.

Excellentissimo principi et domino magnifico Domino Henrico dei gracia Regi Anglie et Francie Illustri Domino Hibernie suus si placeat humilis et devotus Johannes Abbas Monasterii Croylandie quicquid poterit spiritualis obsequii ac terrem [*sic*] cum omnimodis reverencia et honore. Ad comparendum una cum prelatis et proceribus regni vestri in instanti parliamento vestro apud Westmonasterium die Conversione Sancti Pauli proximo futuro tenendo ad tractandum cum eisdem ad consenciendum hiis que communi consensu ad Ecclesie sancte regni et status vestri utilitatem ordinabuntur ibidem dilectos nobis in Christo Dominum Nicholam Dyxson, Willelmum Tresham, Thomam Kirkeby clericum, Johannem Louth, et Johannem Stanlowe coniunctim et divisim et quemlibet eorum per se et in solidum attornatos meos et nuncios speciales ordino, facio et constituo per presentes ratum habituri et gratum quicquid iidem attornati mei, seu unus eorum, nomine meo in premissis duxerint seu duxerit faciendum. In cuius rei testimonium Sigillum meum presentibus apposui. Dat' apud' Croyland terciodecimo die mensis Januarii anno regni vestri vicesmio.